D0139692

Rousseau's Republican Romance

Rousseau's
Republican Romance

Elizabeth Rose Wingrove

PRINCETON UNIVERSITY PRESS

PRINCETON, NEW JERSEY

HOUSTON PUBLIC LIBRARY

R01239 81806

Copyright © 2000 by Princeton University Press
d by Princeton University Press, 41 William Street,
Princeton, New Jersey 08540
n the United Kingdom: Princeton University Press,
Chichester, West Sussex
All Rights Reserved

Wingrove, Elizabeth Rose, 1960–
Rousseau's republican romance / Elizabeth Rose Wingrove.
p.   cm.
Includes bibliographical references and index.
ISBN 0-691-00996-1 (cloth : alk. paper)
ISBN 0-691-00997-X (pbk. : alk. paper)
1. Rousseau, Jean-Jacques, 1712–1778—Contributions in political science.
2. Rousseau, Jean-Jacques, 1712–1778—Contributions in republicanism.
3. Rousseau, Jean-Jacques, 1712–1778—Views on sex role. I. Title.
JC179.R9W55 2000
320'.092—dc21
99-41737

This book has been composed in Baskerville

The paper used in this publication meets the minimum requirements
of ANSI/NISO Z39.48-1992 (R1997) (*Permanence of Paper*)

www.pup.princeton.edu

Printed in the United States of America

1   3   5   7   9   10   8   6   4   2

TO KELLY

Contents

Acknowledgments

I AM PLEASED to acknowledge the Rackham School of Graduate Studies at the University of Michigan, for a Summer Fellowship, and the Office of the Provost at the University of Michigan, for an award from the Career Development Fund for Women; these awards contributed in tangible ways to the completion of this book. I am also pleased to acknowledge the ARTFL Project, co-sponsored by the Institut National de la Langue Française and the University of Chicago and maintained online by the University of Chicago: their databases facilitated my research at several crucial junctures. An earlier version of chapter one appeared as "Sexual Performance as Political Performance in the *Lettre à M. d'Alembert*" in *Political Theory* 23 (November 1995): 585–616, and appears here in revised form by permission of Sage Publications. An earlier version of chapter six appeared as "Republican Romance" in *Representations* 63 (Summer 1998): 13–38, and appears here in revised form by permission of the University of California Press. Versions of "Republican Romance" were presented at the annual meeting of the American Political Science Association in August 1996, where it received an award from the Foundations in Political Thought section, and at the faculty seminar of the Program in Comparative Studies of Social Transformations at the University of Michigan in October 1996; on both occasions I benefited from the spirited comments of seminar participants.

I was introduced to the pleasures, the pains, and the satisfactions of scholarly pursuits at Reed College, and I acknowledge with respect and affection the many teachers and classmates who constituted that intellectual community. Among my teachers I owe a special debt of gratitude to the late William Lankford, William Ray, Peter Steinberger, and Richard Wolin. I was introduced to feminist political theory by Craig Carr at Portland State University; I thank him both for that introduction and for supporting my early interest in the field. At Brandeis University I was privileged to study feminist political thought with Susan Okin; I thank her for guidance on the dissertation project that transformed into this book, and for her ongoing support and skepticism, both of which have been invaluable as I worked to articulate a theoretical voice. Among my teachers at Brandeis I owe special thanks to Jeffrey Abramson, Jim Hollifield, the late Roy Macridis, Sid Milkis, and George Ross.

Many colleagues and friends have lent their support and encouragement to this project, in some or all of its various incarnations. Elizabeth Bussiere, Jonathan Goldberg-Hiller, David Hasen, Paul Edison, Stephen Engelmann, Sophia Mihic, and Mark Reinhardt have deeply influenced my thinking about political and feminist analysis: I am grateful for their friendship and for innumerable conversations about texts, ideas, and the worldly dimensions of theory. I am also grateful for an outstanding group of junior colleagues with whom I had the privilege of working during my time on the Reed College faculty. I remain especially indebted to those whose advice, good humor, and red wine sustained me over the course of my writing: Géraldine Deries, Jacqueline Dirks, Chris Lowe, and Anita Sande. I thank colleagues at the University of Michigan for their comments and suggestions on the manuscript: Liz Anderson, Arlene Saxonhouse, Sid Smith, Domna Stanton, Abby Stewart, and Jackie Stevens. It is a special pleasure to acknowledge the debt I owe to my friend Don Herzog, who read and commented on multiple versions of the manuscript: I have been sustained by his intellectual and personal generosity. Glenn Perusek endured anguished recitations of ill-formed ideas and always helped me to see things a bit more clearly. Bill Paulson generously responded to various questions concerning translation. Ann Lin provided emotional, intellectual, spiritual, and nutritional solace at every step along the way. Ted Guthrie regularly punctured my lofty formulations and fed ideas back to me with gentle precision. I am also pleased to acknowledge my debt to William Rohm, who persuaded me to take seriously the complexities of "consensual nonconsensuality" and who I hope will forgive the bookish ends to which I have put his convictions and insights. Some time ago, Joan Bolker helped me find my way back to the writing life: I remain profoundly grateful for her kindness and wisdom.

My writing group in Ann Arbor, also known as the Fellow Flaming Bitches, saved me on more than one occasion: I thank Catherine Brown, Kali Israel, and Yopi Prins for giving me perspective, provocation, and reassurance, and at all the right times. I thank Tracy Strong for comments and suggestions and for his encouragement even, or especially, in the face of our disagreements. Kirstie McClure's attentive reading constitutes a model of scholarly generosity and erudition: I thank her for suggestions and criticisms that made the book better. I am grateful to Christine Di Stefano for comments that prompted me to rethink the conclusion and to Peter Steinberger for insightful comments on an earlier version of this manuscript. I am also indebted to an anonymous press reviewer, for comments that afforded me the opportunity to sharpen my argument and dig in my heels.

My students at Reed College and the University of Michigan have contributed to this book in various ways: by challenging my assumptions, offering their own wonderful alternatives, and never letting me forget what is at stake in canonical reiteration and feminist analysis. I am indebted to Ryan Hudson for her kind and skillful assistance in preparing the manuscript; Khristina Haddad for helping to ensure that there would be no ripped bodices on the cover; Pierre Landry for assistance in decoding bibliographic software; Steve Maizie for help with an earlier version of the manuscript; Mark Knoll for enduring my inelegant response to computer crises and for making them go away; and Gina Bloom, for her generosity of spirit, mind, and time when I needed it most.

Over the course of writing and rewriting this book I have been sustained by the loyal friendship of Rick Boney, Pat Cross, Rebecca Cross, Pam Crow, Gaby Donnell, Clarissa Howison, Steve Lindsay, Anne Schwab, and Nora Stern. I am deeply grateful for their compassion, good humor, and cheerful refusal to let my scholarly pretensions take up all the space in my life. My parents, Philip and Ida Dennis Wingrove, and my sisters, Lelia Wingrove and Suzanne Wingrove-Haugland, have been an ongoing source of support: I thank them for encouraging me to take risks and for the inspiration they have given me in the form of their own creative endeavors. My brother, Mark Wingrove, taught me the value of laughter, the meaning of compassion, and the power of love: I write

A Note on Texts and Translations

ALL REFERENCED TEXTS by Rousseau appear in *Oeuvres Complètes de Jean-Jacques Rousseau*, 5 vols. edited by Bernard Gagnebin and Marcel Raymond, Bibliothèque de la Pléiade (Paris: Gallimard, 1959–95), and the translations are mine. The one exception is *Emile*; referenced material from this text appears in *Emile: or, On Education*, translated by Allan Bloom (New York: Basic Books, 1979). In addition, I refer to editorial and translation notes that appear in *La Nouvelle Héloïse*, 4 vols., edited by Daniel Mornet (Paris: Hachette, 1925); *The First and Second Discourses*, translated by Roger D. Masters and Judith R. Masters, edited by Roger D. Masters (New York: St. Martin's Press, 1964); *The Political Writings of Jean-Jacques Rousseau*, with Introduction and Notes by Charles E. Vaughan, 2 vols. (Cambridge: The University Press); and *Politics and the Arts: Letter to M. d'Alembert on the Theater*, edited and translated by Allan Bloom (Ithaca, N.Y.: Cornell University Press, 1960). In preparing my own translations, I have also benefited from consulting the following: *Confessions*, translated by J. M. Cohen (Baltimore: Penguin, 1953); *The First and Second Discourses and Essay on the Origin of Languages*, edited and translated by Victor Gourevitch (New York: Harper and Row, 1986); *La Nouvelle Héloïse*, translated by Judith McDowell (University Park: Pennsylvania State University Press, 1968); *Julie, or, The New Heloise*, translated and annotated by Philip Stewart and Jean Vache (Hanover, N.H.: University Press of New England, 1997); and *Rousseau: The Basic Political Writings*, edited and translated by Donald Cress (Indianapolis: Hackett, 1987).

Rousseau's Republican Romance

How to Engender a Political Subject

> [It is] an invariable law of nature which
> gives woman more facility to excite the
> desires than man to satisfy them. This causes
> the latter, whether he likes it or not, to
> depend on the former's wish and constrains
> him to seek to please her in turn, so that
> she will consent to let him be the stronger.
> Then what is sweetest for man in his victory
> is the doubt whether it is weakness which yields
> to strength or the will that surrenders.
>
> *Emile*

CONSENT IS an ambiguous thing. What guarantees the absence of coercion? When must consent be expressed directly, and when can it be assumed? And what constitutes a direct expression? These questions loom large for social contract theorists, who typically respond with appeals to process and form: what makes political consent authentic is power rightly instituted and reason rightly understood. Rousseau's social contract is taken to be exemplary on this score: by casting citizens as the authors of every law that constrains them, the general will ensures that they are only ever self-coercing, and therein lies "the harmony of obedience and liberty."[1] But what is philosophical brilliance, or legerdemain, in *On the Social Contract* assumes an intractably tangible form in Rousseau's depictions of the romantic dyad. There the expression of will takes place in a physical exchange whose "sweetness" derives precisely from the confusion of coercion and consent: desire intensifies in the ambiguous interplay of force and will. For this reason a woman's sexual submission, like a citizen's obedience to the general will, is consistent with consent because her desire, like his interest, materializes only through relations with another whom

---

[1] *Du Contrat Social*, in *Oeuvres Complètes*, vol. 3, 427 (hereafter *Social Contract*).

she has "let" be stronger. A show of force is necessary to the expression of will, and consent is always consent to the terms of one's domination.

We know this, of course, from the *Social Contract*'s oft-cited paradox of citizens who are "forced to be free." To preserve the coherence and the promise of Rousseau's account of a genuinely self-ruling citizenry, many interpreters have sought to contain this paradox within a metaphysical or naturalistic frame. Thus some of the more enduring political theoretical approaches to Rousseau cast him as a proto-Kantian working through reason's necessitations, a protoliberal grappling with the tensions between man and citizen, and a proto-Freudian fantasizing a return to wholeness.[2] But these interpretations inevitably minimize his claim that the freedom democratic politics makes possible entails domination. Taken as a whole, his writings do not allow us to resolve this paradox by appeal to the domination of self-authored law, or the domination of private by public interest, or the inner domination of our fears and desires, because those writings insistently inscribe domination onto the daily practices of republican men and women. "Clothe reason in a body," he advises would-be educators in *Emile*. "Make the language of the mind pass through the heart, so that it may make itself understood."[3] By making the language of consent pass through the experience and expression of desire, Rousseau's republican romance reads the paradoxes of democratic self-rule into citizens' sexual interaction.

In this book I reassess Rousseauian consent in light of these erotic and romantic designs. At first blush there appears to be an isomorphism between political and sexual experience. On the one hand there is the citizen, who in his political practice maintains a twofold identity vis-à-vis the state: when he participates in the articulation of the general will as a legislator, he is ruler, and when he receives its pronouncements through the execution of law, he is ruled. These two positions are given as absolutes: he is alternatively sovereign or subject.[4] On the other hand there is the heterosexual couple, which in Rousseau's telling also affords the man a

---

[2] See, for example, Cassirer, *The Question of Jean-Jacques Rousseau;* Shklar, *Men and Citizens;* Starobinski, *Jean-Jacques Rousseau.*

[3] Rousseau, *Emile,* 323.

[4] Rousseau, *Social Contract,* 361–62, 433.

twofold identity, as husband/father and as lover: in the first position he rules absolutely over his family, but as a lover, he must be ruled. This corresponds to the woman's twofold identity in which she alternatively assumes dominant and submissive roles: as a wife and mother, she is subordinate to her husband, while as mistress, she rules.

Both the man and the citizen thus appear embedded in relationships of what I will call consensual nonconsensuality, meaning the condition in which one wills the circumstances of one's own domination. If, for the citizen, this condition is the formal consequence of living under the rule of law, for the heterosexual couple it organizes daily practice: consensual nonconsensuality authorizes the erotic violence Rousseau accords to men (and which he distinguishes from "real rape"),[5] the father's domestic absolutism, and the lover's sexual submission to his mistress. The difference between a public, institutional expression of consensual nonconsensuality and its private, embodied enactment seems substantial. But in reading through Rousseau's stories, this structural similarity between sexual and political relations looks increasingly like their mutual constitution: in every account he provides, the possibility of securing a stable republican community turns on the interaction between men and women and, likewise, the proper organization of sexual desire turns on securing a stable political rule.

This is certainly the case for Emile, whose moral education is organized around the concomitant articulation of a sexual and social order: the student is led to imagine similarity, difference, and the prospects of rule simultaneously, in the form of masculine and feminine objects. So, too, with St. Preux's exemplary masculinity and Rousseau's own "bizarre" sensuality: for both characters, the (self-)narration of autonomy wends through expressions of a servile desire. And in his multiple depictions of the republic, whenever Rousseau's citizens appear they are acting like husbands and wives, fathers and mothers, sisters and brothers, or tremulous lovers and "imperious mistresses."[6] These roles are critical in what he describes as his "most cherished" work. Le Lévite d'Ephraïm,

---

[5] *Emile*, 359.

[6] The term is Rousseau's, introduced in the narration of his own sexual imaginary and what he refers to as his "bizarre taste" in being dominated; see Rousseau, *Confessions*, in *Oeuvres Complètes*, vol. 1, 16–17.

which tells an epic tale of political fracture and (re)union in terms of rape, murder, marriage, dismemberment, and homosexual desire. In this story of a general will made material on and through sexed bodies, we will see only a more graphic display of what proves true throughout his work: that sexual interaction is not *like* political interaction, nor are its identities preparatory in the sense of being prior to or separate from politics; rather, his republicanism consists in the proper performance of masculinity and femininity.

In developing this argument I part company with, on the one side, interpreters whose central concern is the fit, or lack thereof, between Rousseau's sexism and his democratic principles more generally.[7] How does gender hierarchy survive his egalitarianism? Can his instrumental deployment of feminine wiles conform with his celebration of citizen probity? And what about that autocratic head of household who magically transforms in public into a democratic citizen? These are the sorts of puzzles that have presented themselves to democratic feminist critics, by which I mean those critically engaging a tradition of democratic political thought in which Rousseau occupies a pivotal, if problematic, location.[8] I also part company, on the other side, with interpreters who find evidence that his gender scheme is the necessary counterpart to his political principles, rather than their simple contradiction. Precisely what Wollstonecraft refers to as Rousseau's "unintelligible paradoxes" concerning women suggests that the heterosexual re-

---

[7] Major works on this score include Okin, *Women in Western Political Thought*, chaps. 5–8; Okin, "Women and the Making of the Sentimental Family"; Lange, "Women and the 'General Will' "; Keohane, " 'But for Her Sex. . .,' "; Pateman, " 'The Disorder of Women,' "; Pateman, "Women and Consent,"; Landes, "Rousseau's Reply to Public Women." For an account of how Rousseau's inconsistencies stem from his own fear of female sexuality, see Wexler, " 'Made for Man's Delight.' "

[8] Feminist analyses of consent theory and its uncertain application to women owe much to the work of Carole Pateman, whose readings of democratic theorists, including Rousseau, emphasize the links between gender relations and the relations of citizens to their state; see Pateman, "Women and Consent." My analysis pursues Pateman's insight that "relationships of consent in everyday life" can shed light on the problems of democratic theory (150), but I construe both those problems and the "exemplary" nature of women's compromised consent (162) differently. See also Pateman, *Problem of Political Obligation*.

lationship complements republican relations by offering a division of moral and social labor, and together the two realms sustain coherent, if unstable, structures of power and interdependence.[9]

These two approaches—emphasizing, alternatively, contradiction and complementarity in Rousseau's sexual politics—work from the received scholarly wisdom that differentiates between his politics and his sex. In Judith Shklar's widely accepted interpretation, this differentiation corresponds to a choice Rousseau presents between living as a man or living as a citizen: while the former remains unfit for politics, the latter requires man's radical "denaturing." Feminist interpreters have contested this oppositional framing, but they have been less critical of its differentiating terms. To be sure, the natural and the institutional, the private and the public, the emotional and the rational, are widely recognized as plastic, and reversible, valuations. But pursuing what I have suggested is the mutual constitution of republicanism and gendered sexuality entails provisionally holding suspect any move that disaggregates and orders what Rousseau presents as experientially coincident. However clear and serviceable an analytic distinction between sexual and political interaction, in the lives of Rousseau's republicans that distinction collapses in the common practices of enacting one's sexuality. The interpretive question then becomes: How best to conceptualize this "collapse" as an integrated whole?

Posing this question in the context of current scholarship highlights an important difference between those who emphasize gender's functional dimensions and those who emphasize its symbolic dimensions. I want to address that difference here as one of levels of analysis. The first approach, inaugurated by Susan Okin's work, emphasizes the utility of the patriarchal family: women's privatization and domestication follow from the need for child rearers, for securing paternity, and for creating a public space emptied of

---

[9] Wollstonecraft, *Vindication of the Rights of Women*, 98. Among important studies that emphasize the significance of sexual complementarity, from both deeply critical and appreciative perspectives, I include Elshtain, *Public Man, Private Woman*, chap. 4; Schwartz, *Sexual Politics of Jean-Jacques Rousseau*; Bloom, "Introduction" to *Emile*; Weiss, *Gendered Community*; Thomas, "Jean-Jacques Rousseau, Sexist?"

potentially disorganizing sexual desire.[10] The second approach, influenced by psychoanalytic theory, emphasizes how and what women signify in Rousseau's work: with their engulfing powers, beguiling sexuality, and skillful dissimulations, women always signal the precariousness of a community of robust and guileless (male) citizens.[11] Here "woman" is an object of exchange in the symbolic economy, where, as Linda Zerilli puts it, she serves as a "scapegoat precipitated by the disorder in men: that feminine other within the citizen-subject who '[w]ill always be marked by the uncertainty of his borders.'"[12]

Setting aside obvious differences in theoretical and linguistic idiom, these two interpretive stances diverge in how they envisage the political stakes in Rousseau's gender scheme: while the functional approach works at the level of women's social labor and material contribution—what women, procreatively and sensually, *do* with, for, and/or to men—the semiotic approach emphasizes the meanings attached to maternal and sexual identity: how woman appears as symptom, an always overdetermined sign of male anxiety. Attending to the problem of Rousseauian consent requires moving between these levels of analysis, because he represents and attempts to resolve that problem in his bodily designs: in their daily interactions men and women substantiate the paradox that autonomy is sustained through relations in which one dominates and submits.[13] Through a gender politics that encompasses both how desire is imagined and how it is enacted, Rousseau anchors his republicanism in the passionate intentions of sexed creatures. The political stakes in masculinity and femininity thus encompass both how they organize social interaction and how they symbolize political ideals.

I use the term *performative sexuality* to suggest this twofold, functional material and semiotic, approach. As emphasized in Judith

---

[10] See Okin, *Women in Western Political Thought*, pt. 3. See also Lange, "Rousseau: Women and the General Will," 41–52; Pateman, " 'The Disorder of Women' "; Pateman, *The Sexual Contract*, 96–102.

[11] See Kofman, "Rousseau's Phallocratic Ends," 46–59; Zerilli, *Signifying Woman*.

[12] Zerilli, *Signifying Woman*, 19. Zerilli is quoting Kristeva, *Powers of Horror, 63*.

[13] I present in its most paradoxical and pungent form what might appear more benign, philosophically and physically, when it is assimilated to the Aristotelian interchange of ruling and being ruled; this is how Joel Schwartz casts sexual

Butler's early and influential account, the representation of sexual identity as performative denies the possibility of an essentialized origin or meaning.[14] Further, it emphasizes that sexuality is never a certain or static state but entails a perpetual reproduction that turns on how and what people do. But my use of the term does not correspond to any particular anxiousness about the status of the subject as unified and fixed. While I share the antifoundationalism that animates these concerns, I am more anxious about questions of governance, of modern political authority and rule, and here my antifoundationalist commitment urges me away from subject-(de)centering projects and toward the relations that structure the community. In this sense a performance model trains our attention on practice, the actions and reactions of individuals, rather than on their inner (in)stabilities. And while this is politically apt inasmuch as what matters most within the context of the state is not what people think but what they do, it will bring to mind for some the unhelpful anticipation that a performing subject might be "only" acting, pretending to be what he or she might otherwise not *really* be. In this context I find detours into authenticity as problematic as those into decentered selves: intriguing but potentially depoliticizing. As I use the term, *performance* offers a means of conceptualizing how citizen-subjects behave with respect to their needs, desires, and fears, even as we recognize the inconstant foundations of these impulsions.

On the other hand, performance, unlike behavior, connotes theatricality, by which I mean a mode of action in which the self-cum-actor represents itself to others through gestures, poses, and words, and successful communication depends on good depictions. My analysis draws on this model of (self-)representation in several respects, but not to propose that gender, for Rousseau or for us, is "nothing more than a way of speaking, a matter of words and clothes."[15] These contingent, improvisational, and specular dimensions of gender should not obscure the less contingent material bases on which they work. I don't mean that bodies constitute either the origins of or limits to sexual identity, but that they

---

relations between men and women; see *The Sexual Politics*, 13. My substantial disagreements with him are addressed at several points below.

[14] See Butler, *Gender Trouble*. See also Butler, *Bodies That Matter;* Butler, *Excitable Speech.*

[15] Zerilli, *Signifying Woman*, 164 n.

are the site of gender's construction. Thus the materialism that interests me has less to do with anatomies than with conduct, and what matters politically in sexual performances is that males act like men and females act like women. That they do not always do so is clear: effeminate courtiers, those intrepid Spartan mothers, and the gender inversions of the salon all attest to the precariousness and motility of gender. But what holds it in place, so to say, what on Rousseau's telling can operate as a natural sign, is the physical body.[16] To be sure, his appeals to nature as the source and substance of gender difference are entirely insufficient: as Penny Weiss and others have persuasively shown, Rousseau clearly reveals, even if he then re-veils, the social and political expediency that drives his account of femininity and masculinity.[17] And precisely for this reason, bodies serve as natural signs only to the extent that they are political sites, where the showing of difference depends more on theatrics than on science.

To present the issue somewhat differently and in the language of the *Discourse on Inequality*: one might characterize performative sexual identities as a response to the troublesome distinction between "being" and "seeming to be"; they represent Rousseau's attempt to collapse that distinction in the ostensibly unmediated unity of "doing." Here the critical thrust of performativity lies in its intimations of unreflective interaction: for an audience, what matters is what moves, and this is a question of surface productions. For this reason Rousseau presents his citizens, to his readers and to themselves, as participants in a sexual *spectacle* whose publicity is critical to its success.[18] We need not evaluate the viability of his lovingly imagined Spartan originals, where bare-breasted

[16] Rousseau's position owes much to what Thomas Laqueur has argued are "new" natural scientific accounts of sexual difference emerging in the eighteenth century. See Laqueur, *Making Sex*. While Laqueur places Rousseau squarely on the side of the "new" natural science, I take his position to be far more ambivalent.

[17] See Weiss, *Gendered Community*, chap. 3: "Anatomy and Destiny: Rousseau, Antifeminism, and Woman's Nature."

[18] Often translated as "theater" or "scene," *spectacle* has richer connotations in French. The 1798 edition of the *Dictionnaire de l'Académie Française* offers the following definition: "said of any matter that attracts notice or attention, that engages the eyes" (2:598). See also the translator's note in *Politics and the Arts: Letter to M. D'Alembert on the Theater*, 150. Throughout the text I will use italics to designate words left in the original French.

and unmolested Lacedaemonian maidens gave witness to, as they renewed, the purity and the innocence of community *mœurs*,[19] and whose nude Olympians remain Rousseau's sign of the "good man."[20] If republicanism then thrived on the publicity of naked citizens, for his time Rousseau proposes a politicization of dancing, ritualized courtship, and carefully costumed self-display, in public festivals staged specifically to that end. The fact that these contemporary entertainments seek to erase altogether the distinction between spectator and *spectacle* does not mean that they preclude theatricality.[21] On the contrary, they effect what might be called a generalization of the theatrical experience, by gathering men and women together publicly to play the roles of themselves. When in this way the paradox of their consensual nonconsensuality is inscribed into citizens' daily sexual practice, republican virtue and sacrifice become as compelling, as natural, as erotic desire itself, and as immune to the challenges of reasoned reflection or calculation.

Recognizing the extent to which Rousseau's democratic project would restrict citizens' deliberation underscores a final dimension of performative analysis, that it explores discursive productions. From this perspective any inquiry into his sexual politics must also interrogate his rhetorical strategies, how his narration of desire and difference performs what it represents, or, to borrow from J. L. Austin, how in doing things with words Rousseau would do things with bodies.[22] My focus on material signs is faithful to Rousseau's own developmental scheme of language and communication, which accords blood, bodies, tears, and gestures a primary symbolic role. My focus is also consistent with the primacy he accords to figural language. In retracing the first meanings to metaphoric utterances—to acts of naming that simultaneously initiate identity and difference—he discloses how literalness is itself a

[19] *Mœurs*, alternatively translated as "mores," "customs," or "manners," suggests a habituated moral practice; see translator's note in *Politics and the Arts*, 149.

[20] See Rousseau, *Discours sur les Arts et les Sciences*, in *Oeuvres Complètes*, vol. 3, 8 (hereafter *Discourse on Arts and Sciences*). For Rousseau's discussion of Spartan maidens' public nudity, see Rousseau, *Lettre à d'Alembert*, in *Oeuvres Complètes*, vol. 5, 133 (hereafter *Letter to d'Alembert*).

[21] Rousseau's ambivalence about theatricality is treated extensively in Marshall, *The Surprising Effects of Sympathy*. See also Coleman, *Rousseau's Political Imagination*.

[22] See Austin, *How to Do Things with Words*.

11

function of symbolization: the notion of an originary meaning, true only and essentially in itself, is the first metaphor.[23] This logic of literalness is precisely the logic of bodily "self-evidence," the baffling claim that a representation (the sexually distinct body) can generate or sustain its own meaning (the politico-moral imperatives of masculinity and femininity). Rousseau's emphasis on origins thus locates the search for an empirical—material, naturalistic—truth within the realm of language and symbolization more generally. No appeal to physically entailed moral and political design, his own included, eludes the moment of rhetorical constitution, and it is through his narrative constructions that Rousseau massages meaning into and out of sexual difference.

The story he will tell, time and again, is a romance: the "romance [*roman*] of human nature," of the "species's" natural history, of republican heroism and devotion.[24] In all of these stories he gives form to sexual creatures whose experiences of desire, sacrifice, and rule coincide with the republican exigency of consensual nonconsensuality. That the form these creatures take is gendered masculine or feminine matters greatly, but not in differentiating between those who submit and those who rule. The heterosexual dyad organizes a distribution of dominance and submission that subjects both individuals to both conditions. And while their respective subjections are not equivalent—the disparities are as profound as bodily integrity and political opportunity— we will misunderstand both the practices and the logic of his heterosexuality and his politics if we insist on reading the differences as the whole. In the conclusion I discuss directly the implications of these interpretive commitments for feminist theory, and specifically for the problem of providing satisfactorily complex accounts of masculine power *and* feminine desire. My primary focus

[23] My language echoes Ernesto Laclau and Chantal Mouffe, who, in exploring how discursively produced identity is always partial and open, write: "This being so, all discourse of fixation becomes metaphorical: literality is, in actual fact, the first of metaphors"; *Hegemony and Socialist Strategy,* 111. They do not mention Rousseau's *Essay on the Origin of Languages,* but the tradition in which they are working has fully assimilated his insights. I discuss some of these assimilating moves—for example, through the work of Jacques Derrida—in subsequent chapters.

[24] *Emile,* 416; *Discours sur l'Origine et les Fondements de l'Inégalité, in Oeuvres Complètes,* vol. 3, 135 (hereafter *Discourse on Inequality*).

in reading Rousseau is teasing out how, in their asymmetrical capacities for autonomy, republican men and women together give form to the worldly—institutional, bodily, sentimental—conditions of his consent. This is true at the level of the individual, where what is experienced as the immediacy of passion in fact mediates, for men and for women, the paradoxical political imperatives of submission and control. It is also true at the level of the community, where Rousseau stages a gender *spectacle* that negotiates intrasocial organization and national identity through fantasies of bloodline, maternal solicitude, and "natural" desire.

On both levels, the interpenetration of sensuous and moral design suggests a somatic dimension to citizenship nourished by a Romantic sensibility: its imaginative transports serve well the affective demands of consensual nonconsensuality. In this Rousseau's republicanism differs markedly from a civic humanist version whose stoic sensibilities posit a very different masculine ideal. As sketched by Stephanie Jed, in this earlier version of republicanism political liberty depends on successfully containing citizens' emotional and sensuous impulses, and thus it depends on maintaining a wall of separation between private and public, and feminine and masculine, realms of experience and meaning.[25] Jed's intriguing reading of philological practice points to the historical and textual dimensions of this separation: in the reception of legends of the rape of Lucretia, she argues, one finds a language and a logic of castigation—of cutting off, chastising, contamination—that effects the discriminations upon which the politics depends.[26] Here republicanism takes the shape of a dispassionate masculinity, negotiated textually through encounters with stories that sever heroism from sentiment, and just rule from bodily griefs. Rousseau's republicanism, by contrast, demands a wholly embodied masculinity. Unlike the evacuation of emotion and desire necessary to "chaste thinking," consensual nonconsensuality moves through a libidinal order where feeling it makes it real, and liberty, no longer the consequence of restricted passions, depends on their excess.

[25] Jed, *Chaste Thinking*.
[26] Ibid., see especially chap. 1, "*Tum Brutus castigator lacrimarum*, The Cruelty of Brutus and the Politics of Philology," 18–50. See also page 8, where Jed introduces the "conflicting lexical families of terms" through which the central figure of "chaste thinking" is constituted.

This shift in gender ideals provokes questions about the political ideals they embody. Both the civic humanist and Romantic versions of republicanism champion self-rule, but the former figures it as the fruit of a masculine reason divorced from pathos, while the latter imagines a political virility born of servile desire. It would be handy to attribute this transformation to the influence of individualist ideologies, naturalistic materialisms, changing relations of production, and other abstractions which, however unwieldy, help to characterize the change in politico-cultural context. Certainly these large-scale, ideological and historical frames illuminate some thematic differences, for example, the civic humanist emphasis on the qualities and dispositions of the soldier versus a Romantic emphasis on artistic self-display, the former's ideals of honor and action versus the latter's tropes of virtue and authenticity. But these illuminations do not, in and of themselves, clarify the logic and process that effect a structural correspondence between sexuality and politics. Indeed, they risk obscuring that mutuality to the extent they telescope the analysis into a comparison of masculinities. Because my subject is not sexuality per se but the political work gender does for republican theory, the more relevant comparisons are those articulated within a narrative frame that connects political liberty to sexual desire and eroticized violence, rather than comparisons drawn between the historical, textual, and social contexts in which different narratives are produced.

In Rousseau's stories, the stoicism associated with an earlier republican tradition contrasts sharply with the sensuous and sentimental appeal of moral experience. Precisely because citizenship includes a corporeal dimension, a retreat from bodily experience signals a retreat from the pleasures and pains on which community and individual identity depend; the result is a moral detachment that suffers both despotic brutality and slavish reserve with equanimity. In this threat to republicanism, dispassion is the mark not of gender but of an unworldly—bestial or divine—indifference, and the image of a stoic withdrawal typically suggests the failure, rather than the culmination, of his sexual politics.[27] Consider Rousseau's own version of Lucretia's rape—an unfinished

---

[27] For a contrasting case that underscores the complementarity of stoicism and masculine sensibility, see Ellison, *Cato's Tears*.

and unpublished tragedy *La Mort de Lucrèce*—which transforms her rapist Sextus into a former suitor, the subject of her affections prior to her arranged marriage to Collintus.[28] The extant text is too fragmentary to sustain extensive analysis, but its opening moves are striking: when the exemplary chaste heroine is introduced through a sentimental discussion of her past desire for her future rapist, the reader is on notice that the terms of her, and thus Rome's, redemption from tyranny cannot be detached from a bodily grammar of consent.[29] We are also on notice that the perverse demands of *la patrie* attach to women not only as objects of purity and possession but also as desiring subjects.

Women's incorporation as willing and wanting agents, like men's embrace of romantic excess, follows the logic of consensual nonconsensuality. But it also provokes performance anxieties: both *salonnières* and high-society coquettes appear in Rousseau's stories as willing women whose influence is wholly pernicious. This is not, however, because they induce masculine submission, but because the submission they induce impedes, rather than invigorates, republican self-rule: by appealing to their vanity and pride, aristocratic women keep men foppish and fragile. Again the issue is less the disorder of sexual roles per se than the political order that builds upon and sustains them; and unlike consensual nonconsensuality, which facilitates a self-authored submission, for Rousseau the social-sexual quiescence of ancien régime mores inescapably subjects men to the tyrannic order of courtly hierarchy, luxury, and ambition. Rousseau's sneering dismissal of worldly women thus heralds his rejection of monarchical masculinity: both the republican and the aristocrat prostrate themselves before "imperious mistresses," but the former is bending to the sovereignty of his own rule, while the latter is (still) quivering before the king.

Rousseau's monarchical version of masculinity, like his stoic account, can throw his republican ideal into sharp relief, but most compellingly by highlighting the political relations that each affords. "Whether a monarch governs men or women ought to be

---

[28] Rousseau, *La Mort de Lucrèce*, in *Oeuvres Complètes*, vol. 2. The tragedy consists of a completed act 1, an incomplete act 2, and several pages of fragmentary dialogue.

[29] Compare this figuration of the body as a perpetual site of, rather than object of, political expression with Jed's discussion of chastity in *Chaste Thinking*, 43–47.

rather indifferent to him," Rousseau observes, "provided that he be obeyed; but in a republic, men are needed."[30] The concern about gender slippage that surfaces in his every discussion of ancien régime mores, the fear and derision provoked by men made into women and women made into rulers, always registers a concern about political rule, and what we see articulated in his contrasting masculinities are different regimes of desire and will that undermine, deny, or promote the democratic possibilities of self-rule.

I will argue that these possibilities do not reduce to the proper elaboration of a true masculinity, understood as a bodily property; instead, they emerge from a distinctly republican organization of heterosexuality, a categorically attenuated order of desire and identity that engenders political subjects as it engenders men and women. And I will show that the sites of (hetero)sexuality's[31] organization are multifold, exceeding the bounds of public and private ritually invoked as definitive. What Rousseau's political, fictional, and autobiographical writings trace is an *éducation sensible* that trains bodily and material practices by organizing experiences of love and power; in this way citizens will come to grasp his republicanism by feeling its compulsions in their daily lives, and the sense they make of themselves—of their "inner" drives, desires, and needs: in short, their nature—is coincident with the sense they make of republican society and rule.

The still orthodox, political theoretical approach to Rousseau maintains that "natural" differences reflect and incorporate every other difference of moral and social significance in his political thought. The general and the personal, the common and the unique, the contrived and the unrefined: grasping these two positions is in each case facilitated by the natural design that Rousseau allegedly tenders to his readers. Within this orthodoxy

---

[30] *Letter to d'Alembert*, 92.

[31] The parenthetical break is intended to signal the simultaneously attenuated and definitive status of heterosexuality: it would be a mistake to take this particular form for the general type, and it would be a mistake to make any claims about the general type that exceed the "evidence" of this particular form. I am couching this matter in terms consistent with my political philosophical approach, but I take it to be a central and unsettled axis of queer theory. For a discussion of the term *queer* as it is used in contemporary politics and theory, see Duggan, "Making It Perfectly Queer," in Duggan and Hunter, *Sex Wars*.

sexuality assumes an important position inasmuch as it includes attributes that straddle the nature/society divide. As an identity and a desire, sexuality seems to provide a lens onto our inner and most private selves, even as it inserts us into a social order that antecedes and exceeds those selves. In challenging orthodox approaches to Rousseau's use of nature and natural sexuality, my primary interest is not to debunk his insipid biologism but to elucidate a sensuous philosophy that gives republican morality a material form. This complication of our understanding of bodily significance offers a better account of how sexual difference matters to Rousseau's republicanism and to political theory more broadly: neither a source of enduring truths nor an object of colonization and resistance, the body remains a figure of political possibility. Ultimately, then, my study of Rousseau's sexual politics elaborates a mode of political analysis, one that attends to the principles and relations of governance inhering in textual, material, and bodily representations.

In chapter one I introduce the problem of consensual politics by revisiting Rousseau's search for origins. I challenge the conclusion that his appeals to nature are definitive on this score, and I propose instead that we see nature as a site at which his politics unfolds. This proposition arises from an attention to the narrative structure of the *Discourse on Inequality* and to the recursive logic sketched by that structure. I show how, rather than a linear progression of discrete causes followed by contingent effects, the *Discourse on Inequality* conforms to a narrative circularity in which ends are always present at beginnings, and the beginning reappears at the end. Thus I argue that the dominant and submissive relationships on which the *Discourse* ends propel its multiple transformations of nature: from the beginning, material and cognitive changes reflect the political imperatives that frame the story as a whole and nature always gives testimony to the laws—positive, cultural, conventional—that subject it. What mediates this circularity, what identifies and orders the categories of *before* and *after,* are pity and self-love: these "natural operations" organize the sociosexual differences that constitute Rousseau's political (d)evolution. I argue that the centrality of pity and self-love, which are none other than the structures of sensuous and sentimental awareness, underscores the political significance of *sensibilité*. Differently inflected than its English cognate in steady circulation at the time,

17

sensibilité for Rousseau suggests an always embodied awareness of pleasure, pain, and difference.[32] I argue that the promise of a conventional politics—of an ending different from that sketched in the *Discourse*—hinges on the development of a republican *sensibilité*, a sentience made sentiment that can feel the paradoxical complementarity of coercion and consent.

In chapter two I make explicit the gender implications of the sociosexual (d)evolution outlined in chapter one by turning to the stories of Emile and Sophie. Rousseau's educational projects incorporate a moral and social awareness into sexual awareness: Emile and Sophie understand their interest and their will as they identify their sexual desire. Here we encounter the first "principle" of sexual difference, that one "be active and strong, the other passive and weak," that one sex "will and be able" and the other "put up little resistance."[33] But in the course of their courtship, marriage, and separation, it appears crucial that these roles are regularly transgressed: a masculine servile desire proves central to sustaining ruling relationships in the republican romantic dyad. Their respective freedoms thus emerge in the performance of a dialectic of (sexual) control whose logic derives from the political vision the couple is intended to inspire. And as presented in *Les Solitaires*, the unpublished sequel that covers their postmarital lives, when their performance fails, so does the political vision.

In contrast to the didactic narrative I trace in chapter two, in chapter three I read *Julie ou La Nouvelle Héloïse* and the *Confessions* as examples of experiential narration. As cultural objects that helped to materialize an eighteenth-century reading public, these books were a means of fashioning the political and sexual *sensibilités* represented within them. But as exercises in self-inscription, Rousseau's epistolary novel and his autobiography represent not only exemplary characters but also the practices through which those characters are produced. I argue that *Julie* thus represents the paradoxical process of self-constitution that obtains in reading, writing, and interpretive exchange more broadly: the story both depicts and discursively performs a dynamic of consensual

---

[32] See Wilson, "Sensibility in France in the Eighteenth Century"; Barker-Benfield, *The Culture of Sensibility*; Mullan, *Sentiment and Sociability*; and Todd, *Sensibility: An Introduction*.

[33] *Emile*, 358.

18

nonconsensuality. It depicts a heterosexual passion that is continuously reconfigured: from the innocence of youthful excess, to the trepidation of illicit gratification, to the exquisite severity of deprivation, to the abiding satisfactions of a platonic form. This transformative process is both cause and effect of new familial demands and social expectations experienced by the lovers, Julie and St. Preux, and with each change they become increasingly autonomous and politically reliable characters. But the novel also underscores how their rectitude remains dependent on their passionate excess; its process of moral maturation ties self-rule to an imaginary extravagance. I conclude this chapter by turning briefly to Rousseau's own self-creation in the *Confessions*. I resist the tendency to read this book as revealing, more or less accurately, a personality whose weaknesses and insights offer a critical lens into his political commitments. I argue instead that the *Confessions'* stories of moral and social awakening reproduce the rhetorical and thematic dimensions of consensual nonconsensuality; thus his own developmental account is scripted by a dynamic in which self-rule emerges through an encounter with, that is also always a creation of, his own political *ordre sensible*.

Rousseau's depiction of the republican state is developed more fully in chapter four. In particular I consider the *Discourse on Political Economy*, whose explicit focus on executive governance sidesteps the knotty issues of conventionality and (thus) legitimation. The essay opens with a series of distinctions—domestic versus public economies, paternal versus political rule, familial versus civic identities—that specify its proper domain. But over the course of the essay these distinctions are thoroughly undermined by a rhetoric that presents citizens as brothers, states as mothers, and political communities as moral bodies animated by a "sublime ardor." Rousseau's gender ideology reflects the reality of his republican state: it is both other and the self, both the cause and the culmination of citizenly desires. He thus attempts to practice that "inconceivable art" by which men are placed in "subjection in order to make them free," not by laying down the law but by provoking familial fantasies of a common flesh and erotic fantasies of passionate service.[34] And in so doing he aims to counter the "danger-

---

[34] Rousseau, *Discours sur l'Économie Politique*, in *Oeuvres Complètes*, vol. 3, 248 (hereafter *Political Economy*). Rousseau concludes that this "inconceivable art" is "the work of the law."

ous *spectacles*" of mesmerizing politicians, oratorical zealots, and babbling sophists. Rousseau's rhetoric of a hazardous, both populist and despotic, theatricality propels us toward his democratic solutions of surveillance and counterillusion: the state figured as family and special friend. The symbolic, the merely cultural, thus becomes profoundly, indistinguishably political: the metaphors of the *Discourse on Political Economy* prove to be performatively metonymic, inasmuch as governance strategies are contiguous to citizens who act like "natural" men and women.

The relationship between symbolic and political practice is the subject of chapter five, where I step back from the content of the romantic dyad to consider its constitutive dimensions. My focus here is on performative structures, discussed directly by Rousseau in his writings on theater and language. While these themes have received extensive attention from literary critics, my goal is to explore their implications for political practice. I argue that while Rousseau rejects the theater as a historical institution, he embraces the manner in which it structures sexual interaction: both its "imagined" identifications and its publicity are necessary to forge the gender-differentiated citizenry he claims merely to discover, and celebrate. The model of theatricality is thus precisely the model of his sexual politics, both of which rely upon good scripts and good actors in order to succeed. But while the theater enlists actors who, given another script, could act otherwise, in Rousseau's romantic dyad success is anchored in intentional bodies that never could: their meanings are as self-evident as the desire they provoke. A similar strategy of representation-as-embodiment appears in the *Essay on the Origin of Languages*, where we find the account of language's figural origins. "When passion holds our eyes spellbound," Rousseau writes, we imagine and thus give conceptual form to illusions whose status *as* illusion we later acknowledge by the term metaphor. This first, figural language reappears, he insists, when we are moved by "the same passions as had produced it."[35] I argue that as long as Rousseau's republicans are "spellbound" by heterosexual passion, then gender's figural representations—masculinity and femininity, rulers who love to be ruled, a "no" that means "yes"—can sustain a republican sensibil-

---

[35] Rousseau, *Essai sur l'Origine des Langues*, in *Oeuvres Complètes*, vol. 5, 381–82 (hereafter *Essay on Languages*).

ity. For this reason, Rousseau's citizens will always appear to act like men and women, in the watchful realms of both state and home.

In chapter six I deploy the arguments of the preceding chapters in a reading of Rousseau's "most cherished," and today almost unknown, text *Le Lévite d'Ephraïm*. This posthumously published story illustrates, in spectacular form, the structural and thematic importance of consensual nonconsensuality for thinking about politics. Taking its plot and some of its language from the Book of Judges, *Le Lévite d'Ephraïm* addresses questions of retribution, justice, freedom, and obedience through a story of motivating and murderous passions. By showing how Rousseau's organization of a libidinal economy is simultaneously his organization of sovereignty, *Le Lévite* lays bare the conceptual and narrative limits of differentiating between his sex and politics. How, I ask, can we identify in this story where republican loyalty triumphs over erotic passion, or where personal desire is intelligible absent a context of community need? How do *Le Lévite*'s political imperatives make sense absent its gender imperatives? What, finally, is "unromantic" about this story of rape, evisceration, forced seduction, and sodomy deferred?

The intentional perversity of this final question frames my conclusion, where I offer some observations about the persistent puzzle of women's desire. If Rousseau's is a compelling account of how the democratic concept of consent is an effect, produced by the "reiterative practice" of gendered sexuality, then aren't women's bodily integrity and political voice *structurally* destabilized within a republican discourse?[36] What remains of the prospects for women's autonomy and for a noncoercive heterosexuality, given the structural imperative of instability? These questions are provoked by a generation of feminist scholars whose sometimes brilliant and sometimes infuriating (and often both) analyses have made sexual identity and desire pressing political concerns; my study complicates those scholarly provocations by taking seriously Rousseau's account of consensual nonconsensuality and thus by proposing that we see political identity and governance as pressing

---

[36] My formulation borrows from Butler, who characterizes performativity as "the reiterative and citational practice by which discourse produces the effects that it names"; see *Bodies That Matter*, 2.

sexual concerns. I resist the will to relevance that makes the import and meaning of Rousseau's work a function of its contemporary applicability, and my aim in concluding is to neither salvage nor savage his political thought. But I do insist that there are creative misuses to be made of his central insights, that consent makes sense only in its material enactments, and that it remains unintelligible when divorced from worldly—institutional, bodily—conditions.

I want to touch briefly on one of these creative misuses, by making explicit my claim concerning the untenability of foundationalist arguments in Rousseau's work. This claim sets itself against not only the settled habits of reading him as a theorist of nature and authenticity but also more recent feminist challenges that see in his gender visions a source, a reason or unreason, for his democratic prescriptions: the putative truth of women's desire, disorder, solicitude, and/or delicacy remains the linchpin of his communal order. This appeal to priority relationships is consistent with Rousseau's location within Enlightenment political philosophy and its abiding concern to reconcile empirical and moral principles. Do experience and observation confirm man's moral and political capacity? Can a rational sociopolitical order be deduced from natural law? Just how enlightened can a body politic be?

Rousseau's responses to these questions notoriously undermine the terms in which they are posed: he dismisses empirical method, rejects rationalism as the hallmark of human progress, and, when asked to consider the implications of natural law, tends to change the subject. Today's readers are no more comfortable with these shaky foundations than were readers in eighteenth-century France, and if at the time the political philosopher Rousseau was often dismissed as a self-indulgent Diogenes, many interpreters today take as their task the resolution of his apparent paradoxes. In the process, they rehearse the move to get beyond (or before or behind) his politics in order to fix its origins and causes: perhaps civil right derives from natural right, or citizenly virtue originates in familial virtue, or political principles emanate from moral truths "engraved upon the heart."

It is awkward, of course, to reassert the very priority claims that Rousseau repeatedly calls into question, but at stake is the coherence of his democratic vision. And to be sure, there is textual support for these efforts: both his rhapsodic appeals to nature and his appropriation of the social contract model leave us with the definite sense that Rousseau's redemptive vision insists upon settled significations of moral causes and effects. The trouble is that no such priority claim holds for very long in his work when it is read as a whole. Nature, bodies, mind, heart: each potential source proves to be thoroughly infused with politics, meaning the social, conceptual, and not infrequently physical struggles over modes and means of governance. So they entail questions of authority and not just power, and they implicate the state and not just subjects.

Rousseau's thoroughly political account of sex, virtue, liberty, and reason suggests that individual identity and agency are not meaningful separate from the structures of government and community which those individuals must legitimize with their consent. Coming to terms with this claim need not resurrect the specter of Rousseau as an incipient totalitarian or, even less, a sneaky or confused polemicist. It requires only that we take seriously and explore thoroughly his most intriguing, irritating, and insistent claim about democratic politics: the freedom it makes possible requires domination. This paradox of intention and capacity conjures up the vexations of both structuralism and its poststructuralist issue. While I do not intend to enter directly into these contemporary debates in what follows, one upshot of my argument, one creative misuse of Rousseau's prescriptions, is that the perceived tension between structure and act—between determining conditions and undetermined choice—is not an epistemological crisis of social theory that arises in the wake of Marx and Freud. It arose as such from efforts to theorize an individualism consistent with new standards of political legitimacy: consent.

Savage Sensibilities

> Not in corrupt things, but in those which are
> well-ordered in accordance with nature, should
> one consider that which is natural.
>
> Aristotle, Politics

> Just as I was about to sink upon a breast which
> seemed about to suffer a man's lips and hands
> for the first time, I perceived that she had a
> malformed nipple. I beat my brow, looked
> harder, and made certain that this nipple did
> not match the other. Then I started wondering
> about the reason for this malformation. I was
> struck by the thought that it resulted from
> some remarkable imperfection of nature,
> and after turning the idea over in my head, I saw
> as clear as daylight that instead of the most
> charming creature I could possibly imagine I
> held in my arms some kind of monster, rejected
> by Nature, men, and love.
>
> Confessions

IMPOSSIBLE BEGINNINGS

The Aristotelian epigraph to Rousseau's *Discourse on Inequality*, quoted here, anticipates that essay's central concern: we can determine what nature authorizes only by looking at how it has been contrived. Alterations, transformations—in short, "ordered things"—give evidence of an ordering principle that precedes or transcends them, and sometimes the evidence is corrupt. This is a teleology troubled by history and by the coincident possibility that human artifice fulfills and perverts natural ends. Aristotle's justification of natural slavery, from which the epigraph is drawn, finds evidence of this perverted fulfillment in the artifice of law: he is troubled by the convention that enables conquerors to enslave the conquered because it authorizes slavery as the outcome of force rather than innate disposition.[1] Here the legitimacy of masters and slaves depends on how these natural categories have been politically construed, and thus whether the body politic is "in accordance with nature" is fundamentally a matter of representation. Similarly, Aristotle points to natural signs of the differences between rulers and ruled in their bodies—the former are marked by an upright carriage, while the latter are stocky and strong—but this turns out, again, to be only an intention: "Nature indeed wishes to make the bodies of free persons and slaves different [as well as their souls] . . . [y]et the opposite often results, some having the bodies of free persons while others have the souls."[2] This is a naturalism that emphasizes the artistry necessary to politics and the artifactual dimension to bodies, and, in the process, repeatedly relocates nature to a point beyond observation: although it remains a regulative ideal for both states and bodies, nature is not reliably evident anywhere.

Aristotle's discussion of slavery reappears in the *Social Contract*. Claiming that he has reversed cause and effect, Rousseau writes that it is wrong to conclude that slaves were born as such when it is the conditions into which they are born that make them slaves: both their bodies and their dispositions are shaped by social and political experience: "Aristotle was right, but he took the cause for the effect; Every man born in slavery is born for slavery; nothing is more certain. In their chains slaves lose everything, even the desire to escape. They love their servitude the way companions of Ulysses loved their degradation. If there are slaves by nature, it is because there have been slaves against nature."[3] Here political relationships neither perfectly nor imperfectly realize natural design. They instead alter that design. Like Aristotle, Rousseau appeals to nature as a regulative ideal rather than as grounds of confirmation; unlike Aristotle, he recognizes nature as a site of political constitutions, or rather, of perpetual reconstituting.

When nature is identified as both cause and effect, the question of what bodies represent intensifies. How to determine the meaning of that natural sign, bodily difference, when this, too, is subject

---

[1] Aristotle, *Politics*, 1.6.
[2] Ibid., 1.5.1254b26–32.
[3] *Social Contract*, 353.

to politics and culture? "An insolent air belongs only to slaves," Rousseau writes in a discussion of Emile's comportment, "independence has nothing affected about it."[4] He illustrates the point with a story taken from Helvétius, where a man's timid glances, uncertain bearing, and hanging head are taken as announcements of his political subjugation. What Rousseau deduces, however, is a refreshing absence of courtier affectation, thus the manly exterior of an honest citizen. Turning Aristotle on his head, Rousseau writes: "I have never seen a man who has pride in his soul display it in his bearing."[5] For Rousseau the body inescapably signals a state of mind, but interpreting the bodily signals returns us, again, to sociopolitical analysis.

And then there's that monstrous nipple. Rousseau writes that initially he saw "the divinity" in the presence of the Venetian courtesan Zulietta: her beauty, generosity, and goodness together made her "Nature's masterpiece and love's." But after reflecting on her abased condition—she's a "slut" (*salope*) who sells herself even to sea captains[6]—he is sure this condition must correspond to some repulsive flaw, which he promptly finds, and just in the nick of time. On display here is a nature that Rousseau readily reads as politically loaded, even as it appears poised to "suffer" contact "for the first time." We do not need to draw on the testimony of Casanova, who neglects to mention any such physical irregularity in his account of Zulietta, to interrogate this well-placed discovery of coincident natural and moral corruption.[7] It is not a question here of finding causes or origins but of preserving a correlation between the natural and the human. The slave's insolence and the courtesan's malformity both preserve that correlation by offering embodied signification of political and moral process. Rather than relocating nature to a realm beyond observation, Rousseau will insist that it bear witness to the well-ordered, or ill-

---

[4] *Emile*, 337.

[5] Ibid.

[6] *Confessions*, 321.

[7] Casanova, *History of My Life*, vol. 1, 145. Casanova reports that he failed to seduce Zulietta: she had sought privacy with him only to plot a dance party jest. Irritated but undaunted, he recounts that he lost control as they cross-dressed for a quadrille and ejaculated on Zulietta's shoes (146). It is unclear why, in making reference to this same incident, Jakob Huizinga characterizes Casanova as having "sampled her favours"; see *The Making of a Saint*, 85.

ordered, politics at work on it. On this account, nature is both humanity's unknowable prehistory and its inconstant, historical subject.

The question, then, of what nature "intends" initiates a perpetual circularity. And while Rousseau's narrative structures, with their confident movement between a *before* and an *after,* seem to deny this circularity, his tendency to undercut or ironize claims about natural law suggests otherwise. The title of the *Discourse on Inequality*, for example, displaces natural law textually by omitting any reference to it or its authorizations despite the prominence of those concerns in the Dijon Academy's original question.[8] Sometimes the displacement is analytic: Rousseau begins the essay by distinguishing between "natural or physical" and "moral or political" inequality, and then he sets the former aside as irrelevant. It is tautological, he insists, to speak of the "source" of natural inequality, and further, efforts to find "essential connections" between political and natural inequality are simply not suited to those "who seek the truth"(131). Most insistently, however, Rousseau displaces the issue of nature's intentions rhetorically, by figuring the question of origins as one of subjection: "Precisely what, then, is at issue in this discourse? To mark, in the progress of things, the moment when, right taking the place of violence, nature was subjected to the law"(132). This proposes an explanation not of where we came from but of how we got here, how politics takes hold of nature and, in the process, transforms its lawlessness into a disciplined and disciplinary order. To suggest that nature can confirm or discomfirm the reasonableness of political practice is paradoxical in the extreme: nature is already subjected to that which it would authorize.

Rousseau's insistence on the paradox of originary stories is not subtle: a state of nature is one which "no longer exists," he writes, "which perhaps never existed, [and] which will probably never exist, and yet about which it is necessary to have accurate notions in order to judge properly about our present state" (123). The problem is clearly not limited to the time elapsed between a then and a now, the difficulty of retrieving what we, nevertheless, can

---

[8] The original question read: "What is the origin of inequality among men and is it authorized by natural law?" *Discourse on Inequality*, 129. Also see editors' discussion of the title, 1300. Subsequent citations will be given in the text.

assume is there. The challenge is to reconstruct the unconstructed, and this in order to judge properly of our current constructions. The dizzying impossibility of the task is matched only
by its urgency in Rousseau's *Discourse*: after a preface, an introductory discussion, and a part one, each of which speculates on the
insurmountability of the difficulties he faces, Rousseau proceeds
in part two to tell that impossible story. Having put aside the facts,
he launches into historical fiction: we were originally independent, strong, and minimally passionate, no more prone to aggression than to fall in love or crave luxuries. Without language or
community there were neither the means nor the impetus to reflect and compare, and in this consisted a natural goodness. With
increasing contact and interdependence, reasoning capacities
awakened, needs multipled, and bodies became enfeebled. Thus
otherwise simple creatures become subject to many miseries with
the advent of property, passions, language—in short, civilization—
and foremost among these is inequality, a misery instituted with
our consent to a government and thus to its laws.

The move toward historical fiction invites a formalist reading,
one that approaches the familiar story of the Fall as a trope: more
significant than its accuracy is how it organizes the dilemma of
reconstructing the unconstructed. The question that frames Rousseau's inquiry into inequality's orgins is, How do we come to authorize it? Conventionality is, from the beginning, what is assumed
and what must be explained, and it is figured as the capacity to
authorize power differences that are undefined and thus unrecog-
nizable in nature. So here, reconstructing the unconstructed
means giving form to an identity and an agency that can produce
a social contract, but that also require a realized contract—a political order—to be at all intelligible: conventionality authorizes the
inequalities without which the capacity for consent is itself unthinkable. (Little wonder why Rousseau cautions that reliable in-
quiries into a "natural" state require "even more philosophy than
is generally supposed" [123]!) But these logical and ontological
impossibilities can be accommodated within a narrative structure
that provides a temporal and causal ordering of the political and
the natural, and the ideal and the material. From *within* this story
one can retrace the developmental-degenerative process and
identify its relatively discrete moments of discovery and decay.
Considered as a whole, however, the narrative begins where it

ends: with Rousseau's insistence on the freedom and the inequality that politics entails. The steps in between, those marking the distance from an unadulterated nature to the unadulterated barbarism on which the *Discourse on Inequality* ends, give form to the relationships of power and difference that conventionality requires to mean anything at all. An inescapable conclusion is that the capacity for political agency obtains in conditions of unequal power, beauty, and/or merit: in embodying these differences, Rousseau's nature bears witness to his politics.

I argue that the *Discourse*'s circular movement from animality to humanity and back again, where "the notions of good and the principles of justice again vanish" (191), is threaded together by a dialectic of control in which consent and coercion emerge concomitantly.[9] There is no one point in Rousseau's tale where the appearance of power ruptures community or self: on the contrary, each step in this savage passage from sentience to consciousness, from isolation to community, is marked by the coincident discovery of difference, pleasure, and power that is framed as an anticipation of domination and submission, which is to say, as an anticipation of the exercise of will. That possibility is fully realized only with the contract, the political moment proper that makes both equality and inequality possible, and in the same gesture: consent. But the political and moral imperative of conventionality, whose institutional form is the rule of law, is iterated in the savage's earliest "discoveries" of species, sexuality, and compulsion: those first identifications, preferences, and attendant loss of control constitute a world whose organizing principle is consensual nonconsensuality.

While in subsequent chapters I consider in detail Rousseau's attempts to redeem that principle's distinctly *republican* potential, here my goal is to sketch how the *Discourse on Inequality* ties an emerging sense of self and world to the imperatives of ruling relationships: in other words, how the capacity to (self-)identify and to act unfolds in a context of domination. In their bodies and minds, Rousseau's savages must substantiate the political impera-

---

[9] Rousseau introduces the metaphor of circularity when the *Discourse* arrives at the despotic stage of political (d)evolution: "Here is the final stage of inequality, and the extreme point that closes the circle and touches the point from which we started" (191).

tive of consent, which is to say, they must substantiate inequality. In an important sense, then, their sequential "discoveries" of love, labor, and economy urgently anticipate the juridical structures of Rousseau's state. In what follows I will retrace these retrospective anticipations of difference and power, beginning where Rousseau begins, with "the first and most simple operations of the human soul," pity and self-love. Indeed, the *Discourse*'s narrative strategy can be understood as a function of these natural "operations" inasmuch as they establish the possibility of representational thinking: they allow us to know politics by allowing us to know—to order, alter, contrive—something we (then) call nature.

PERFECTING PITY

Recall the tale: in the beginning was the savage, a creature of minimal self-awareness unburdened by reason or passion. Like other animals, the savage is an "ingenuous machine," endowed with senses to renew its strength and preserve itself (141).[10] Unlike other animals, the savage is endowed with a faculty of self-perfection, a "distinctive and almost unlimited" faculty that, over time, "develops all the others" (142). Residing "as much in the species as in the individual," a faculty of self-perfection guarantees that the savage's natural condition is a dynamic one: together with the spur of circumstance, perfectibility portends continuous change. From the moment Rousseau imagines his savage, it is already on the way to becoming something else.

Hypothesizing a moment prior to any such change, an exercise Rousseau likens to the "conditional reasoning" of physicists imagining the world's beginnings (133), he identifies two essential characteristics: *amour de soi*, or an "ardent interest in our well-being and self-preservation," and pity, or a "natural repugnance to seeing a sentient being, especially our *semblables* [p]erish and suffer."[11] Both self-love and pity anticipate distinctly human quali-

[10] I use the impersonal pronoun here to underscore the absence of gender in Rousseau's initial presentation of the state of nature.

[11] *Discourse on Inequality*, 126. The term *semblable* is generally translated as "fellow" or "fellow-man" and, occasionally, "equal." I will leave this term in the origi-

ties, and thus the social and cognitive development always ready to take hold of the savage. However paradoxically, they do not necessarily entail the notion of *selfhood*: Rousseau emphasizes that they are present in all living creatures, the simple concomitants of *sensibilité*, necessary to a condition in which the body is the only instrument of survival. *Amour de soi* "moves every animal to be vigilant in its own preservation"; it in no way depends on an awareness of social positional goods that is the linchpin of *amour propre*, or egotism. Pity moves animals to be disturbed by the sights, sounds, and smells of imminent death; it in no way depends upon the tenderness, sentimentality, or reflection that compassion implies.

These impulses—to secure what the body needs and to be repelled by signs of its destruction—first appear in the preface when Rousseau takes up the conundrums of natural law. If such a law exists, he writes, "not only must the will of him who is obliged by it be capable of knowing submission to it, but also, for it to be natural, it must speak directly [*immediatement*] by the voice of nature" (125). And what can be heard prior to all reflection are the compulsions of the sensate body, which he labels self-love and pity. Rousseau observes that this should end an old dispute regarding animals' participation in natural law: "Since [animals] share to some extent in our nature by virtue of the sentient quality [*sensibilité*] with which they are endowed, one will judge that they should also participate in natural right, and that man is subject to some sort of duties toward them. It seems, in effect, that if I am obliged not to do any harm to my *semblable*, it is less because he is a rational being than because he is a sentient [*sensible*] being" (126). Neither rationality nor freedom nor the equality these might imply obligates respect. Rather, it is *sensibilité*—a condition of sensuous awareness shared by all animals—that undergirds natural obligation if it exists, naturally, at all.

But how can a savage "be capable of knowing submission"? Incapable of distinguishing between self and other, must and might, or force and duty, it feels the compulsions of natural law the way it feels hunger, thirst, and exhaustion. Submission is the certain posture of a creature intent on meeting its needs. It becomes un-

---

nal French in order, first, to underscore the connotations of resemblance and, second, to leave open the issue of the "fellow"'s gender.

certain only when positive law subjects nature, mediating the here-tofore immediate compulsions of sentience. As self-love and pity become *relative* sentiments, marking distance and difference be-tween selves, what the body needs and what prompts repulsion at its sufferings are shaped by the play of well- and ill-ordering politics.

The difference becomes clear in contrasting Rousseau's de-scriptions of pity in the state of nature and in human society. He writes that savage pity is impelled by the sensations of a fellow creature's pain. The example he uses is cattle entering a slaughter-house, where the "horrible *spectacle*" of suffering is sufficient to engender a sense of immediate danger. Here the intensity of the spectator's reaction is rooted in its *in*ability to differentiate itself from other beings: "Commiseration will be all the more energetic as the witnessing animal [*l'animal Spectateur*] identifies more inti-mately with the suffering animal [*l'animal souffrant*]. . . . Now it is evident that this identification must have been infinitely closer in the state of nature than in the state of reasoning. Reason is what engenders egocentrism [*amour propre*] and reflection strengthens it. Reason is what turns man in upon himself [and what] separates him from what bothers and afflicts him" (156).

But pity is transformed with the onset of individual conscious-ness. The development of individuality mitigates the sensation of danger by introducing the notion of distance between selves: only then is it possible to say, with the philosopher's keen sense of dis-tinctions, "perish if you will, I am safe and sound" (ibid.). In that situation pity requires the transgression of boundaries, the ability to put oneself in the place of suffering where one is not.

These are the terms in which *Emile* presents pity, where at issue is the child's uncertain awareness of *semblables*:

> To become sensitive and pitying the child must know that there are beings like him who suffer what he has suffered, who feel the pains he has felt, and that there are others whom he ought to conceive of as able to feel them too. In fact, how do we let ourselves be moved by pity if not by transporting ourselves outside of ourselves and identi-fying with the suffering animal by leaving, as it were, our own being to take on its being? We suffer only so much as we judge that it suffers. . . . Thus, no one becomes sensitive until his imagination is animated and begins to transport him out of himself.[12]

---

[12] *Emile*, 222–23.

What the savage experiences as continuous with its own sentience must be imaginatively (re)constructed by the individuated subject. The pedagogical-political strategy in *Emile* is precisely to manage these reconstructions: "To excite and nourish this nascent *sensibilité*... what is there to do other than to offer the young man objects on which the expansive force of his heart can act?"[13] By structuring the identification of *semblables*, these representations also structure self-love that, in a being of reason and reflection, always weighs relative position: "Pity is sweet because, in putting ourselves in the place of the one who suffers, we nevertheless feel the pleasure of not suffering as he does."[14] Pity is a function of bodily identification; for the civilized savage, cognizant of the distance between self and other and attuned to their relative advantages, this entails a complex mediation of imagined pleasures and pains.

In the *Discourse on Inequality*, Rousseau both identifies and performs this complexity. He identifies it in his discussion of theaters[15] as an illustration of pity's process and power: "Every day," he writes, audiences are moved to tears by representations of misery, the actual infliction of which they often witness impassively or even themselves provoke (155). Whether this contradiction is only apparent or whether it derives from the experiential differences of theater and politics is discussed in the *Letter to d'Alembert*; here Rousseau's goal is simply to gesture toward the "everyday" evidence of pity's enduring force and form. The complexity of pity's mediations is performed in a discussion of Mandeville; Rousseau notices "with pleasure" that Mandeville must adopt an uncharacteristically vibrant style in order to depict compassion. In recounting the "pathetic image of an imprisoned man who sees outside a ferocious beast tearing a child from its mother's breast, shattering the frail limbs with its murderous teeth, and ripping with its claws the child's palpitating entrails," Rousseau appreciatively reproduces Mandeville's gruesome imagery in the service of evoking anguish (ibid.). And indeed, Rousseau's reproduction embroiders the original: there is no mention of a mother or her breast in Mandeville, whose scene opens with "a thriving good-

---

[13] Ibid., 223.
[14] Ibid., 221.
[15] The original French is *les spectacles*.

humor'd Child at play, of two or three Years old."[16] While Mandeville's original offers rich descriptions of the "smoking blood" and the "crackling of the bones" at this "horrid banquet," Rousseau's reimagined scene of maternal despair and desire promises an even more excessive pity.[17]

For Rousseau, the complex pleasures of the sensational are inaccessible (and irrelevant) for those in whom sentience alone guarantees right action. "Nature commands every animal, and beasts obey" (141): in political terms, nonreflective animals are ruled by instinct, or the body's mechanistic response to the senses, whereas the ability to *dis*obey belongs to creatures who can live outside themselves in the flux of memory, imagination, and history. Indeed, freedom of a distinctly spiritual proportion, about which the "laws of mechanics explain nothing," is first manifest as resistance to nature: "Man feels the same [natural] impetus, but he knows he is free to acquiesce or resist" (ibid.). Of course, bodily needs always remain the "foundations of society," and no society is conceivable without a foundation in their satisfaction, as Rousseau elsewhere reminds us.[18] What the *sensibilité* of a perfected pity suggests is not that we reject, deny, or transcend bodily compulsions but that we reimagine them. Perfecting pity thus means that what was instinctive becomes the effect of reflection and desire, an ethical pose that hinges on the ability to seem to be other than what one is, and the perfect pity is always transgressive. For a being of (self-)consciousness, social order and mutual security depend upon these imagined identifications that put us in another's body to feel its suffering and our own relief.

But what makes these identifications possible also threatens them: as self-love becomes subject to the play of comparison, choice, and preference, pity confronts the imagined possibility of a zero-sum relation between discrete selves. Sustaining sympathy for those whose suffering and success often appear inversely related to our own is a difficult proposition, and isolation is a perpetual threat where reason iterates the distance between self and other. In this context it appears that perfecting pity must also mean fortifying it against the forces of egocentrism, thereby strik-

---

[16] Mandeville, *The Fable of the Bees,* vol. 1, 255.
[17] Ibid., 255–56.
[18] *Discourse on Arts and Sciences,* 6.

ing a balance between a reason that serves self-interest and a feeling that takes us closer to our *semblables*. This conclusion has been reached by many of Rousseau's interpreters who find support in *Emile*'s analysis of pity, discussed previously. Tracy Strong, for example, identifies pity as the crucial counterweight to *amour propre*: it is the faculty that permits "acknowledgment of other minds, the possibility of which was essential to keep Emile from falling under the domination of *amour propre* [and which] required from Emile an act that is not simply that of bodily observation; it is also an act of thought. . . . It is in the ability to be beside one's body that reflection and true philosophy develop."[19]

But this interpretation ignores the structural and experiential similarities between *amour propre* and pity, both of which entail an awareness of *relative* identities and situations. As David Marshall puts it, "Each is structured by an act of identification through which one transports oneself to someone else's place, a comparison of the self with an other turned *semblable* in which one forgets oneself and imagines the point of view of the other."[20] Rather than drawing a parallel between the innocence of *amour de soi* and a pity that tempers *amour propre*, it is more accurate to say that pity is the vehicle through which egotistical interest and vanity are configured: it is pity that forges the necessary ties between selves and their senses. Indeed, pity *counteracts* self-interest only in the natural state, where its sentient immediacy functions as do laws, *mœurs*, and virtue for the civilized savage: "By moderating, in each individual, the activity of *amour de soi*, [pity] contributes to the mutual preservation of the entire species" (156). But when existence is no longer immediate, when social interaction is necessary to create and sustain an expansive self's "sentiment of existence," pity structures the relationships of comparison and recognition through which pleasure and suffering assume their meanings and thus self-interest assumes its form. The categories that Strong deploys as oppositions—*amour propre* and pity, sensuousness and "true philosophy," body and mind—are on this account better understood in their experiential similarity.

Rousseau's perfecting pity does not suppose an insurmountable tension between reason's self-regard and love of others. On the

---

[19] Strong, *Jean-Jacques Rousseau and the Politics of the Ordinary*, 124.
[20] Marshall, *The Surprising Effects of Sympathy*, 150.

contrary, the two emerge coincidentally by means of a *sensibilité* that joins reflective and sensuous capacities: both represent the self to the other, and the other to the self. That these representations, and the identifications and comparisons they make possible, are the occasion of longing, pain, and desire is of fundamental political importance. Our weakness makes us sociable, Rousseau writes, and we "would owe humanity nothing if we were not men."[21] Such are the assumptions of the *Discourse on Inequality*, which tells the story of increasing sociability as a story of multiplying weaknesses and evolving sexuality. It is the story of an *éducation sensible* where males and females secure moral and social identities as men and women through the (re)organization of their "natural" pleasures and pains: their "sense of self" is constituted by the new needs and desires of an interactive existence. What moral inclinations and sociopolitical attachments ensue—what *political* possibilities emerge—depends largely on how these sexual-political personae are established, which is to say, how their identities incorporate and reflect the inequalities that politics entails, or again, how their "natures are subjected to the law."

I began this discussion of the *Discourse on Inequality* by suggesting, paradoxically, that it must begin where it ends, with the recognition of inequality. One crucial implication is that the social contract's creation of rulers and ruled is a form for perfecting the relationships of difference, dominance, and (inter)dependence that were in some sense already there. I then introduced the mechanisms by means of which these relationships are possible, *amour propre* and pity: by (re)structuring bodily pleasures and pains as socially mediated desires and needs, these modes of identity and distinction structure the civilization process. In the following section I turn to a more detailed look at that civilization process with two goals in view: first, to reconstruct a transforming *sensibilité* that experiences the world as a place of rulers and ruled, and second, to reconstruct a transforming world whose institutions enable and constrain this distinctly human *sensibilité*. In this way I flesh out Rousseau's strategy to inscribe the imperative of conventionality onto the savage and its condition. As Rousseau tells it, submission and domination are the natural concomitants

---

[21] *Emile*, 221. Subsequent citations to *Emile* will be given in the main text.

of human *perfectibilité*, inasmuch as an awareness of will, world, and self entails the recognition, which is the experience, of coercion and consent.

(RE)CONSTITUTING NATURE

Back to that impossible beginning: What is the life of an animal limited to "pure sensations" (164)? Rousseau's brief description suggests a self-contained equilibrium: "The products of the earth furnished him with all the necessary assistance [*secours*]; instinct led him to make use of them. Hunger and other appetites making him experience by turns various manners of existing, there was one appetite that invited him to perpetuate his species; and this blind inclination, devoid of any sentiment of the heart, produced only a purely animal act. This need satisfied, the two sexes no longer recognized each other, and the child no longer meant anything to his mother as soon as he could do without her" (ibid.).

Appetites prompt all "manners of existing," which are enacted in turn and without consequence. Eating, coupling, giving birth, growing up: each is experienced as immediate, none generates its own impulsions. To the extent these "manners of existing" involve others they remain objects, incapable of provoking a lasting impression.

The precise moment of change, that first entry into history, is, predictably, abrupt: "But difficulties [*peines*] soon arise" (165). Tall trees, fierce animals, and competition for limited food "obligated him to apply himself to bodily exercise" (ibid.). The first alteration of the natural condition is thus physical, and it consists in a stronger, fleeter, more agile body. Only then, as their bodies change, do these vagabond gymnasts experience a change of mind: a "mechanical prudence" (*prudence machinale*) emerges from "repeated usage [*application réiterée*] of various beings in relation to himself, and of some beings in relation to others" (ibid.). Swift and slow, strong and weak, large and small become useful bodily comparisons as the savage discovers the diverse ways in which instincts can be satisfied. What results is akin to a species awareness, a differentiation between those animals who exhibit a mechanical prudence and those who do not: "The conformities that time could make him perceive among them [*ses semblables*], his female, and himself made him judge those he did not perceive; . . . he concluded that their way of thinking and feeling was in complete conformity with his own"(166). These first differentiations (re)constitute the world as a place of intentional engagements: "[The savage] found himself able to distinguish the rare occasions when common interest should make him count on the assistance of his *semblables* and those even rarer occasions when competition should make him distrust them" (ibid.). For the mechanically prudent savage, the social frames of cooperation and competition are in place, but they do not yet signify moral positions: the impetus to act remains a simple, animalistic *amour de soi*, the immediate imperatives of a "present and perceptible interest."

A similar portrait of reflective sentience appears in *Emile*'s discussion of childhood development: "Since man's first natural movements are, therefore, to measure himself against everything that surrounds him and to experience in each object he perceives all the qualities which can be sensed and relate to him, his first study is a sort of experimental physics relative to his own preservation, from which he is diverted by speculative studies before he has recognized his place on earth" (125). Rousseau makes these observations in the course of outlining a strategy to conceal human volition and design in the child's first extended worldly encounters. He advises that the tutor instead arrange "exercises of the body" in which the child learns through the physical expedients of weakness, limitation, and immediate need. When it climbs and falls, or runs and tires, the child both learns the dimensions of its world and strengthens and extends the instrument of its grasp upon that world: "These constant exercises, left in this way to the direction of nature alone, in strengthening the body not only do not stultify the mind but, on the contrary, form the only kind of reason of which the first age is susceptible and which is the most necessary to any age whatsoever. They teach us to know well the use of our strength, the relations of our bodies to surrounding bodies, and the use of the natural instruments which are within our reach and are suitable to our organs" (124).

Beyond raising an athletic child, the goal is to manage the proper order in which it makes sense of its "place on earth"—first through sensations and things, then through sentiments and persons: "Since everything which enters into human understanding comes there through the senses, man's first reason is a reason of the senses; this sensual reason serves as the basis of intellectual reason. Our first masters of philosophy are our feet, our hands, our eyes" (125). The relationship between body and mind sketched here suggests a temporal and perhaps causal priority. Our body "reasons" before our mind, and we make sense out of our sensibilities. But repeatedly, and with explicit appeal to the situation of a savage, Rousseau iterates the mutual (re)constitution of the two: "The more his body is exercised, the more his mind is enlightened; his strength and his reason grow together, and one is extended by the other" (118). And when his "body and his mind are exercised together," reason remains yoked to physical imperatives—what "nature" dictates—rather than responding to the opinions and power of others. Rousseau does not ignore the social dimensions of these natural prods—he approvingly cites the example of young Spartans taught how to steal their supper—but more significant than their (re)constituted form is their end: "You will never get to the point of producing wise men if you do not in the first place produce rascals" (119).

And those Spartan rascals were conquerors, captivated by their state and enslaved to their duties, a condition not unlike the stated ends of Rousseau's *éducation sensible*: "Let him always believe he is the master, and let it always be you who are. There is no subjection so perfect as that which keeps the appearance of freedom. Thus the will itself is made captive"(120). Rousseau is emphatic that no overt displays of will be made or recognized; but from the child's first moments of awareness and understanding, the dilemma of rule is already in play. Here the child's will is kept "captive" by the limitations and obstacles of a disinterested nature that is, in reality, wholly mediated by the tutor. This keeps the appearance of freedom because the only perceptible impediments are natural ones, and nature cannot be conceived as opposition: it is immediate, given. Thus the pride that mastery produces does not challenge the nonreferential quality of *amour de soi*: so long as satisfaction is limited to "immediate and palpable interest[s]," the child will avoid the invidious pleasures of comparison. The situation is identical for the mechanically prudent savage, whose "first glance [d]irected upon himself" produced "the first stirring of pride," but initially only by virtue of being in the "first rank" of species (*Dis-*

course on Inequality, 166). The richer possibilities of vanity and egotism await an awareness of individuality.

That claim is staked in the course of a "first revolution" that brings about "the habit of living together" (168). Now "husbands and wives"—no longer mere *mâles* and *femelles*—grow accustomed to different activities ("the first differences in the manner of living of the two sexes was established"), and with this division of labor, both "lose something of their ferocity and vigor" (ibid.). The opportunity for *intraspecies* comparison comes only within the newly interactive, interdependent, and sexually differentiated community: "Each one began to look at the others and to want to be looked at himself, and public esteem had value; the one who sang or danced the best, the handsomest, the strongest, the most adroit or the most eloquent became the most highly regarded. And this was the first step toward inequality and, at the same time, toward vice" (169). Recall how the first contemplations of mechanical prudence confirmed sameness: "Their [*semblables*'s and *femelle*'s] way of thinking and feeling was in complete conformity with his own." By contrast, the first contemplations of love create opposition: frequent contact and prolonged exposure engender an economy of esteem organized by erotic regard. Self-love now demands individual recognition, which, on Rousseau's telling, is pursued through balletic and vocal performance. Now the pertinent bodily comparisons are beauty and grace.

The result is a gender identity, a sense of self secured through heterosexual practices. By this I mean, first, that identity is tied to the bodily representation of sexual difference: displays of feminine and masculine forms, of strength and grace, exhibit difference and elicit preference, and in so doing give shape to *amour propre*. This means, second, that identity is tied to the social-sexual roles through which the community is organized: an expansive sentiment of existence takes shape as savages take up the practices of either hunters or "hutwives."[22] On both counts—as a function of bodily performance and of a division of labor—gender secures individuality; indeed, the former provides the conditions of intelligibility for the latter.

[22] The term is Susan Okin's. See her extended discussion of Rousseau in *Women in Western Political Thought*, chaps. 5–8.

Gender also promotes production: "In this new state, with a simple and solitary life, very limited needs and the implements they had invented to provide for them, since men enjoyed great leisure, they used it to procure many kinds of commodities unknown to their fathers" (168). Now endowed with "softer" bodies, the civilizing savages recognize multiple sources of pleasure: adorning their clothes with thorns and their bodies with paint, embellishing their bows, and carving the occasional "crude musical instrument" (ibid.). The development of industries, more extensive divisions of labor, and the exchange of commodities all follow rapidly on the experiences of love, lassitude, and cohabitation. The result is a proliferation of enacted and expressed preferences that again (re)constitute self-interest, now lodged within complex social interactions that determine relative holdings of goods and merit. In matters of both love and economy, the individual's satisfaction turns on others' interests: "He must therefore incessantly seek to interest them in his fate, and to make them find their own profit, in fact or in appearance, in working for his" (175). This means also that the newly indeterminate world of multiple possibilities and positions affects the structuring of *self*-presentation: "It was necessary, for his advantage, to show himself to be something other than what he in fact was" (174).

And what, "in fact," is he? Rousseau's fiction gives form to his fact: the possibilities of *being* and *seeming to be* emerge coincidentally, and self-love rests precariously on the capacity for (mis)representation. Of course, to some degree this follows naturally as a consequence of any system of signification: what is reflection and what is distortion are always functions of the meanings *made*, rather than something particular to the referent—here, what one is "in fact." But within Rousseau's originary tale, the desire and deliberation that make factual *and* fictional self-positioning possible are inseparable from the social practices in which they are embedded; thus love and labor, family and economy, also produce authentic and false identities. Here the system of signification—that which makes representation possible—is simultaneously a structure of social practices and of identity. How Rousseau's savages come to live in the world, as farmers and producers, as men and women, as rulers and ruled, constitutes the framework of authentic and fanciful "senses of self."

This is one reason that I am reluctant to use psychoanalytic models to read Rousseau's politics. To be sure, my claims that he inexorably ties identity to (mis)representation and gender to individuality are prominent within that tradition, as well as in psychoanalytically inspired readings of Rousseau. But his anthropological account begins and ends with social roles and practices, and in so doing it makes gender and other opportunities for self-(mis)representation inseparable from the effects of worldly and material structures. These links between sexuality, sexual difference, and social forms, and their collective vulnerability to historical variation, are often obscured by the timelessness of theories of mind.

Consider, for example, Jean Starobinski's seminal analysis, which shows a keen attention to Rousseau's always constructed state of nature and to the historical, literary, and logical challenges of differentiating his "natural" from his "human." But in concluding from this that every portrait of the savage is simultaneously a portrait of man, Starobinski reads self-awareness, intentionality, and masculinity—the social accoutrements of *man*—back into Rousseau's depiction of an original, historical simplicity.[23] He thus deduces that Rousseau's complex and contradictory naturalism is driven by his desire for transparency, and nature is the placeholder for a moment, an imagined moment, when everything *is* always what it appears to be: "That appearance and reality are two different things and that a 'veil' covers our true feelings—this is the initial scandal that Rousseau encounters, this is the unacceptable datum for which he will seek the explanation and cause, this is the misfortune from which he longs for deliverance."[24]

Implicit in this insistence upon self-exposure is the assumption that there is someone there to witness it. "Lifting the veil" is a meaningful gesture only if there is someone there for whom authenticity can be displayed and who, further, takes some interest in it. But there is no audience in the state of nature: "Each particular man regards himself as the only spectator who observes him, as the only being in the universe that takes an interest in him" (219). Rousseau's savage is incapable of acknowledging an other's self-exposure. Further, it has nothing *to* expose, a situation that

---

[23] See "Rousseau and Buffon" in Starobinski, *Transparency and Obstruction*, 328.
[24] Ibid., 5.

renders it unsuited to the ideal of self-communion that Starobinski reads in Rousseau. Thus, while he depicts isolation in the language of engagement—the self who is spectator to itself—Rousseau's earliest vision of nature is defined by the absence of any such possibility. Sometimes when *being* and *appearing* are indistinguishable, the result is not a confident communication where "mind meet[s] mind in perfect harmony," as Starobinski suggests, but an oblivious silence.[25] For natural man to be *authenticated*—which is to say, for the possibility of self-revelation—boundaries must be erected that can then be trespassed.

None of this is news to Starobinski, who reads in Rousseau's appeal to nature a tortured refusal to grasp the existential reality of intersubjectivity. On his interpretation Rousseau rejects the risk, doubt, and ultimately, the difference entailed by intersubjectivity, instead retreating into nostalgic and then fantastical versions of self-sufficiency, on the one hand, and utopian conjurings of a transparent political community, on the other. Thus lurching between solipsism and a narcissistic collectivism (community as reflection of self), Starobinski's Rousseau offers a fundamentally regressive, if brilliantly articulated and always provocative, condemnation of the inauthencities of modern life. Furthermore, the freedom that Rousseau champions and bemoans is existential: radical in its depth, precarious in its success, and self-referential to the core. By holding out, impossibly, for transparency, Starobinski's Rousseau wants self-determination without the mediations that are its necessary conditions.[26]

Whether or not this is so (and perhaps the sheer power of Starobinski's interpretation minimizes the salience of that question), its emphasis on transparency obscures the mediation strategies Rousseau *does* recognize, the manner in which freedom *is* grounded. His triumphs and defeats of the will are never only imaginary and psychological events: they are always embodied affairs whose logic and process are politically organized. These material and institutional dimensions of identity are less readily visible in interpretations that emphasize the radical possibilities and insecurities of an existential freedom. For all its nuance, Staro-

---

[25] Ibid., 12.
[26] Asher Horowitz makes similar observations about Starobinski's interpretation of Rousseau; see *Rousseau, Nature, and History*, 25–26, 30.

binski's interpretation encourages us to imagine a disembodied protagonist who has little to offer us politically, and thus it unavoidably reiterates the logic of a long tradition of humanism that ties "authenticity" to inner and natural states, over and against material opportunities and conditions. But this misses much of the action in Rousseau's account, as well as its radical possibilities: the inner dramas of his isolated subjects overwhelm the ordering and ordered world of historical agents.

To understand *that* world is to move beyond the systemic necessitations of consciousness: it is to consider that authentic identity is less about sustaining, or creating, an undivided unity with the self than it is about sustaining, or creating, the social, erotic, and productive practices through which that self can be identified *as* authentic. It might appear in the *Discourse on Inequality* that these authenticating practices are found at the stage described by Rousseau as a "golden mean [*un juste milieu*] between the indolence of the primitive state and the petulant activity of our *amour propre*" (171). At this point (inter)action is motivated by "reciprocal affection and freedom," and the material world has not yet been reconstituted as property; thus inequality of *power* is minimally experienced, expressed, or, indeed, comprehensible.

But this stage, like every stage in Rousseau's recursive tale, is not static, and he imagines it simultaneously with its overdetermined transformation: its displays of sexual difference and preference were "the first step toward inequality and, at the same time, toward vice"; its creation of new commodities was "the first source of the evils they prepared for their descendents." Furthermore, vulnerability to offense increases as self-love and the senses extend, and in this "nascent society" only the "terror of revenge" restrains potential aggression (170). Unless and until criminality is conceived—which is to say, physical trespass is (re)configured as legal trespass—the conditions necessary to authenticity are lacking. In the end, gendered bodies and gendered labor are insufficient: a body of law is required to extend the citizens' *sensibilité* over the entire community.

STATE POWER AND SERVILE DESIRE

Identifying common cause in the establishment of an overarching authority follows "naturally" for every individual who must "interest [others] in his fate and [m]ake them find their own profit, in fact or in appearance, in working for his" (175). A juridical order gives form to these personal, and general, imperatives by fixing the terms of mutually profitable engagement and by generating, through threat of sanction, an interest in the fate of others. And because this juridical (re)constitution of interest identifies the individual as a member of a political community, the publicity of the latter is inseparable from the former's agency: to weigh, judge, and choose as a rational being is to recognize one's place and purpose within a legal order. Thus "authentic" individuality is conceivable only as a function of one's standing within a body politic that is "the people."

The mutual constitution of polity and person is thematic in the *Social Contract* and the *Discourse on Political Economy*, both of which use the imagery of bodily metamorphosis to describe the instituting of law.[27] This theme also surfaces, albeit in a very different language, in the brief history of government found in the *Discourse on Inequality*, where Rousseau insists that state authority could never have originated in arbitrary power. The reason for this, he argues, is that arbitrary power could never account for political right, which, as both an idea and an act, depends on a shared capacity and circumstance to recognize or create inequality (179–83). In other words, political power denotes a relationship of obligation; whether that relationship is between princes and subjects or between republican citizens, it entails a shared awareness of the twofold imperatives to rule and obey. Arbitrary power, by contrast, characterizes encounters between selfless savages. Rousseau concludes that the actual, historical instances of arbitrary rule must be derivative forms of an institution—government—whose emergence can only be understood in terms of the concurrent appearance of "a people." There is no politics absent a people, and there is no people absent conventionality.[28]

It would seem that the body of law that proved necessary "in the end" is where Rousseau's story must also begin. And indeed, the ordering, enforcing power of government is a prerequisite to the expanding and complexifying *sensibilité*—the continually (re)-constituted desires and interests—that move this plot along. Consider the gender differentiation through which erotic and familial

---

[27] See *Social Contract*, 362–64 and *Political Economy*, 244–45.

[28] This parallels to some extent Locke's two-step contract: the first agreement (unanimous and unrenounceable) establishes civil or political society, and the second (majoritarian and renounceable) establishes the form of government. See Locke, *Second Treatise of Government*, 374–77, §95–99.

regard is sustained. While in Rousseau's narrative, sexual identity and preference predate any formal act of conventionality, the nature of those choices is intelligible only within the sociopolitical context of the heterosexual family: "Instead of saying that civil society is derived from paternal power, it should be said on the contrary that it is from civil society that this power draws its principle force. An individual was not recognized as the father of many until they remained assembled around him. The goods of the father, of which he is truly the master, are the bonds which keep his children dependent on hi[m]" (182). *Mâles* and *femelles* become men and women as they enter into social-sexual relationships whose shape and direction depend upon the legal guarantors of paternity and inheritance.[29] The security of familial membership and finance thus frames erotic choice: positive law provides the structures that provoke lasting impressions—that is, sexual and parental recognition.[30]

Clearly, one cannot sustain the conclusion of Rousseau's narrative linearity, that the institution of government is a response to changing bodily and psychic needs: the denominative and regulative power of law shapes the perception of those needs and the experience of their satisfaction. Like love, the family, and economic exchange (and, indeed, recapitulating those relations), the state realizes "authentic" individuality by structuring the social practices of desire and reflection. Thus what appears in the *Discourse on Inequality* as a break from what preceded it is better understood as yet another in a series of continuous reconfigurations.

[29] Much more can (and will) be said on this topic; paternity and the familial form are central themes in chapter three. At this point my goal is simply to point to, first, the centrality of political practices and institutions to Rousseau's (re)constituted originary state, and, second, the inseparability of political imperatives and embodied practices. A similar paradox of "beginning where one ends" could be sketched with respect to property, which Rousseau insists is "only conventional and of human institution": in the *Discourse on Inequality* it features as both cause and effect of political organization.

[30] Rousseau raises the possibility that desires are shaped by law in a passage from the *Discourse on Inequality* that addresses the difference between physical and moral love: "It must first be agreed that the more violent the passions, the more necessary are laws to contain them; but beyond the disorders and the crimes that they cause daily among us, which are enough to show the insufficiency of the laws in this regard, it would still be good to examine if the disorders weren't born with the laws themselves" (157).

The political recognition of "ruler" and "ruled," the sensuously reflective recognition of "desired" and "despised," and the mechanically prudent recognition of "strong" and "weak": these are all iterations of the relationships of difference and power through which *amour de soi* becomes *amour propre*. Together they reveal how dominant and submissive practices are written into Rousseau's story of political will and, in the process, are simultaneously naturalized and civilized. These practices structure our transforming *sensibilité* even as they constitute the structure of a newly politicized world that legitimizes them through the mechanism of collective consent. The imperatives of ruling and being ruled were always what perfected pity and (re)constituted self-love. They are, from the beginning, how we envision our interests and desires.

We would thus anticipate that pity and self-love, and the bodily sensibility to which they give form, remain central to the experience of Rousseauian citizenship. And this is consistent with his rhetorical moves toward the end of the *Discourse on Inequality*, where a final depiction of political will presents us with citizens "consent[ing] to wear chains in order to be able to give them in turn to others" (188). Rousseau invites the reader to imagine how oppressions would multiply "as a consequence of the very precautions taken against [them]" and how "bizarre rules in a code of honor" would develop such that citizenly duty became warped and fatal: "There would come a time when one would hear [citizens] say to their country's oppressor: '*If you order me to plunge my sword into my brother's breast or my father's throat, and into my pregnant wife's entrails, I will do so even though my right hand is unwilling*'" (190). Political devotion becomes coincident with despotic terror, through the voice and on the body of a zealously submissive citizen. And this depiction of abject republicanism borrows its script from Lucan: the passage is from book 1 of *Pharsalia* (or *Civil War*), and the voice is Laelius's, responding to Caesar's plea to march on Rome and, in the process, persuading the other soldiers to imitate him.[31] Here the political and literary functions of pity converge, in the form of multiple reiterations of sadistic and masochistic excess: Rousseau is reenacting an epic reenactment of a republic's internecine ruin, as a means of warning his readers to

[31] See Roger Masters's note 56 in Rousseau, *The First and Second Discourses*, 242. See also Lucan, *Lucan's Civil War.*

beware the seductions of being ruled. This is to say that he exhorts them to beware the seductions of violence, by exploiting a passage whose entire rhetorical thrust—its pitiability—hinges on just these seductions. And while the pathos induced in Lucan's readers might have transported them back, away from the debauched present of Nero's regime and toward a moment prior to their republic's decay, Rousseau speaks to his monarchical audience in the voice of depravation in order to incite desire for a republican future. In both cases, political identification moves through a language of passion whose violent and *sensible* excesses initiate a dynamic of pity. In this sense Rousseau's exhortation performs what it decries, by engendering a pathos for the criminal and the fantastic: "there would come a time" when citizens take the imitation for the original, or the theatrical for the real, and that time is now.

The narrative descriptions with which Rousseau ends this section of the *Discourse* are equally ferocious, building from images of farmers in arms to a total social chaos from which the tyrant's body emerges: "It is from the bosom of this disorder and these revolutions that despotism, by degrees raising its hideous head and devouring all it had seen to be good and healthy in all parts of the State, would finally succeed in trampling underfoot the laws and the people, and in establishing itself upon the ruins of the Republic. The times that would precede this last change would be times of troubles and calamities, but in the end everything would be engulfed by the monster, and peoples would no longer have chiefs or laws but only tyrants" (190–91).

The bloody *spectacle* Rousseau paints is enough to arouse even the most complacent reader; indeed, it borrows language from the earlier defense of pity—from both the image of Mandeville's mangled and eviscerated child and the image of horses repulsed by the prospect of "trampling a living body"(154). Rousseau appeals to the readers' *sensibilité* to establish the fraudulence of the contract: if we can feel what is right, we will shun the pleasures of civic bacchanalia and enchaining others. But what is here despotic is elsewhere divine: "The means to place men in subjection in order to make them free" and "to use the goods, the manual labor, even the very life of all its members in the service of the state without forcing them and without consulting them," Rousseau writes in *Discourse on Political Economy*, is an "inconceivable art" whereby the human imitates the divine.[32] In a context where the contract's inevitable (so the *Discourse on Inequality* warns) degeneration is not at issue, Rousseau finds only a "marvel" (*prodige*) and a "salutary tool" (*organe*) that renders subjection and liberty inseparable one from the other.[33]

The difference between this rapturous embrace of paradox and the *Discourse on Inequality*'s dire warning of terror is, of course, the latter's focus on potential abuse, most notably in situations of extreme wealth and poverty. In that context what seduces citizens are neither appeals to godlike acts of self-creation nor wrenching testimonies of self-dividing loyalties, but anxious references to vulnerability and sober petitions for justice. Here is Rousseau limning the sentiments of political prudence in *Discourse on Inequality*:

> Let us unite . . . [t]o protect the weak from oppression, restrain the ambitious, and secure for everyone the possession of what belongs to him. Let us institute regulations of justice and peace to which all are obliged to conform, which make an exception of no one, and which compensate in some way for the caprices of fortune by equally subjecting the powerful and the weak to mutual duties. In a word, instead of turning our forces against ourselves, let us gather them into one supreme power which governs us according to wise laws, protects and defends all the members of the association, repulses common enemies, and maintains us in an eternal concord. (177)

At first glance this formal recognition of governmental power does suggest a benign self-rule, a reasoned bid for juridical compensation and reciprocal self-restraint. But the Kantian logic cannot anesthetize the Hobbesian practice: the desire for justice has as its object an authority whose right to command is absolute and whose domination organizes the world. Here the morally redemptive aspect of politics—its *willful* reconstitution of might—coincides with its disciplinary aspect: because autonomy is embedded in the political structures and worldly routines of governance, it is attained through the *practices*, never only the *idea*, of submission. Thus the reasoned decision to enter into a social contract is also a sensible desire to do so, and the experience of submission it entails also provides the experience of fulfillment. In this sense

[32] *Political Economy*, 248.
[33] Ibid.

the *Discourse on Inequality*'s blindly obedient subject ready to dis-
embowel his kin is only a derivative form of the republican in
whom the state must always provoke a servile desire, and the heady
excesses of despotism are continuous with the patriotic fervor of
republicanism: both suggest a desire for citizenship that binds individual pleasure to the transports of a shared pain. Not a depravity, a deformation, or an excess, servile desire is rather the apex
of the developmental trajectory of pity and self-love through
which we are made moral, and men.

Rousseau's conception of pity and its relationship to erotic desire has been definitively treated by Derrida, who claims that the
relationship is one of perverse complementarity: on the one hand,
amorous passion dilutes the social bonds by narrowing attachment
and attention to a single person; but on the other hand, because
it incites jealousy and other immoderate desires, erotic regard
consistently veers toward the brutality that arouses pity.[34] Derrida
concludes that *moral* as opposed to physical love—what Rousseau
describes as "determin[ing] the desire and fix[ing] it exclusively
on one single object" (157–58)—is a perversion of *natural* pity,
which then (re)appears as supplemental: if not for pity's tempering, dissipating effects, the furies of moral love (both the passionate and female varieties) would threaten humanity, life, and
virility:

> Is it by chance that, like many another supplement, the natural and
> prereflexive sentiment of pity, which "contributes to the preservation
> of the whole species," protects us from, among other deadly menaces,
> love? Is it by chance that pity protects man (*homo*) from his destruction
> through the fury of love, to the extent that it protects man (*vir*) from
> his destruction through the fury of women? . . . [P]ity protects the
> humanity of men and the life of the living to the extent that it saves
> . . . [t]he virility of man and the masculinity of the male.[35]

While Derrida identifies the "virility of man" and the "masculinity
of the male" as products of socialization, he simultaneously reads
in Rousseau a transhistorical, even metaphysical, account of feminine and masculine *desire*. Derrida's assertion of a similarity between Rousseau's account of sexual struggle and Hegel's master-

[34] Derrida, *Of Grammatology*, 171–92.
[35] Ibid., 175.

slave dialectic emphasizes that it is a historical, and not biological, phenomenon: "it is a war of consciousness and desires, not of needs or natural desires," he insists.[36] But this war is, inexplicably, heterosexually organized; it is the possession of women, Derrida observes, that motivates and sustains the move into and through history: " 'Moral love,' not having any biological foundation, is born of the power of the imagination. All the depravity of culture, as the movement of difference and preference, is therefore related to the possession of women. One must know who will have the women but also what the women will have. And what price will be paid within that calculation of forces."[37] Derrida's move into a gendered history is abrupt, and in a familiar manner it functions to (re)constitute what preceded it: the natural and immediate desires of physical love, that which culture and society must grasp through "the movement of difference and preference," are heterosexual.

There are by now, I hope, several self-evident reasons for resisting this verdict, but for present purposes let's notice how it limits an analysis of the political possibilities of pity and erotic desire. In particular, Derrida's renaturalization of heterosexual desire relies upon oppositions which I have suggested are themselves a function of Rousseau's politics.[38] Power and submission, masculinity and femininity, sensuous superfluity and reasoned control: moral and political capacities emerge within these binaries and remain dependent on their *simultaneous* negotiation. Thus, rather than seeing our "humanity" endangered by sexual excess, we need to consider how the two are inextricably intertwined: in all their domineering, monstrous immoderation, Rousseau's women make his natural virility possible. On this interpretation it is the orchestration, not the repression, of the "deadly menaces" of enslaving passions that sustains reasonable, compassionate men. And pity, neither compensatory nor supplemental (in the Derridean sense), organizes and generalizes this understanding of submission and pleasure. It is the touchstone of a servile desire,

[36] Ibid., 180. He writes: "Setting not only men against women, but also men against men, this war is historic; It is not a natural or biological phenomenon."

[37] Ibid., 181.

[38] For feminist engagements with Derridean method, see "Choreographies: An Interview with Jacques Derrida"; and "Women in the Beehive: A Seminar with Jacques Derrida."

a *sensibilité* that ties fulfillment and self-love to the imagined brutalities of another's rule.

Of course, Derrida is right to notice deeply Hegelian themes in all this. Both the confrontations that nurture self-consciousness and the historicization of those encounters anticipate Hegel in important respects. But, as I have tried to underscore in this chapter, Rousseau's phenomenology moves through a protagonist who, unlike Hegel's *Geist*, knows itself and its world only as an embodied, sensuous creature. On a quick glance the contrast might not seem compelling: after all, the outcome of the Hegelian conflict of consciousness depends on the two combatants' respective reaction to the prospect of death, and the initial loser ultimately "wins" only insofar as his transformation of the world through (forced) labor and his persistent awareness of mortality reveal his will to him.[39] But Rousseau's version of how will and world are learned relies on the particular, bodily interactions of what, following Asher Horowitz, we might call "biological men."[40] These are beings moved less by the wonders of invention or "the prospect of hanging"[41] than by the need to sustain a sentiment of existence that turns on social and sexual engagements. What for Hegel is *actualization* (the making concrete of an always present Idea) is for Rousseau *reconstitution* (a dynamic transformation of historical *and* sensuous proportions). In this sense the Hegelian dialectic of (self-)consciousness finds a more politically robust because embodied and erotic, and a more historically nuanced because contingent, progenitor in Rousseau's account of conventionality and sexual-social becoming.

[39] See "Independence and Dependence of Self-consciousness: Lordship and Bondage," in Hegel, *Phenomenology of Spirit*, 111–19.

[40] See Horowitz, *Rousseau, Nature, and History*, especially chap. 3, "Rousseau's Historical Anthropology." On page 65 Horowitz describes Rousseau's concept of free agency as "primarily a biological category rather than an ontological one predicated of an independent substance." Horowitz's very interesting point is that Rousseau provides a "historicity of human nature" (32) in which social—sensuous and economic—interaction provides the evolutionary context for human capacity. In making the argument Horowitz draws several contrasts between Hegel and Rousseau; see, for example, 65 and 72. He does not address or explore the possibility of gendered "becoming" in Rousseau's account.

[41] The phrase is Samuel Johnson's, quoted by Charles Taylor in his discussion of the *Phenomenology*; see Taylor, *Hegel*, 155.

Similarly with Rousseau's insistence on the institutional context of moral agency, which in many ways anticipates Hegel's *Sittlichkeit*. For both thinkers judgment occurs within a social matrix that structures comparisons, obligations, and choices: the ordering and ordered interactions of family, civil society, and state give substance to ethical life and decision making. But whereas Hegel's tripartite arrangement of nested identities and relations—for example, the husband within the producer within the citizen— suggests a discrete positioning of freedoms, needs, and affections, Rousseau's republicanism requires its citizens to perpetually reenact conventionality's twofold imperatives of submission and domination.

The same issue surfaces in Hegel's critique of the general will. Rousseau, he observes, has failed to differentiate between the consistently subjective and particular dimension of will, on the one hand, and the objective and universal dimension of reason, on the other; Rousseau thus falsely assumes that the contract can sustain an identity between personal and political will.[42] The result is a sovereign who exhibits all the excesses of an individuality that takes itself to be everything. In the *Philosophy of Right,* Hegel points to the Terror as the logical and tragic consequence of this failure to distinguish between the potential capriciousness of individuality and the reasoned restraint of an always differentiated collective.[43] In light of our current considerations, however, it is not clear that the central issue dividing Hegel and Rousseau is the adequacy of contractarian thinking and practice; rather, what seems more salient is that Rousseau does not rely upon accretive, historical, and ideological "moments" to contain the problem of domination. Rousseau's approach thus exposes what Hegel's attempts to adorn with metaphysical mysteries: whatever else one might say about its ability to allay the absolutism of a distinctly *political* power, the differentiated citizenry portrayed in the *Philosophy of Right* daily reenacts domination and unfreedom across its multiple, public and private, sites.[44]

[42] See Hegel, *Philosophy of Right*, 33, 156–57.

[43] Ibid., 157. "The result is that [Rousseau] reduces the union of individuals in the state to a contract and therefore to something based on their arbitrary wills, their opinion, and their capriciously given express consent."

[44] This point is not new and is not necessarily Marxian; Heidi Ravven, Seyla Benhabib and others have analyzed the unfreedoms of gender in Hegel's

The paradox of a love that is inseparable from violence, of confrontations that set the stage for communions, and of consent that is consonant with coercion weaves through Rousseau's stories of human and sexual becoming. There is no single recognition, frozen in institutional form, that can overcome what is subject to dynamic, quotidian renewal and irruption. To be sure, the *Social Contract* does offer an instantaneous rendition of what the *Discourse on Inequality* parses over a millennia of unretrievable anthropology, namely, the mutual constitution of moral freedom and political constraint.[45] But because, as I have suggested, that mutual constitution turns on a transforming *sensibilité* that coordinates bodily pleasures and pains, it must be (re)constituted anew in the lived practices—social and material—of every citizen.

"To suffer is the first thing he ought to learn . . ."

In the following chapters I explore how this perpetual (re)constitution occurs in the lives of particular individuals, and how gendered sexuality figures centrally in that process. In so doing I turn to several stories of developmental-degenerative transformation, all of which make multiple and contradictory appeals to nature. The analysis offered in this chapter indicates that these appeals must be approached with great care, not in the interest of uncovering their incoherence but to work out their role in sustaining Rousseau's republicanism. Here I part ways with the many political interpreters of Rousseau who remain gripped by the primacy of nature in his thought, by its impossible, romantic irreducibility. While this grip has been loosened recently by feminist attentions to his textual and conceptual inconsistencies concerning natural sexual difference, still the tendency has been to dismiss Rousseau's use of nature as instrumental, a prop inserted periodically to buttress an otherwise shaky argument. But from my perspective this conclusion makes it difficult to see how nature functions in the complex negotiation of the paradoxes of political origins and of democratic politics in particular. I am suggesting that, perhaps

thought. See Ravven, "Has Hegel Anything to Say to Feminists?" and Benhabib, "On Hegel, Women and Irony."

[45] See *Social Contract*, especially Book I, chaps. 6 and 8, 361, 364–65.

ironically, we will understand better Rousseau's republicanism and the sexual ideologies on which it depends by taking nature seriously as a designated realm of action and meaning: his politics is most significantly on display there.

In the division of labor that characterizes Rousseau scholarship, it is the literary critics who have most fruitfully mined his originary stories, by taking seriously the process and the paradox of his reconstructed unconstructed. For Starobinski this circularity suggests the movement of consciousness, of a self yearning for deliverance from a state of alienation that is, in the final instance, the very condition of its existence. For Derrida, Rousseau's impossibilities are the stuff of language and its representational imperatives: the "dream of a full and immediate presence" is sustained only by a series of *suppléments,* those compensatory substitutions whose intermediary function is quietly forgotten, or violently denied. De Man, too, finds Rousseau articulating and suppressing the suspicion that "human specificity may be rooted in linguistic deceit."[46] On his interpretation the *Discourse on Inequality* presents (and performs) a theory of rhetoric in which the figural (a state of nature) establishes the only terms in which the literal (a political world of institutions and contracts) can be forged: "Far from being a suppression of the political, [l]iterature is condemned to being the truly political mode of praxis."[47] The ambiguity of de Man's "condemnation" is instructive. By suggesting both that literature loses its status as purely expressive act and that politics loses its field of independent self-generation, his analysis appears to lead inescapably to the conclusion that meaningful change—of the political *or* literary sort—is only ever an aesthetic possibility.

This interpretive strategy does not usually sustain the attention of Rousseau's political analysts. This is not only because, as I suggested earlier, they resist recognizing nature *as* figural but also because they are keen to understand the tangibility of state power. The conclusion reached by many political theorists is that the "violence of the letter" loses significance when the object of inquiry is governmental violence. But I want to challenge this conclusion in my reading of the *Discourse on Inequality*, by suggesting that the story's recursive logic gives form to a distinctly political impera-

[46] de Man, "Metaphor (Second Discourse)," 211.
[47] Ibid., 212.

tive: namely, the naturalization of consensual nonconsensuality through the (re)constitution of humans as rulers and ruled. Thus, alongside the paradoxes of consciousness, language, and literality, I want to place the paradox of law and its originary moment of conventionality: the *autonomous* man strives to overcome, through the contract, the relationships of domination and submission that are necessary to produce the very context in which his *auto* and his *nomos* become intelligible.

This gloss on conventionality expresses a logical necessity and a historical contingency: the possibility of consent is premised on the possibility of coercion, and yet both of these possibilities emerge only in the particular practices of sensuously motivated creatures. Rousseau's republican project and his vision of an "authentically" autonomous citizen turn on this awareness of variable practices. To be sure, the experiential coincidence of rule and pleasure is constant: both the "natural" slave who loves his chains and the "unnatural" citizen who loves his republic are created and sustained as such by a servile desire. What is different is how the republican's *sensible*, social, and ethical development is managed, choreographed, and contained in the context of a romance. This is the story of Emile, a little savage who develops into an autonomous man, not *despite* his encounters with worldly difference and power but as a consequence of them. This is the story of St. Preux, whose slavish love appears first to endanger, but then engenders, his commitment to social institutions and practices. And this is the story of Rousseau, who roots his own social and ethical development in the genesis of a twofold desire for "imperious mistresses" and for injustice avenged.

In each of these cases, learning how, what, and when to suffer is central to the maturation process. "To suffer is the first thing he ought to learn and the thing he will most need to know," advises Rousseau early in Emile's educational design.[48] And unlike the situation of the Stoic or the flagellant, Emile's experience of suffering is woven into his experience of (hetero)sexual love, with the result that the first (or so the *Discourse on Inequality* suggests) expressions of desire fuse his understandings of pleasure and pain. In this context of imagined identities and mutual need, the will emerges in a play of difference that "naturalizes" obsessive

[48] *Emile*, 78.

desires, devouring passion, and sensuous agonies. When rightly accommodated within a romantic dyad, these initiating experiences of consent and coercion contain the possibility of degeneration which the *Discourse on Inequality* depicts as the outcome of a fraudulent contract. But that essay also depicts reason and desire developing only through social and sexual roles that structure them. The (hetero)sexual romance that seems to precede the life and the logic of the state will in fact remain a persistent political concern, and Rousseau's recursive republicanism will remain forever wedded to a transformative *sensibilité*.

Object Lessons

> One desires without knowing what. The blood
> ferments and is agitated; a superabundance
> of life seeks to extend itself outward. The
> eye becomes animated and looks over other
> beings. One begins to take an interest in those
> surrounding us; one begins to feel
> that one is not made to live alone. It is thus that
> the heart is opened to the human affections
> and becomes capable of attachment.
>
> *Emile*

SENSING THE DIFFERENCE

Rousseau's portraits of men, women, and the relationships that sustain them as such respond to and reconstitute the problem of political origins outlined in the *Discourse on Inequality*. They respond to that problem inasmuch as they depict difference, interdependence, and desire as aspects of a natural developmental process: the experiences of power and compulsion upon which democratic political agency depend are provided by the experience of sexual maturation. In this way Rousseau's story of bodily and cognitive perfectibility incorporates the imperatives of conventionality: the encounter with dominant and submissive positions is as natural, inevitable, and ultimately irresistible as erotic desire itself. These depictions of sexual identity and experience continue the problem of the *Discourse on Inequality* inasmuch as they also betray the impossibility of originary stories and unmediated identities. As in the case of Rousseau's civilizing savage, his men and women attain their self-awareness only through a perpetually (re)constituting *sensibilité* that presupposes an already ordered and ordering world.

In this chapter I turn directly to Rousseau's account of sexual subjection and, in particular, to its illustration in *Emile*. In reading that text as an exercise in engendering republican men and women, I join those feminist theorists who question the centrality of biologism in Rousseau's thought.[1] But after displacing biological determinism as the linchpin of Rousseau's sexual politics, one should not then ignore bodies and their sexualities as crucial sites of its enactment. Such ignorance might seduce us into imagining sexual difference as epiphenomenal, an ideological conceit whose reality is only as solid as the consistency of its naturalistic justifications (which, given Rousseau's notorious inconsistency, is not very solid at all). And this epiphenomenalism might in turn invite us to celebrate the difference and the distance between his broader, sociopolitical goals and his sexual prescriptions, understood as contingent means to achieve those ends.

My concern is that this disarticulation of ends from means misrepresents both: inasmuch as the bodily practices and identities of republican citizens—their objective, sensate pleasures and pains—*are* Rousseau's political ends, his republicanism is inseparable from his gender ideology. With this conclusion I mean to call into question the reasonableness of evaluating—redeeming or refuting—Rousseau's political contributions while neglecting his account of gender. But I mean more urgently to suggest that any account of those broader political contributions must come to terms with the evidence, so to speak, of his gender romance. This evidence obtains in stories of sexual maturation that link erotic desire to doubt, violence, fear, and sexual difference, and that link masculine and feminine self-awareness to the particular, material and institutional forms of interdependence and governance that characterize a republican state. In this sense the *éducation sensible* to which Emile and Sophie are subjected can illuminate a political theory whose ends and aims—a stable and secure state, a general will—always appear at a distance from them: their apparently stateless educations should not blind us to the civic

---

[1] Penny Weiss, for example, has persuasively argued that in justifying his sexual politics and its gender distinctions Rousseau does not rely exclusively or even primarily on anatomical or physiological evidence; see *Gendered Community*. Weiss further insists that Rousseau's broader theoretical commitments give the lie to his periodic appeals to natural difference: for him, cultural and, most specifically, educational influences are always paramount.

dimension of their "superabundant" lives and transforming *sensibi-lités*.[2]

In retracing the stories of Rousseau's natural man and woman, we will find once again that putative origins and foundations are already shot through with the political imperatives whose legitimation initially motivated the originary search; Rousseau's story of sexual subjection also ends up where it starts, with the worldly entailments of consensual nonconsensuality. Instinct, body, law, contract, state: each offers an object lesson in the process of engendering republican subjects. But so, too, recognizing this persistent circularity points to the multiple presentations and locations of political identity in Rousseau's developmental tale, including those that find form in his archetypal natural woman, Sophie. Taking Sophie seriously as a political actor is not easy to do for readers with feminist sensibilities, and more often than not she appears in their interpretations either as a perversely stunted character or a tragically divided one.[3] Others have had less trouble imaging her whole: some interpreters have seen a strong resemblance between women's skillful dissimulations and the "hidden and personal" rule of Rousseau's magistrate, and thus they have deduced an authenticity to feminine will and power.[4]

My intention is to take seriously the form of subjectivity that Sophie's sexual and social roles provide (and that means taking seriously her opportunities for moral and political action), without subscribing to the wildly implausible conclusion that her metaphoric resemblance to magistrates and queens indicates

[2] This challenges, of course, a widely accepted reading of *Emile* as the story of the naturally virtuous man whose education opposes all that is required of the politically just citizen. Judith Shklar has offered the most influential and enduring argument that this distinction is fundamental to Rousseau's political thought; see *Men and Citizens*.

[3] For the latter see Okin, *Women in Western Political Thought*, chap. 8; for versions of the former see Wollstonecraft, *Vindication of the Rights of Women*, esp. chap. 5 ("Animadversions on Some Writers Who Have Rendered Women Objects of Pity, Bordering on Contempt"); and Keohane, " 'But for Her Sex.' "

[4] Joel Schwartz's influential account of Rousseau's sexual politics paints a fully realized Sophie whose political power is no less real or admirable for being relegated to the private realm; see *Sexual Politics*, 43–44. Allan Bloom also insists upon the authenticity of Sophie's will and independence, although he does not suggest that there is anything specifically political about either; see his introduction to *Emile*, 22.

a relative symmetry, if not equality, of sexual power and control. My concern is less about the authenticity of any will that must remain private and personal[5] than it is about a logic of resemblance that works only to the extent we sustain a strict differentiation between its terms—here, between the feminine and the state functionary, the private and the public, the natural and the political. But holding too tightly to these distinctions makes it difficult to grasp how Sophie herself embodies a grammar of interpreted consent and thus how, in their sexual-social dynamic, Emile and Sophie enact a political relationship that is not just like (or even not much like) Rousseau's democratic republicanism but that is continuous with it.

Otherwise put: the rhetorical logic of Rousseau's heterosexual narrative is metonymic insofar as it fashions contiguous political sites, each of which (re)defines the terms of governance. To take one example that I will flesh out later, Rousseau's republicanism materializes through a family form and a moral economy of desire and dependence that together entail a compulsory heterosexuality, but also and critically, an enforced ambiguity in Sophie's (sexual) consent; these entailments—sexual difference and the ambiguity of women's will and desire—function in turn as sites of political (re)constitution. As a result, states come together and come apart (quite literally, one wants to say) through the sexual practices that constitute a Rousseauian romance. On this interpretation, women's bodies and babies are objects of political scrutiny and care because they appear to be materializations of will.

By imagining men's and women's interests, pleasures, and pains on the model of consensual nonconsensuality, Rousseau imagines how sex might matter to a political order, and in so doing he lays bare what Linda Zerilli calls the "emphatically performative" aspect of all political theory: "It uses language to determine what shall count as a matter for political concern and debate; it uses tropes and figures to bring about certain effects in the reader."[6] In Zerilli's analysis this general truth is nowhere more evident than in Rousseau's sexual significations, rhetorical productions that code chaos, dread, culture, and solace—political anxieties and their res-

---

[5] I take this concern to be central to Weiss's critique of Schwartz; see *Gendered Community*, 100.

[6] Zerilli, *Signifying Woman*, 4.

olutions—as disordered and subsequently disciplined femininity. Zerilli underscores how a narratively deployed dialectic of control, one that threads together the author and reader on the common ground of the text, is central to understanding Rousseau's republicanism. I want to add that the dialectic of control represented *in* the text is also of central importance, inasmuch as it depicts a similarly emphatically performative aspect to *politics*, whose key "tropes and figures" emerge as feminine and masculine forms. What contemporary feminist theorists often present as a discrete choice—between granting the symbolic production of all sexual difference or holding onto its prediscursive determinations—cannot be easily parsed as such in Rousseau's thought. Ironically, we can better assess Rousseau's rhetorical strategies and achievements when we keep "embodied social referents" in the forefront of our analysis.[7]

In what follows I turn directly to the question of sexual difference as it is presented in *Emile*, first in the general context of social and cognitive development and then in the particular context of Sophie's education. In both cases we will see the reappearance of rhetorical strategies and thematic content from the *Discourse on Inequality*: what the previous chapter retraces as pity's perfection might here be called the perfection of sex. But perfection suggests an impossibly complete and static condition, and Rousseau's romance never ends, although it moves around quite a bit. I consider how that never-ending story moves in the context of Emile and Sophie's marriage, and I conclude by considering how the story of its failure, depicted in *Emile*'s unfinished sequel, *Emile et Sophie, ou Les Solitaires*, reiterates to some extent the degenerative moves toward the end of the *Discourse on Inequality*. In both cases, the sensible transgressions through which conventionality takes

---

[7] Here I am quoting Zerilli, who appears to be offering readers precisely this choice, between examining "woman as she is symbolically produced and deployed rhetorically" or treating her as "an embodied social referent or as a term whose meaning preexists its figuration [and] narrative invocation"; ibid., 4. While Zerilli's interpretation never loses sight of the political and social world into which Rousseau's texts would intervene, her methodological choice (psychoanalytically inspired semiotic analysis) always dictates the referential logic of sexuality and sexual difference: woman, she argues, is deployed in response to crises of signification ("woman becomes a marker and a scapegoat for the utter failure of meaning, for sociosymbolic bedlam" [8]).

shape culminate in the excesses of despotism. But the differences between the two are equally instructive: while the *Discourse* repels its readers with a zealously fratricidal Laelius, Emile enslaved offers us a beguiling portrait of heroism, moderation, and justice incarnate.

To What Does Sex Refer?

Book V of *Emile*, where Rousseau takes up the subject of girls' education and, in particular, the education of Emile's intended, Sophie, opens with a discussion of the source and the meaning of sexual difference. The passage merits extended quotation:

> In everything not connected with sex, woman is man. She has the same organs, the same needs, the same faculties. The machine is constructed in the same way; its parts are the same; the one functions as does the other; the form is similar; and in whatever respect one considers them, the difference between them is only one of more or less. In everything connected with sex, women and men are in every respect related and in every respect different. The difficulty of comparing them comes from the difficulty of determining what in their constitutions is due to sex and what is not. On the basis of comparative anatomy and even just by inspection, one finds general differences between them that do not appear connected with sex. They are, nevertheless, connected with sex, but by relations which we are not in a position to perceive. We do not know the extent of these relations. The only thing we know with certainty is that everything that man and woman have in common belongs to the species, and that everything that distinguishes them belongs to the sex. From this double perspective, we find them related in so many ways and opposed in so many other ways that it is perhaps one of the marvels of nature to have been able to construct two such similar beings who are constituted so differently [*d'avoir pu faire deux êtres si semblables en les constituant si différemment*].[8]

A marvel indeed: similarly constructed and yet differently (re)-constituted, and in a manner "we are not in a position to perceive." What, and where, is sexual difference? A comparative anal-

---

[8] *Emile*, 357–58. Subsequent citations will be given in the text.

ysis is beyond our grasp, and even careful inspection leaves us baffled. But similarities and differences abound, and if their causes and connections—their meanings—are irretrievable, they are not, for all that, unimaginable. For this we need a doubled vision: from one perspective, two "machines" with identical parts and functions, and from the other, two sexes determined by their relational difference ("in every respect related and in every respect different"). The difficulty introduced in the previous chapter as the need to contrive nature in order to know it reappears here, together with an insistence that the difficulty can be negotiated: despite the appearance of differences unconnected to sex, "the only thing we know with certainty" is that all meaningful similarities mark the species, and the only meaningful distinctions are of sex. But it is a curious certainty that is sustained by the evidence of "marvels" (or "perhaps" marvels), which themselves become apparent only through a doubled vision.

Similarly marvelous and certain are the political effects of natural difference. "These relations and differences must have a moral influence," Rousseau continues, "this conclusion is evident to the senses [*cette conséquence est sensible*]; it conforms with our experience" (358). Confidently (or perhaps just urgently) asserting the reality of what we would call gender, Rousseau here displaces the question of nature as origin by reframing it as a question of representation: physical diversity bears witness to the moral differences that we imagine there and that are confirmed by our sensuous experience.

It follows that without such imaginings, which in Rousseau's developmental schema means prior to pity's perfection and the emergence of *amour propre*, sex makes no sense. This is the position Rousseau stakes out at the beginning of Book IV, which opens with Emile at age fifteen. Heretofore "alone in human society" (208), he now stands poised to leave childhood, and thus to enter the realm of moral relations: "We are, so to speak, born twice; once to exist and once to live; once for our species and once for our sex. Those who regard woman as an imperfect man are doubtless wrong, but the external analogy is on their side. Up to the nubile age children of the two sexes have nothing apparent to distinguish them: the same visage, the same figure, the same complexion, the same voice. Everything is equal: girls are children, boys are children: the same name suffices for beings so much alike" (211).

Puberty's prehistory is one of ungendered existence. This is certainly the case for the prepubescent Emile, who "does not feel himself to be of any sex" and "to whom men and women are equally alien" (219). Like the savage in its condition of mechanical prudence, Emile's minimal awareness of difference is consonant with his minimal sense of self: "*amour propre*, the first and most natural of all the passions, is still hardly aroused in him" (208). Thus hardly able to imagine—to fear or desire—distinctions, Emile is incapable of perceiving sex.

Everything changes with the "moment of crisis" that marks the passage out of childhood (211). Repeating the sequence and the signifying scheme sketched in the *Discourse on Inequality*, Rousseau identifies bodily change as the first mark of a cognitive and social revolution: a breaking voice, a coarsening beard, eyes that "find a language and acquire expressiveness," a mind in constant agitation. These mark the emergence of sexual *sensibilité*, which (leaving nothing to the imagination) Rousseau reiterates "is the second birth of which I spoke earlier. It is now that man is truly born to life and now that nothing human is foreign to him" (212). Up until this point, Rousseau continues, the tutor's task has been "a child's game. It takes on true importance only at present" (ibid.). This truly significant iteration of educational practice is persistently anticipated throughout the preceding three-quarters of the book, an anticipation that again echoes the rhetoric of the *Discourse on Inequality*. Difference, desire, domination, an expanding self and sensuousness: from the beginning Rousseau is persistently alerting his reader to these multiform threats and inevitabilities. In this sense Emile's "moment of crisis" on the way to adulthood, like the savage's on its way to civilization, is multiple.

In *Emile*, however, the significance of a specifically sexual iteration is underscored by Rousseau's announcement that a "new plan" is needed to replace the "ordinary educations" that have heretofore sufficed. The tutor's challenge is not only the power and pace of this "stormy revolution"; it is also that the child "becomes sensitive [*sensible*] before knowing what he is sensing [*avant de savoir ce qu'il sent*]" (ibid.). Emile's vision is doubling; the question is, What sense will he make of these sensibilities? What certainties will he find there? In Rousseau's chronology, it is only as we arrive at this second, truly impossible beginning—namely, puberty—that any distinctions that matter become apparent. Only then do we enter into and perceive relations of meaningful difference and similarity.

> The study suitable for man is that of his relations. So long as he knows himself only in his physical being, he ought to study himself in his relations with things. This is the job of his childhood. When he begins to sense his moral being, he ought to study himself in his relations with men [*par ses rapports avec les hommes*]. This is the job of his whole life, beginning from the point we have now reached.
>
> As soon as man has need of a companion [*une compagne*], he is no longer an isolated being. His heart is no longer alone. All his relations with his species, all the affections of his soul are born with this one. His first passion soon makes the others ferment. (214)

The move in this passage from identifying a moral imperative to study "relations with men," to identifying all such relations as coincident with (hetero)sexual awareness, is swift: that the reorientation from things to men (who may or may not be concurrent with "humanity") is effected by the need for *une compagne* might be one of those things we all just know "with certainty." But Rousseau was not always so certain. In the earliest draft of *Emile* he had written and then crossed out the following sentences, at precisely the moment of transition between the two paragraphs just cited: "If I am asked how it is possible for the morality of human life to emerge from a purely physical revolution, I will answer that I do not know. I base myself throughout on experience and do not seek the reasons for the facts. I do not know what connection there may be between the seminal spirits and the soul's affects, between sexual development and the sentiment of good and evil. I see that these connections exist. I reason not to explain them but to draw out their consequences."[9]

What the *Discourse on Inequality* seeks to contain within a narrative linearity is met here with a shrug of indifference. Or maybe not: that the sentences survive only *sous rature* suggests an ambivalence on Rousseau's part about drawing attention to the problem. His admissions are perhaps too reminiscent of his own criticism of Locke, who had made the claim that (hetero)sexual unions in the state of nature are monogamous and of relative permanence: "Monsieur Locke" employs "moral proofs," Rousseau observes in

---

[9] Cited in the Pléiade editors' introductory discussion to *Emile*, lxxx.

a note to the *Discourse on Inequality*, which "serve to give reason to existing facts rather than to prove [*constater*] the real existence of those facts." But Rousseau, too, has only observed a correlation between moral and natural "facts": apparently "seminal spirits" occasion moral difference, but the "real existence" of spirit and difference, and of a causal link between the two, remains unprovable.

When the gap between observation and explanation cannot be bridged, one reasonable response is to abandon, or evade, the question of verification and work instead in the realm of representational effects. This is not, of course, to abandon or evade nature, but, again, to re-imagine it. And what Rousseau imagines there, in the form and on the person of pubescent youths, is a dyadic complementarity that fuses desire and struggle:

> In the union of the sexes each contributes equally to the common aim, but not in the same way. From this diversity arises the first assignable difference in the moral relations of the two sexes. One ought to be active and strong, the other passive and weak. One must necessarily will and be able; it suffices that the other put up little resistance. Once this principle is established, it follows that woman is made specially to please man. (358)

Rousseau's first principle of sexual difference establishes domination and submission as its certain postures. Masculine audacity on the one side, feminine timidity on the other: these are presented as the proper dispositions whereby natural relations of difference find moral representation, or rather, it is how moral relations of difference find natural representation. Of course, Rousseau never completely abandons the search for sensible foundations, and thus after presenting his first principle of sexual "attack and defense," he mounts a brief but wide-ranging apologia during which he appeals, alternatively, to the law of nature "prior to love itself," the nature of true love which "does not admit of real violence," the (counter)examples offered by other species, the differential capacities of men and women to arouse and satisfy their desires, the intentions of the "Supreme Being," the laws of Deuteronomy, and, finally, the precariousness of paternal identity (358–63).

To displace the authority of natural origins in accounting for Rousseau's sexual politics, it ought to be sufficient to notice this erratic and often esoteric use of evidence, or even the tone of escalating urgency that ends, as does a similar discussion of femi-

67

nine modesty in the *Letter to d'Alembert*, with a bald appeal to social expediency.[10] But this does not appear to suffice. Repeatedly readers are drawn toward reclamations or denunciations of the accuracy of Rousseau's natural scientific observations. Successful copulation depends on male arousal, whereas female performance is "guaranteed"; women's insatiable passion threatens to overwhelm men; men's greater physical strength underlies their political dominance: none of these assertions sheds much light on the moral and political dynamic that sexual interaction represents.[11] (Which is not to say that they do not contribute to that representation: anatomy and biology are always rich resources for signs.) But in the final instance, Rousseau's claims about sexual difference cannot be reduced to his natural scientific commitments because they cannot be understood without reference to desire, and desire entails the mediating operations of pity and self-love, as well as a social and political order in which those operations unfold. And surely my claims on this score cannot be reduced to an attack on the *reality* of sexual difference or, to paraphrase Rousseau, the "existing facts" of sexual difference; indeed, just because we imagine masculinity and femininity on our persons and through our practices, their reality is singularly secure.

[10] *Letter to d'Alembert*, 77–78: "As if all the austere duties of the woman were not derived from this alone, that a child should have one [*un*] Father!"

[11] Joel Schwartz entertains all three possibilities; see his *Sexual Politics*, 34, 38, 87. With regard to the first two assertions, Schwartz takes some pains to distinguish between females' sexual *capacity* and their *desire*, a distinction he insists Rousseau also made: while the former refers to different procreative roles, the latter refers to the relative intensity or constancy of passion (see his note 32, p. 158). Schwartz questions the "biological basis" of claims about female insatiability, but he underscores the scientific status of the claim about capacity. I find Schwartz's position somewhat confusing. On the one hand, he traces Rousseau's understanding of women's relatively unlimited capacity to a comment in the *Discourse on Inequality*, that human females do not "have times of heat and exclusion"; but Rousseau makes this observation to support his claim that the procreative impulse does not of itself give rise to competition between men: the opportunity to satisfy individual impulse and to meet the need for species reproduction is always available. On the other hand, Schwartz wants to link different sexual capacities to the anatomical requirement of an erection: only men run the risk of a failed sexual (thus reproductive) performance. But this argument assumes a biological knowledge Rousseau might not have had about the relationship between orgasm and conception; see Laqueur, *Making Sex*, 2–3, 146–48, 181–92.

The tutor's "new plan" made necessary by Emile's "stormy revolution" concerns precisely these newly imagined possibilities of feminine and masculine persons and practices. Rousseau writes that, with a "carefully raised young man," the first sentiment he will experience is friendship rather than love: "The first act of his nascent imagination is to teach him that he has *semblables*; and the species affects him before the (female) sex" (220). This announcement is followed by an extended discussion of pity, "the first relative sentiment which touches the human heart" and thus the means by which Emile will learn of his *semblables*. Rousseau continues that the carefully raised young man will learn about humanity through the objects that the tutor presents to him, "objects which swell the heart, which extend it to other beings, which make it find itself everywhere outside of itself" (223). Provide the student with the opportunities to imagine proper similarities, Rousseau advises, and he will identify with his kind. Consistent with the introduction of pity as Emile's mode of identification, his imagined similarities and thus his (re)constitution of his kind (*man*) turn on perceived weaknesses and pain. It is the "sad picture of suffering humanity that ought to bring to his heart the first tenderness it had ever experienced" (222).

But, inevitably, these first forays toward others introduce the possibility of comparison and, with this, the possibility of vanity and pride. Self-awareness and self-doubt emerge coincidentally: "Since my Emile has until now looked only at himself, the first glance he casts on his *semblables* leads him to compare himself with them. And the first sentiment aroused in him by this comparison is the desire to be in the first position. This is the point where *amour de soi* turns into *amour propre* and where begin to arise all the passions which depend on this one" (235). Here reproducing the language and the chronology of the *Discourse of Inequality,* Rousseau depicts his Emile moving ever closer to politics as he moves from a species awareness to a sense of individuality, and exactly when he begins to "feel himself in his *semblables*," he begins to position himself relative to them. And as was the case for the savage, this indiscrete moment wherein *amour de soi* becomes *amour propre* is the moment of moral awareness: "Now comes the measurement of natural and civil inequality and the picture of the whole social order." But of course, this measurement is impossible to the extent that all one sees and feels is resemblance: "We must show him men by means of their differences, having already showed him them by means of the accidents common to the species" (ibid.).

And the measure of that difference, and thus of the "whole social order," is sex. Because entering the moral and social order requires this "second step into manhood," the object that will swell his heart, that will take him closer to and hold him apart from his *semblables*, must be a woman: her difference consolidates their similarity. What *Emile* represents through a panoply of bodily and sensible particularity is a recapitulation of the developmental trajectory of the *Discourse on Inequality* in which communality, desire, and dependence are established through alternating pleasures and pains. In both instances, what we pity and what we fear—what we think that we want and what we feel that we need—take their shape through our sexual-social interactions. Another impossible beginning: to become attached to his *semblables* man must not know women, but identifying those *semblables* to whom he will attach himself requires that women be known. Otherwise put, knowledge of an original—of a temporally prior (asexual) humanity—derives from secondary sexual differences, and we can only know "with certainty" where we came from through the process of imagining where we are now.

GUYS AND DOLLS

> "Your heart," I say, "needs a companion. Let us go seek her who suits you. We shall not easily find her perhaps. True merit is always rare. But let us neither be in a hurry nor become disheartened. Doubtless there is such a woman and in the end we shall find her, or at least the one who is most like her." With a project that is so appealing to him, I introduce him to society. What need have I to say more? Do you not see that I have done everything? (328)

Entry into the social order is fraught with dangers, and Emile must be forearmed. Rousseau's "expedient" is to initiate the search for a beloved, a search that will serve to make "agreeable and dear to him the qualities he ought to love" and to properly dispose his sentiments "with respect to what he ought to seek or to flee" (329). That this project depends upon a wholly imaginary object is precisely what makes it expedient. "What is true love itself [*le veritable amour lui-même*]," Rousseau continues, "if it is not chimera, lie, and illusion?" True attachment could never rest on exact knowledge: "If we saw what we love exactly as it is, there would be no more love on earth." And what, "exactly," *is* that real love object? Something about which Rousseau would prefer there be no illusions: "By providing the imaginary object, I am the master of comparisons, and I easily prevent my young man from having illusions about real objects" (ibid.). The vertiginous slide from illusion to reality and back again offers a compressed account of how Rousseau's fiction gives form to his facts: "from the hope to the supposition, the path is easy" (ibid.). Here the fiction gives form not only to Emile's real love object—"in the end we shall find her, or at least the one who is most like her"—but to his real social relations: in the end, it is his social and moral awareness that are constituted through the imagined feminine form.

It follows that this image that generates its original ought not to be a "model of perfection which cannot exist" (ibid.). Sophie, like Emile, will be an ideal of ordinariness. She must have "defects," Rousseau insists, but defects that "suit [Emile], please him, and serve to correct his own." And in order that this illusion be given "a greater air of truth," Rousseau gives her a name: " 'Let us call your future beloved Sophie. The name Sophie augurs well. If the girl whom you choose does not bear it, she will at least be worthy of it. We can do her the honor in advance.' If, after all these details, you neither affirm nor deny her existence, but slip out of it by evasions, his suspicions will turn into certainty. He will believe that you are keeping a secret about the spouse who is intended for him. . . . He can be exposed to society almost without risk" (ibid.).

Emile's protection consists in the successful "enchaining" of his imagination by an engendered sentiment of sexual longing: the sense he makes of the social world will always be subject to (dis)-confirmation by his illusions of women (which were first the tutor's, which were first Rousseau's, which were themselves always [re]constitutions of his own social sense).[12] The claim seems to

---

[12] The subject of Rousseau's own sexual illusions is taken up in the following chapter. Here we might flag two possible referents for the name Sophie, his choice to signify illusory perfection. The first is Mme Elisabeth-Sophie-Françoise d'Houdetot, sister-in-law of Rousseau's patron Mme d'Epinay and mistress of his

be that Emile is now prepared to enter a new realm of "society," or the cities, salons, theaters, and other spectacular spaces where Rousseau finds the "scandalous morals of our age" on view, as well as the "contemptible men who form the scum [*la crapule*] of our youth" (335). Here learning the ways of society means learning of taste, gallantry, and other complex social relations where displays of self distinguish rank and class. Femininity and the masculinity it makes possible—all the differences that matter, we have been apprised—make sense only at this moment, as they make sense *of* this moment: the social debut is also a sexual debut and, prior to the "nubile age," Emile's world is ungendered.

But that can not be right: the moment of social awareness, of entry into the moral order and thus into a world of self-display and sexual difference, begins with Emile's earliest sense of self. How early is that? We could retrace the recursive logic of discovering what was already there, previously described in my reading of the *Discourse on Inequality*, and consider again the impossibility of the savage's story that is nevertheless rehearsed daily, in the life experiences of every creature that becomes human. Or we could muse on the insight of contemporary feminist theory that seeing oneself as unmarked by gender—identifying oneself as the universal—is the sign of masculinity: it is thus precisely Emile's

---

friend Saint-Lambert. Rousseau writes he felt for her the "first and only love in all my life" (*Confessions*, 439). Mme d'Houdetot is usually associated with Julie, the heroine of *La Nouvelle Héloïse*, which Rousseau was writing at the time they first met: his own rendition suggests that he came to love Mme d'Houdetot by seeing in her his imagined Julie (440), a sequence that reproduces how Emile comes to fall in love with Sophie. Rousseau's personal address to Mme d'Houdetot was "Sophie," and his *Lettres Morales* (also referred to as *Lettres à Sophie*), portions of which reappear in the "Profession of Faith of the Savoyard Vicar," were composed for her (see *Oeuvres Complètes*, vol. 4, lxiii–lxiv). A second possible source is (more) literary: the pseudonymous "Sophia," author of the 1739 tract "Women Not Inferior to Man," which appeared as Part 1 of the widely read "Beauty's Triumph; or the Superiority of the Fair Sex Proved," in 1751. At the very least one can assume that *Emile*'s audience would be familiar with Sophia's writings; see Mornet, "Les Enseignments des Bibliothèques Privées," 449–96. While Sophia's contribution to the *querelle des femmes* insists that "there is no inward or outward" sexual difference "excepting what merely tends to giving birth to posterity," she also emphasizes sexual complementarity and the virtuous contributions women make to society through the care of children, and in particular, their capacity to nurse, e.g., "in a peaceful, orderly state the major part of Men are useless in their offices, with all their authority; but Women will never cease to be useful while there are Men, and those Men have children"; in Jones, ed. *Women in the Eighteenth Century*, 226–28.

ignorance of gender that marks the existence of his (sexual) self-understanding. Or we could turn directly to the story of Sophie and of Emile's introduction to her, a story that appears in *Emile*'s final chapter with the prefatory claim that "we have come to the last act in the drama of youth," but which Rousseau composed prior to the book's other chapters.[13]

As I have already suggested, that story begins with its own gesture toward gender that introduces and then dismisses the problem of natural origins: "Observe how the physical leads us unawares to the moral, and how the sweetest laws of love are born little by little from the coarse union of the sexes" (360). This birth (a second? a third?) of sweet law gives form to the sexual *spectacles* through which women can be known as such. Again we read that this difference will first be made manifest in material form: "since the body is born, so to speak, before the soul, the body ought to be cultivated first" (365). He continues: "For man this aim is the development of strength; for woman it is the development of attractiveness" (ibid.).

This first cultivation produces, predictably enough, a preoccupation with bodily form, on the part of Rousseau and the women he imagines. Perhaps for this reason his discussion of Sophie's education is introduced by an appreciation of Spartan girls, gracefully displayed at public festivals. By offering a "charming *spectacle*" that counterbalanced "their indecent [because naked? because strengthening?] gymnastic," these maidens simultaneously acquired "salutary exercise" and "a continual desire to please." Their delicate drapery is presented in sharp contrast to the "gothic shackles" that allow French women to "counterfeit their waists" (366). It is unattractive, Rousseau advises, "to see a woman cut in half like a wasp; that is shocking to the sight and it makes the imagination suffer" (367). Rousseau can imagine, although he "dares not pursue," the reasons that women are motivated to so armor themselves: "a drooping bosom, a fat stomach, etc." He agrees that these are "most displeasing," but they are nonetheless "what nature pleases" women to be (although not, apparently, until after the age of forty, thirty at the inside) (ibid.).[14]

---

[13] *Confessions*, 521. See also Lange, "Rousseau and Modern Feminism," 96.

[14] These imaginations of the feminine form echo Rousseau's discussion of theatrical dress in the *Letter to d'Alembert*, where he considers the claim that the nakedness of savage women is evidence of their minimal modesty: French women

At issue, then, in cultivating girls' bodies is how they will function as signs. This is why the first educational concern that Rousseau discusses is their practice of self-adornment, which begins with their first play. "The doll," Rousseau writes, "is the special amusement of this sex" (367). This is because dolls are "useful for ornamentation": "But, you will say, [the girl] adorns her doll and not her person. Doubtless. She sees her doll and does not see herself. She can do nothing for herself. She is not yet formed; she has neither talent nor strength; she is nothing. She is entirely in her doll and she puts her coquetry into it. She will not always leave it there; she awaits the moment when she will be her own doll" (ibid.).

This is a girl's "very definite primary taste," Rousseau assures us. It is also an object lesson in the development of *amour propre*: to be "entirely in the thing" is to be "nothing," and to be "formed" is to become one's "own thing." Here the tutor adheres to the plan outlined earlier for Emile: provide the child with objects "which make it find itself everywhere outside of itself." Give the girl a doll, then "follow and regulate" her "taste" for it: "It is certain that the little girl would want with all her heart to know how to adorn her doll, to make its bracelets, its scarf, its flounce, its lace" (ibid.). Using the girl's attachment to this love object as expedient, the tutor can manipulate her proper interests and activities: "Once this first path is open, it is easy to follow; sewing, embroidery and lacemaking come by themselves." Once accustomed to adornment and skilled in its means, the girl is on her way to becoming a self-adorning woman. She will soon desire to dress, coif, and adorn her own body, just as she once derived pleasure from performing those acts upon her doll.[15]

Coquetry is the first of Sophie's "defects" that will prove useful and satisfying to Emile, and thus to their social and moral order:

"are even less so," he observes, "for they are dressed" (79n.). He then refers readers to the *Letter*'s closing depictions of Spartan maidens, whose dancing naked forms caused less agitation than the décolletage of actresses: "the immediate power of the senses is weak and limited; it is through the intermediary of the imagination that they make their greatest ravages" (122).

[15] There is an interesting parallel between Rousseau's discussion of the right use of dolls in raising girls and Simone de Beauvoir's discussion of this same subject in *The Second Sex*, 313–14. In both cases, early play is seen as critical to teaching girls the lessons of femininity and survival, and in both cases, the doll plays a crucial role in this process.

through it she is enabled to stage the bodily *spectacles* that engender sexual difference, together with the desire for it. This education in vain practices initiates Sophie's own agentic capacity inasmuch as it introduces a difference between *being* and *seeming to be.* That it makes these differences matter in acts of bodily display—first the doll's, then hers—suggests a self-generation that we know is not possible: veiling, too, is meaningful only when there is an audience to witness it. But Sophie must not become a slave to fashion: while she "loves adornment and is an expert at it" (393), she uses this expertise to create an unadorned simplicity that distinguishes her from those whose dress advertises social rank and privilege. Rousseau insists that "we are not our clothes" (372); but he also insists that we lose our savage innocence when we put them on.[16] We can then (re)constitute that innocence only in the form of sexually differentiated selves. This means dressing to give evidence of an unrehearsed naturalism.

Rousseau's invective against showy ornamentation and the elaborate ceremonies of *la toilette* is thus a rejection of ancien régime social conventions, but not, as Charles Ellison suggests, a rejection of costuming strategies themselves.[17] In an insightful reading of Rousseau as a critic of the modern city, Ellison argues that, because Rousseau both "refuse[s] to use dress to create distinctions between public and private life" and recognizes how "dress mediates relations between self and others," it follows that "girls' taste for adornment and ornamentation, met partially by a fascination with dolls, must be repressed at an early age."[18] Here we reencounter Starobinski's Rousseau, a naturalist obsessed with the transparent and what is "real"—the natural body—over and against what is merely "appearance." But why is Rousseau's preferred simple dress any less symbolic than "gothic shackles"? Isn't the latter rejected precisely because it "makes the imagination suffer"? And why conclude that bodies are more simple, thus less symbolic? Surely, for Rousseau, the body serves to symbolize simplicity. Indeed, Sophie's ability to seduce through her bodily displays—"no one could have a better figure, a more beautiful complexion, a whiter hand, a daintier foot" (393)—is the result of a most careful costuming strategy: "She is ignorant of what colors are fashion-

[16] See *Letter to d'Alembert,* 79 (quoted in note 14).
[17] Ellison, "Rousseau and the Modern City."
[18] Ibid., 518–19.

able, but she knows marvelously which look well on her; there is no girl who appears to be dressed with less study and whose outfit is more studied . . . [a]nd one would say that all this very simple attire was put on only to be taken off piece by piece by the imagination" (394). What appears as a "defect"—coquetry—establishes a symbolizing practice that substantiates sexual difference; it is precisely through her choreography of a bodily transparency that Sophie makes the moral order intelligible, and desirable.

But this runs the risk of seeing in women's coquettish displays an authentic self-representation. Linda Zerilli's ingenious analysis of a "linguistic and sartorial contract" at the core of Rousseau's politics is particularly attentive to this problematic possibility.[19] She writes: "The narcissistic pleasures the masculine subject denies himself (the tutor forbids his pupil) are projected onto the feminine other who is compelled to love adornment, to make herself a fetish."[20] Although Sophie might appear to be engaged in signifying practices, her self-adornment marks her only as a thing: "She may never signify herself as speaking subject, as producer of signs—that is, if she is to remain in her function as sign."[21] Leaving aside for the moment whether Rousseau actually denies masculine self-display (I argue later that he does not),[22] I want to suggest that the paradoxical condition of both being a sign and producing signs is at the core of Rousseau's sexual politics. Not only is this consistent with the *Discourse on Inequality*'s account of how moral and political agency is sustained, but it is critical to the political expediency of a gendered *sensibilité*: one signifies political imperatives through the body-as-sign. For all the narcissism it appears to entail, Sophie makes her body matter, and in so doing she substantiates the moral order of difference.

It is tempting, watching Sophie get dolled up for Emile, to conclude that this is nothing but self-effacement. It is difficult to read

---

[19] Zerilli, *Signifying Woman*, 19.

[20] Ibid., 45. In this way, Emile's (natural?) desire to be seen is satisfied through a "vicarious pleasure" in seeing, an expedient which, Zerilli adds, risks leaving him "caught in a kind of psychic cross-dressing, that is to say, in a destabilizing identification with his own woman-as-spectacle" (48).

[21] Ibid., 47.

[22] Zerilli makes a similar point in a discussion of Polish *spectacles*, where she concludes that "masculine self-display is not in any way forbidden by Rousseau but rather strictly regulated" (ibid., 56). Zerilli and I differ in our

Rousseau's pronouncements that girls "ought to be constrained early" (369) and must "always be subjected" (ibid.), and not conclude that his engendering is a thinly disguised annihilation of women's capacity as agents. But my goal is not to retrieve or redeem some authenticity to Sophie's self-expressions. It is to understand how, for Rousseau, political and moral agency is possible *only* in the context of, through the enabling *and* constraining structures of, social interaction and material, bodily practices. It is to understand how subjection is *always* a feature of political and moral agency. After identifying those subjecting interactions and practices as gendered, it is not, then, helpful to dismiss them as artificial and illegitimate. That they are undoubtedly both is (oddly, I admit) beside the point, because we can better understand how they structure republican politics, and thus how sexed bodies substantiate consensual nonconsensuality, only if we consider how they make moral agency—both Sophie's and Emile's—possible.

IMAGINING SOPHIE

The importance of women's capacity for self-authored acts is touched upon repeatedly in Book V's early discussion of girls' education. The need to cultivate their wit, the "simple reason" they must develop in order to perform their social roles, and Rousseau's urging that they "be allowed to use a little cleverness, not to elude punishment but to get [themselves] exempted from obeying": these suggest that the living doll will have choices to make, that she will need to perform with relative independence (370).[23] The first such performance comes when she chooses a husband. Rousseau's rejection of the practice of arranged marriages appears in *Emile* in a speech made by Sophie's father. "Marriages made by the authority of fathers are guided uniquely by the suitability of convention and by that of opinion," he explains to Sophie as *she* reaches the nubile age; "it is not persons who are married; it is positions of power and wealth" (400). He continues:

---

conceptualizations of the form, content, and goals of those (bodily and institutional) regulations.

[23] See also *Emile*, 364, 366, 368, 369.

It is up to the spouses to match themselves. Mutual inclination ought to be their first bond. Their eyes and their hearts ought to be their first guides. Their first duty once united is to love each other; and since loving or not loving is not within our control, this duty necessarily involves another, which is to begin by loving each other before being united. This is the right of nature, which nothing can abrogate. Those who have hindered it with so many civil laws have paid more attention to the appearance of order than to the happiness of marriage and the morals of the citizens. You see, my Sophie, that we are not preaching a difficult morality to you. It leads only to making you your own mistress and having us rely on you for the choice of your husband. (Ibid.)

Attachment stems only from true love, and the duty to love truly cannot be commanded: it can only be self-authored. Its authority is rooted in inclinations, which are themselves determined by what is seen and felt. Sophie must authorize her own duty, through her freely imagined desire. To ignore this is to be ignorant of everything that secures political order, over and against its mere appearance. To "make" Sophie her own mistress is therefore to guarantee citizens' morals. But isn't her judgment in matters of marriage— so critical to that institution's moral economy and thus to political stability and order—restricted and constricted by an education in dependence, obedience, coquetry, and the like? No doubt: if she, like Emile, has been rightly raised, then her very bodily inclinations—her romantic *sensibilité*—will be aroused by particular objects (men, virtuous citizens) long "before she knows what she is sensing." But this is a circumscription, not a vitiation, of her capacity for consent: for both women and men, engendering provides the social conditions that organize the very possibility of choice. In this sense Sophie's marital consent simply reiterates the story of conventionality outlined in the *Discourse on Inequality*. Indeed, the preceding passage follows precisely that story's recursive logic: a reinscription of paternal and civil authority onto individual will, which is then reinscribed onto individual desire, which is then reinscribed onto "the right of nature," and all of this made possible through an act of paternal authority.

We are not, then, surprised to read Rousseau's prediction that her father's speech will "remain engraved upon [Sophie's] heart for the rest of her life," in that way becoming an expedient to steer her toward a proper choice—one consistent with her parents' esteem (402).[24] It is perhaps more surprising to see Rousseau announcing a several-page digression into the story of some other Sophie—"a girl so similar to Sophie that her story could be Sophie's without occasioning any surprise"—at precisely the moment when Sophie's freedom is affirmed and it is time for the beloveds to meet. The doubling of Sophie is prefaced with a description of how "the very liberty she has received has the effect only of giving her a new elevation of soul and making her harder to please in the choice of her master" (ibid.). Rousseau then depicts her elevated soul using a pastiche of national gender traits: "Possessing the temperament of an Italian woman and the sensitivity of an Englishwoman, Sophie combines with them—in order to control her heart and her senses—the pride of a Spanish woman, who, even when she is seeking a lover, does not easily find one she esteems worthy of her" (ibid.).

The passage underscores the cultural variability of sexual *mœurs* by identifying feminine *sensibilité* in terms of a national community that both authorizes temperamental difference and secures the freedom of individual desire: it is as subjects of conventional communities that women articulate their need for esteemable masters and, when they are not found, refuse to consent. The imperative of Sophie's freedom and the moral elevation associated with it are intensified by these explicitly political references: her consent to be ruled (re)authorizes the civil and paternal authority that was already there. How else could she be so *sensible*? How else could she be free?

Rousseau's appeal to the natural woman's political and cultural assemblage is followed by the announcement of a digressive tale that he acknowledges is all about expediency. "There are people," he writes, "to whom everything great appears chimerical and who in their base and vile reasoning will never know what effect even a mania for virtue can have upon the human passions." To these people "one must speak only with examples." And whether or not his example appears factual is immaterial: "Whether it is believed to be true or not, it makes little difference. I shall, if you please, have told fictions, but I shall still have explicated my method and I shall still be pursuing my ends" (ibid).

---

[24] Rousseau uses the same phrase—"engraved upon the heart"—to describe how cultural law remains the most important guarantor of the contract and thus the general will; see *Social Contract*, 172.

This fiction ("if we please") involves a young girl who resembles the original Sophie in every way "which would make her merit the name," and so Rousseau will "continue to call her by it"(ibid.). This other Sophie proves unenthusiastic about choosing a mate. She is shopped around—her aunt "made her see society, or rather, made society see her, for Sophie cared little for all this bustle"— and suitors presented themselves, but she remained indifferent. "Why did she not make use of the freedom she was given?" Rousseau asks. "The answer," he responds, "was simple." Much like Emile, she has fallen in love with an illusion prior to the time she is to choose her husband. Her beloved is Telemachus, the fictional hero of Fénelon's didactic tale, and her passion for this unobtainable man makes her incapable of accepting wordly suitors. She knows that Telemachus is a "fiction," but he has become the standard-bearer in comparison with which all real men must suffer: " 'I do not seek Telemachus. I know that he is only a fiction. I seek someone who resembles him. And why cannot this someone exist, since I exist—I who feel within myself a heart so similar to his? No, let us not thus dishonor humanity. Let us not think that a lovable and virtuous man is only a chimera'" (405).

Rousseau tells us that her parents' first response upon learning about Sophie's unreal love was laughter: "They believed they could bring her around by reason." But "reason was not entirely on their side; how many times she reduced them to silence by using their own reasoning against them, by showing them that they had done all the harm themselves." By raising her such that her "heart depend[ed] upon her will," this Sophie's parents are responsible for her predicament: because she has been made her own mistress, she can love only "a man imbued with my maxims, or one whom I can bring around to them." Here, then, is the consequence of her father's commitment to enfranchise the lovers' "eyes and their hearts": these best "first guides" discover duty and will in the pursuit of passion, and they discover passion in what is dutiful and properly willed.

But this follows naturally, we might say, from the logic of Rousseau's sexual subjection. If sexual desire were just about "youthful needs," Rousseau acknowledges, Sophie's choice would be simple; "But a master for the whole of life is not easy to choose" (404). And because "those two choices [satisfying a sexual awakening and finding a master] cannot be separated," a girl must "often lose her youth before finding the man with whom she wants to spend the rest of the days of her life" (ibid.). Such is the predicament of this other Sophie, an example for those who doubt the effects of "even mania." This Sophie's mania consists in her unwavering attachment to an illusion with whom the living cannot compare. To her utter despair, this Sophie has learned that when it comes to men, "everything great" *is* chimera.

This "sad narrative," Rousseau suggests, might well have a "catastrophic end," one that finds Sophie dead, the casualty of a loveless match now demanded by an "exasperated" mother and an "irritated" father. But Rousseau introduces this denouement through a series of five rhetorical questions, each of which situates the relevant catastrophe—the familial disputes, the parents' angry impatience, Sophie's descent "into the grave" at the moment she is to be led "to the altar"—in a deliberative future tense ("Shall I tell [*Dirai-je*] . . . ?" "Shall I portray [*Réprésenterai-je*] . . . ?" "Shall I, finally, paint [*Peindrai-je enfin*] . . . ?") that proposes only to deny: "No, I put aside these dreadful objects [*j'écarte ces objets funestes*]" (405). From a rhetorical perspective this passage, and indeed, the entire digressionary tale, constitutes a *preterition*, or a mode of inclusion that works by way of an insistence on omission.[25] Rousseau "shall not" tell, neither will he paint nor portray, the disastrous end that awaits a Sophie imprudently attached to chimeras. He will instead acknowledge that he has taken a wrong turn: "I went astray myself; let us retrace our steps" (ibid.). The original Sophie must be "resuscitated" with a "less lively imagination" before we can return to Emile's story proper.

So what is the point of this digressionary Sophie? It is perhaps tempting to read in her a cautionary tale about the illusions given to young girls, a sort of Sophie Bovary *avant la lettre*. But this is difficult to sustain, for several reasons. First because, as suggested earlier, the complexity of the digression's rhetorical situation complicates any easy conclusions about its moral. Rousseau refuses to say that illusory love cannot be confirmed by the real thing, even as he seems to be saying just that; he will not paint a "virtuous daughter [treated] like a madwoman" (ibid.) even as he depicts just that; and he will not show how Sophie's search for a man worthy of her subjection is impossible, even as he portrays just

---

[25] Preterition is famously associated with Cicero's oratorical style.

that.[26] If love, virtue, and an esteemable subjection all turn on the power of illusion, then perhaps it makes sense not to just say so; but in a didactic tale, one composed for educators and other "base and vile reasoners," it must be indicated. And we have seen it before: to be stripped of "chimera, lie, and illusion" is to be stripped of "true love" itself, and therefore virtue and the freedom that subjection makes possible.

A second reason to be wary of the conclusion that the other Sophie underscores the need to suppress girlish illusion is that Rousseau himself points in a different direction. After announcing that he will put aside "these dreadful objects" he continues: "I need not go so far to show by what seems to me to be a sufficiently striking example that, in spite of the prejudices born of the morals of our age, enthusiasm for the decent and the fine is no more foreign to women than to men, and that there is nothing that cannot be obtained under nature's direction from women as well as men" (405). This statement introduces both the infinite (re)-constitutability of a naturally directed woman, which is to say, the many useful ways she might imagine her desires, and the possibility of differently constraining (thus enabling) feminine will for Rousseau's time: let enthusiasm for the "decent and fine" counterpoise the excesses born of ancien régime social gallantry. "Pity me [*Plaignez-moi*]," the other Sophie implores: imagine through me the pain of desiring but not finding an esteemable master (ibid.). If this republican (re)constitution of women's will and desire turns on intemperate fantasy and fictitious men, it is, again, understandable that Rousseau wouldn't want to say so too transparently; but the pitiable Sophie and her imperfect freedom are too expedient to ignore completely.

This suggests a third and final reason to suspect any lessons from a doubled and discarded Sophie: subsequent textual references in *Emile* to Telemachus throw into doubt the distinction between the original and its copy. It will turn out that the real Sophie has also read Fénelon and has also been inspired by its lessons of masculine audacity and beguiling femininity. When Emile reluctantly sets out on his journey of political discovery subsequent to meeting Sophie but prior to their marriage, she gives him her *Adventures of Telemachus*, while he gives her his copies of *The Specta-*

---

[26] See Rousseau's own verdict on Ciceronian technique; *Emile*, 343.

tor, so that each can be instructed in what the other needs: Emile will "learn to resemble [Telemachus]," while Sophie will learn "the duties of decent women" (450). It is thus difficult to sustain any strong convictions that preventing an illusory excess is the story's moral, given how the characters continue to rely upon an excess of illusion. And while the "resuscitated" Sophie will have a "less lively imagination," this doesn't prevent her from providing Emile with a script to enact.

Neither does it prevent her from identifying with Eucharis, the nymph beloved by Telemachus, when she first lays eyes on Emile.[27] But of course it is the tutor who initiates the fantasy, with a little help from Sophie's father, who, as the strangers Emile and his tutor eat dinner at their family cottage, compares their arrival to "Telemachus and Mentor on Calypso's island" (414). Emile answers, "It is true that we find here the hospitality of Calypso," to which the tutor adds, "And the charms of Eucharis" (ibid.). Familiar only with the *Odyssey,* Emile doesn't get it; but Sophie blushes "up to her eyes, lower[s] them toward her plate, and [does] not dare murmur." Over the course of the dinner, however, she steals furtive glances at Emile and, in so doing, compares him to the fictitious Telemachus (ibid.).

Lacking the advantage of a literary facsimile, Emile has a harder time placing Sophie. But when her mother speaks her name, he "is wakened with a start and casts an avid glance at the girl who dares to bear it" (ibid.). That she is chaste, coy, obedient, loving, and thoroughly enamored of him are not qualities taken in readily at a glance: "He observes her and contemplates her with a sort of fear and distrust. He does not see exactly the face he had depicted to himself. He does not know whether the one he sees is better or worse. He studies each feature; he spies on each movement, each gesture. In all he finds countless confused interpretations" (ibid.). Each of the "four spectators" at the table takes easy notice of Emile's attempts to reconcile the Sophie before him with the image he has made. His "disturbance" is particularly apparent to Sophie's "penetrating eyes," which see in his eyes a confirmation

---

[27] Pierre Burgelin suggests that this identification with Telemachus's temptress rather than with his sage wife, Antiope, is evidence of the "fatal bent" to Emile and Sophie's relationship, which he likens to Julie and St. Preux's; see Burgelin, "L'Éducation de Sophie," 126–27.

that "she is the cause of his disorder" and, further, that this disorder "is not yet love" (415). But when she speaks, "Emile surrenders." After this it is only a question of "swallow[ing] with deep droughts the poison with which she intoxicates him" (ibid.).

Here is a successful, if deadly, second birth: "It is Sophie's soul that appears to animate him; How his own soul has changed in a few instants!" When she speaks, sighs, or averts her glance, Emile mimics her. Like a savage experiencing its first differences of species and sex, Emile's successful recognition of Sophie introduces him to new anxieties and pleasures of witnessing and self-presentation: "Farewell freedom, naïveté, frankness! Confused, embarrassed, fearful, he no longer dares to look around him for fear of seeing that he is being looked at. Ashamed to let the others see through him [*se laisser pénétrer*], he would like to make himself invisible to everyone in order to sate himself with contemplating her without being observed" (415).

Sophie, by contrast, is pleased: "she sees her triumph; she enjoys it." Her palpitating heart reassures her that "her Telemachus has been found" (ibid.). Emile's awareness of others—as those who "see him" as well as those he might desire, need, and fear—is thus initiated by an attachment to one who is simultaneously obedient and imperious. For both lovers, the discovery of interdependence and individuality obtains in the (re)constitution of bodily expression on the model of their respective object lessons: for Sophie, it is Telemachus; for Emile, it is Sophie. In this way Rousseau's story of sexual maturation represents a choreography of that "crisis that serves as a passage from childhood to man's estate," rather than an account of its origins. As Emile and Sophie imagine sexual difference, they imagine the social order and their places and purposes within it. The conclusion must be that in Rousseau's tale, sexual awareness does not precede social awareness, but rather, the two are coincident: the recognition of sexual identity is a recognition of political forms.

Marital Arts

The dialectic of control that weaves through these shared sexual illusions—the reiterated births, poisonings, animations, triumphs, and subjections—finds a further iteration in marriage, a relationship that exemplifies the problems and possibilities of convergent political and naturalistic rationales. On the one hand, it would seem obvious that Emile's capacity for autonomy depends upon Sophie's obedience: an education geared toward making her pleasing and acquiescent guarantees that he does not risk enslavement to the one on whom he must depend. On the other hand, the recursive logic of the *Discourse on Inequality* and its reappearance in Emile's *éducation sensible* suggests that his subjection is inevitable, inasmuch as it is entailed by political and moral experience. Emile will never know the fierce demands of political duty or the exquisite severity of moral law if he does not feel them. This means that he must also be ruled, a conclusion that returns us to Rousseau's first principle of sexuality, that one of the two "must necessarily will and be able," while the other one resists just a bit.[28] That each of these roles can be played, on occasion, by either men or women underscores the political expediency that drives Rousseau's first principle: it organizes an interaction that is a, indeed *the*, moral relationship through which the social world is envisioned.

In this sense the cross-gendered dimension of Rousseau's order of "attack and defense" (358) highlights how sexual difference secures species similarity: the lover and beloved, the husband and wife, (re)constitute a world of perfected beings who can both dominate and submit. It is not a question here of role equivalence but of a structural logic: inasmuch as femininity and masculinity articulate opportunities for control and submission, they are *together* an iteration of a political imperative made all the more acute by Rousseau's republicanism, namely, the need for a coincidence of consensual and constraining relations. This coincidence, which is the conceit of republican law, finds sensible, realized form in sexual roles only insofar as those roles are periodically transgressed. Emile's masculinity must accommodate his servile desire, and Sophie's imperious authority must on occasion preempt her docile femininity. Here again we find boundaries—of identity, behavior, sentiment—whose violation is an anticipated, even vital, dimension of their initial construction.

The final passages in *Emile*, at the end of Book V, depict the young couple newly wedded, three years after their first encoun-

---

[28] *Emile*, 358.

ter, and headed for the nuptial bed. The tutor takes them aside for a brief chat, hardly indifferent himself to "the sole subject which can occupy them on this day" (475). It is difficult, he explains to the couple, "to prolong the happiness of love in marriage" (476). The problem is that "constraint and love go ill together, and pleasure is not to be commanded" (ibid.). Echoing the claims made by Sophie's father apropos her right to choose a husband, the tutor insists that marital law does not give spousal right of bodily access inasmuch as those "sweetest proofs of love" are such only when the passion is shared: "It is mutual desire which constitutes the right. Nature knows no other. Law can restrict this right, but it cannot extend it. Voluptuousness is so sweet in itself!" (ibid.).

But marriage undercuts the opportunity for these sweet proofs, not because it imposes exclusivity but because it engenders constraint: "It is not so much possession as subjection which satiates, and a man stays attached to a kept woman for longer than to a wife" (ibid.). Here the inconstancy of (men's) desire, which others have read as an indication of Rousseau's anxieties about sexual performance or as a concomitant of his biologistic concerns,[29] seems primarily a function of (women's) occluded consent: Does she really want me, or is she simply doing her duty? The latter, which is all about constraint, deprives the act of its voluptuousness: "How could a duty be made of the tenderest caresses?" (ibid.). This suggests that the cornerstones of Sophie's wifely virtue—compliance and obedience—threaten to undermine the passionate attachment that initially authorized the marriage contract and which (re)authorizes the duties that the contract imposes.

Rousseau's prescription—his "simple and easy" means to avoid this dissipation of desire, thus duty—is to "go on being lovers when one is married" (ibid.). Emile immediately concurs, apparently limited in his comprehension by newlywed puerility.[30] But the tutor insists that he needs time to explain, and in so doing he elaborates a sexual iteration of consensual nonconsensuality that rejects the paternal authority upon which their marriage depends.

[29] See, for example, Schwartz, *Sexual Politics*, 34; and Kofman, "Rousseau's Phallocratic Ends."

[30] *Emile*, " 'Quite so,' Emile says, laughing silently, 'It won't be hard for us' " (476).

What must be rejected is the power and the enervating comfort of an assumed sexual access. The lover, unlike the husband, can never deny his mistress's will: " 'If it is true, then, dear Emile, that you want to be your wife's lover, let her always be your mistress, and her own. Be a fulfilled but respectful lover. Obtain everything from love without demanding anything from duty, and always regard Sophie's least favors not as your right but as acts of grace' " (477). By acknowledging that Sophie remains her own mistress, Emile consents to be ruled: only her desire can authorize the satisfaction of his own. But when the will converges with desire, knowing what is commanded is as difficult as interpreting bodily signs. Using a phrase that will reappear in the *Letter to d'Alembert*, Rousseau writes that Emile must be aware of when Sophie's "heart and her eyes accord what her mouth feigns to refuse" (ibid.). In thus negotiating the difference between what she says and what her body shows, Emile will never make mistakes about his mistress's "secret will" (*volonté secrette*), at least not if he remains guided by "true love" (*véritable amour*) (ibid.), which, we have learned earlier, is "chimera, lie, and illusion."

The couple's initial reaction to the tutor's plan is irritation on Emile's part and shame on Sophie's. But Emile stops protesting when he "consults the eyes of his young wife" and he sees that "beneath their embarrassment they are full of a voluptuous agitation that reassures him about the risk he takes in trusting her." Emile is already learning the grammar of interpreted consent, and once reassured of Sophie's desire, he falls prostrate in front of her: "He throws himself at her feet, ecstatically kisses the hand she extends to him, and swears that, with the exception of the promised fidelity, he renounces every other right over her. 'Dear wife,' he says to her, 'be the arbiter of my pleasures as you are of my life and my destiny. Were your cruelty to cost me my life, I would nonetheless give to you my dearest rights' " (ibid.).

Here the reinscription of civil (marital) law onto individual will identified as sexual desire is affected through an explicitly political language: Rousseau's "simple and easy" romantic prescription is described in this passage as a "law," even though Emile is not to claim any "rights," and Sophie is said to accept her side of this "treaty," even as she is released from her conjugal "duty" (ibid.). And while the centerpiece of this contract is a renunciation of paternal right in the service of preserving initiating desires, the contract's necessary precondition is Sophie's unquestioning bodily devotion. She will decide what Emile gets, but she will only ever get Emile. Here a profoundly political contrivance is used to shore up, indeed, to bring about, a romantic state of affairs, and it is in embodying the multiform postures of those who consent to be ruled that the lovers are preserved in their natural inclinations.

That the distance between Sophie's eyes and her mouth, between her desire and its representation, is mediated by force lays bare the political imperatives that undergird Rousseau's foundational moral experience: through it, the pleasures of rule and of erotic gratification are thoroughly confounded. "What is sweetest for man in his victory is the doubt whether it is weakness which yields to strength or the will which surrenders" (360): but while his sweet doubt about her desire drives his own, the opportunity to doubt and to vanquish emerges only when "she consents to let him be the stronger" (ibid.). As striking as the question of whether anybody's consent or control is authentic here is a recognition of the destabilization of any ground on which that determination could be made. This is because, in Rousseau's sexual politics, as in his republican politics more generally, the satisfaction of one's desire turns on some other's domination. This is true for Sophie, whose coy modesty "asks to be conquered" (477), and it is true for Emile, whose passion must be authorized by the "arbiter of [his] pleasures." Desire for another, articulated within the moral frame of autonomy, or self-imposed constraint, will always blur the difference between choice and compulsion.

An extended marital seduction scene from *Les Solitaires*, the unfinished sequel to *Emile*, demonstrates both the inherent difficulty of determining the "secret will" that is feminine desire and the necessity of making that determination.[31] The scene takes place in Paris, where the couple has moved with their son following their daughter's death. They have become distanced from one another, and Sophie has taken to repeatedly rejecting Emile's sexual advances. He must then determine whether these rebuffs indicate "wise refusals, made to increase the value of that which is given," or "firm refusals that filled [Emile] with love but which [he] was obliged to respect," or "serious refusals of a resolute will, indig-

---

[31] The incomplete sequel consists of two letters from Emile to his tutor.

nant that it might be doubted."[32] They initially appear to him to be the last, a conclusion punctuated by Sophie's reminder of the promise he had made to her on their wedding day. "You can punish me [*me punir*]," she insists, "but you cannot coerce me [*me contraindre*], and be assured that I will never tolerate that" (889). By insisting on her capacity to resist, Sophie threatens to recast Emile's power over her as simple force, a threat that both persuades him to retreat and intensifies his desire: "Perhaps never after ten years of marriage, after such a long cooling off, has a husband's passion been rekindled so hot and so lively; never during my first loves had I spilled so many tears at her feet: it was useless, she remained unmoveable" (ibid.).

But after catching signs of "regret and pity" in her eyes, Emile decides differently. Perhaps what Sophie really wanted was "a little constraint in order to appear to concede to force what she no longer dared to give of her own accord [*gré*]." Thus Emile persuades himself that her "serious refusals" are in fact "wise ones," and he presses himself upon her. But, mid-ravaging, he is disabused of this notion by Sophie's angry command that he "stop, [a]nd know that I am no longer anything to you; another has defiled your bed; I am pregnant" (ibid.).

Here the marital rape fantasy blurs into what one might call, with all its oxymoronic valence, a quasi–attempted rape: the fact that she appeared "moved" by Emile's "ardent caresses" turns out to be a sign of her distress (although whether it was distress about his insistence or about her inability to "succumb" in good faith remains, predictably, unclear [ibid.]). That Sophie's pregnancy later appears to be the consequence of a successful rape (the extant text is strongly suggestive but imprecise on this score)[33] completes the vicious circularity of her embodied consent. She says nothing about the particular circumstances of her impregnation to Emile—who learns about "that which excused her, perhaps even justified her" only after her death—because she knew her "crime" could not be "forgotten": in bearing some other man's child she will produce a bodily challenge to Emile's paternal authority. This is the final and "most horrible" realization that strikes

---

[32] *Les Solitaires*, 889. Subsequent citations will be given in the text.

[33] For a discussion of Rousseau's intended plot resolutions, see Charles Wirz, "Note sur *Emile et Sophie*"; and Schwartz, *Sexual Politics*, 96–97.

Emile in his struggle over the decision to leave her: "in dividing her tenderness between two sons [Sophie] will be forced to divide her attachment between two fathers!" (904). Announcing that he would rather see his own son dead than see Sophie give birth to another man's child, Emile abandons his country, penniless and alone: parental attachment, property, citizenship, and *patrie* are all lost in the aftermath of her revelation.

Sophie's infidelity thus prompts Emile's sexual, social, and political fragmentation. And while her treachery appears, technically, we might say, excusable and even deniable—"nothing forced her to reveal" the perfidious paternity, writes Rousseau (897)—it inevitably defies Emile's autonomy, first, because it raises doubts about the constancy of her desire. Here the promise and the problem of Rousseau's "secret will" are revealed in all their Hobbesian glory: because women are always saying no, the meaningfulness of their consent can always be questioned and always be presumed, and in the end, what matters are the consequences of this consent rather than its authenticity. Or rather, its authenticity can be determined only with respect to its consequences.[34]

A second way in which Emile's autonomy is undermined pertains to the consequence of Sophie's suspect consent: a child, a new object of her attachment and a living testimony to the divisibility of his paternal authority. "Yesterday," Emile laments, "even yesterday at the feet of an adored spouse, I was the happiest of beings; it was love that enslaved me to her laws, that kept me dependent upon her; her tyrannic power was the work of my tenderness, and I enjoyed even her severity" (895). This tender tyranny is the domain of the mistress, but Sophie is also a wife and mother, thus the guarantor of familial integrity. Recall that, on their wedding day, Emile had made his wife his mistress by renouncing every right over her "with the exception of fidelity": in *Les Solitaires* it seems clear that this fidelity is not, in the final instance, a question of intention but of bodily practice, and the sanctity of her will—enslaving, severe—turns on its corporeal representa-

---

[34] Pateman also emphasizes that women's inability to openly announce their desire compromises their ability to withhold consent ("Women and Consent," 154–55). However, she concludes from this that Rousseau's marriage contract reflects the commonly held and often legally confirmed position that "rape is impossible within marriage" (155).

tion. Because she is pregnant, Sophie now embodies a challenge to Emile's absolutism, and in so doing she loses all her tyrannic powers.

The tension between Sophie's role as mistress (arbiter of his pleasure) and her role as wife (subject of his rule) surfaces in Emile's struggle over the decision to leave her. When he is guided by his ever-present desire, Emile believes he can and even must forgive her: a "body too formed by love, too exposed to perils by its charms and to temptations by its senses" is "a woman [t]o be pitied" (897). Identifying in this way with Sophie's well-formed body, Emile is certain that "her heart remained pure," and he is thus able to pronounce more "gentle judgments" upon her (898). But when he considers the situation as husband, things look quite different: "It is with good reason that one faults a husband for his wife's disorder, be it for having chosen poorly or for governing her poorly [and] I myself was an example of the justness of this charge, and if Emile had always been wise, Sophie would never have erred; [o]ne has the right to presume that she who does not respect herself will at least respect her husband, if he is worthy, and he knows how to maintain his authority" (901).

After oscillating several more times, contemplating the situation as, alternatingly lover and then husband, Emile finally arrives at the conclusion noted earlier, that the "imagination" of Sophie giving birth to another man's child "alienated me from her more than everything that had tormented me up until then; from that moment I was irrevocably decided, and to leave no room for doubt I stopped deliberating" (904). (Another marvel: an "irrevocability" whose vulnerability to change requires a disciplined nondeliberation.) The conclusion seems to be that while Emile's moral capacity and political identity are secured through the "natural" passions he shares with his mistress and by the lessons in subjection, domination, desire, and dependence that her enjoyable severity provides, those passions and lessons rely in turn on the authorizing, sanctifying, and enforcing power of the husband-as-peerless-father, which is to say, on the ordering and enforcing power of the state. In the end, the art and artifice of the mistress requires the sanction of paternal authority, and love's tyrannic power is lost, or must be forceably denied, when the law that protects the tyrannized is violated.

PATERNALISM, BARBARISM, FREEDOM, AND THE STATE

The form, function, and justification of paternal authority are presented most succinctly in Rousseau's *Discourse on Political Economy*, which opens with an attempt to distinguish between it and the proper subject of that essay, civil authority. But what emerges from the essay as a whole is the interdependence and interpenetration of the two. Predictably, Rousseau initially introduces the problem as one of origins: "This word [economy] is derived from *oikos*, *house*, and *nomos*, *law*, and originally signified merely the wise and legitimate government of the household for the common good of the entire family; the meaning of the term was later extended to the government of the large family which is the state" (241). In what follows this etymological specification, Rousseau attempts to undercut any apparent similarities between the two forms of government by turning away from their common origin to consider their differing constitutions. Whatever the resemblance between these two bodies politic, he writes, it does not follow that their "rules of conduct" are the same: "They differ too much in size to be capable of being administered in the same fashion. Moreover, there will always be an extreme difference between domestic government, where the father can see everything for himself, and civil government, where the leader can hardly see anything unless through someone else's eyes" (ibid.).

So, too, the father's physical superiority over his children is different in kind from the laws through which state power is established. In the first case, the natural inequality between infant and adult makes it "reasonable" that "paternal power passes for being established by nature," but in the "large family where all members are naturally equal, political authority, purely arbitrary with regard to its institution, can be founded only upon convention" (ibid.). It follows that the duties associated with the latter are of a strictly contractual sort, whereas the father's duties are "dictated to him by natural feelings and in a tone that rarely permits him to disobey."

Rousseau continues that "an even more important" difference stems from the origin and distribution of property within each society: whereas children obtain family property through their patrimony, it is to the contrary in "the large family, where the general administration is established only to assure private property, which is antecedent to it." Thus property rights are differently construed in each situation: within the household they "emanate" from the father; within the state they remain lodged in "the particulars" whose peace and abundance are always primary. And while parental love suggests that the father has a "natural interest" in the happiness, pecuniary and otherwise, of family members, "it is not uncommon for [the magistrate] to seek his own happiness in the misery of others" (243).

As a society, then, the household constitutes a natural hierarchy arranged by differences in age, strength, capacity, and sentiment, while the state constitutes a contrived equality of mutual obligations and always threatened tyrannies. And yet, not only are these two societies consistently referred to as "families"—*la petite* and *la grande*—the source and scope of their respective protective and distributive roles are thoroughly confounded over the course of the essay. Consider, for example, filial submission: "If there are laws for those of mature age, there should also be some for the very young which teach them to obey others" (214). This project, which is nothing other than the teaching of duty, cannot be "abandoned" to "the lights and prejudices of their fathers, since it is of even more importance to the state than it is to their fathers." Indeed, Rousseau suggests that the conflation of paternal rights and duties with those of the state is best understood as a question of semantics: "[Fathers] are merely changing a name, and will have in common, under the name of citizens, the same authority over their children they exercised separately under the name *fathers*, and will be obeyed no less well when they speak in the name of the law than they were when they spoke in the name of nature" (ibid.).

But fathers were always speaking in the name of the law. Patrimony, which secures the child's sustenance, obedience, and future (civic) rights, turns out to be an invention of the state: "As Pufendorf has shown, by the nature of the right to property, it does not extend beyond the life of the property owner and the moment a man dies his estate no longer belongs to him. Thus, prescribing to him the conditions under which he can dispose of them is actually less an apparent alteration of his right than it is a real extension of it" (263). Rousseau adds that while the laws that regulate inheritance are determined solely by the sovereign, it makes good sense to favor the decedent's children, "to whom the right to property would be quite useless were the father to leave them nothing," and who, "moreover, have contributed by their labor to the acquisition of the father's goods." Paternal love and filial attachment are buttressed, if not forged, by the laws of inheritance and the sentiments of the contract.

The same matter is presented without nuance in the *Discourse on Inequality*: "The goods of the father, of which he is truly master, are the goods that keep his children in a state of dependence toward him, and he can make their share of his estate dependent on how well they have merited it by continuous deference to his wishes" (182). Here the pleasure of being obeyed and the tyranny to which that anticipated pleasure might give rise are not the magistrate's dreaded collateral, unavoidably issuing from a contrived equality: they are the "natural" creations of that public contrivance, inscribed onto the father's authority and thus made available to him within the household. Precisely because the law has already spoken, the force and the form of the father's "natural" speech engenders a loving despotism of dependence, gratitude, and need.

Rousseau's significations of household and state, of nature and politics, are similarly unsettled in the *Discourse on Political Economy*'s account of women's familial subordination. The "authority of the mother and father must not be equal," Rousseau asserts, because, first, "there must be a single government and when there are differences of opinion there must be a dominant voice which decides." (Here Locke's position on the family is repeated almost exactly, without occasioning any of the deep concerns that occupy extended notes in the *Discourse on Inequality*.)[35] Second, the father should command because he is not, in the normal course, subject to the "interval of inaction" which, however "slight" her "particular inconveniences" (*incommodités particulières*), a woman will periodically experience (242). Perhaps he is anticipating his audience or perhaps he recognizes the tenuousness of the claim, but Rousseau immediately adds: "It is a sufficient reason for excluding her from this primacy: for when the balance is perfectly equal, a straw is enough to tip it." Finally, a husband must be able to inspect his

---

[35] See *Second Treatise of Government*, 362–64, sections §79–82, much of which Rousseau quotes in note 12 of the *Discourse on Inequality*, 214–19.

wife's behavior "because it is important to him to be assured that the children that he is forced to recognize and support [*nourrir*] do not belong to anyone but him" (ibid.).

These three reasons given for the necessity of masculine dominance in the family all derive, Rousseau tells us, "from the nature of the thing," but it is clear that that thing is politics. In the first and second instances, domestic patriarchy is cast as a response to the imperatives of efficacious rule. Echoing the *Social Contract*'s depiction of government as fundamentally "a means of communication" that requires "a particular self" (*un 'moi' particulier*) of "robust health," Rousseau presents the father's ever-ready, dominant "voice" within the household as simply more expedient.[36] In the third instance (and the only time Rousseau refers to "the husband" [*le mari*] in this essay), domestic patriarchy is justified as protection against nonconsensually assumed obligations: it is because marriage law will "force" him to accept his wife's children as his own that the husband has the right to oversee her conduct.

If it is biology that makes paternity precarious, it is politics that makes it matter. This is clear from the *Social Contract*'s treatment of marriage, which appears in the final chapter on civil religion. Rousseau is cautioning his readers about the consequences of the clergy's dogmatism and ascendent power:

> Marriage, for example, being a civil contract, has civil effects without which it is impossible for a society even to subsist. Suppose then that a clergy reaches the point where it subscribes to itself alone the right to permit this ac[t]. In that case, is it not clear that in establishing the authority of the church in this matter, it will render ineffectual that of the prince, who will have no more subjects than those whom the clergy wishes to give him? Is it not also clear that the clergy—if master of whether to marry or no[t]—in behaving prudently and holding firm, will alone dispose of inheritance, offices, the Citizens, the State itself, which could not subsist if composed solely of bastards?[37]

[36] See *Social Contract*, Book III, chap. 1, "On Government in General," 396, 399.

[37] Ibid., 469. See Pléiade note at 1506–7, and the text of Rousseau's original note in the first version of the *Social Contract* (Geneva Manuscript) "The Marriage of Protestants," 343–44. There Rousseau offers as an example the situation of French Protestants who, following the revocation of the Edict of Nantes, were

Like the prince who is governor of the state, the father who governs the household must have assurances about the number and identity of family members. But in this passage and in the *Discourse on Political Economy*, it is a juridical rather than a romantic *sensibilité* that animates the desire for sexual exclusivity and surveillance. Bastards are a political construction whose site is women's bodies; they both give form to the threat of princely impotence—what state could subsist "if composed solely of bastards"?—and demarcate a naturalistically (re)constituted category of authentic citizenry: those children born to a man's lawful wife. And while this "forces" the husband to recognize and accept what he might not believe is truly his, it also sustains and repopulates the state that is his own. Juridical paternity is perhaps another way of forcing him to be free. But when Sophie refuses to force Emile in this way (recall that "nothing forced her to reveal" that he was not the father [897], she ironically preserves the integrity of a state that creates bastards in order to create citizens: the semantic (re)constitution of *father* as *citizen* depends on the prior (re)constitution of *citizen* as *father*, and (thus) both on the political fantasy of bloodline. (This is not, of course, to deny the reality of biological parentage, but to insist that its meanings are inseparable from juridical forms. For example, when he learns that his exclusive claim to Sophie's body has been violated, Emile certainly doesn't cease to be his son's father: he just wishes his son dead, and then abandons him [904].)

While Sophie's confession preserves the integrity of the political order, it does so at the expense of Emile's membership: the state is saved, but the citizen dies.[38] Or perhaps he just devolves. The story line of *Les Solitaires* following Sophie's revelation traces this political devolution and in so doing, it recalls the circular structure of the *Discourse on Inequality*: in both instances, the "inevitable" abuses of consensual nonconsensuality return subjects to a

---

denied marriage by Catholic clergy: "[Protestants] are permitted to be neither strangers, nor citizens, nor men. Even the rights of nature have been taken from them, marriage is forbidden to them and they are all at once stripped of *la patrie*, the family and its goods, they are reduced to the state of beasts" (343).

[38] Twice in the *Discourse on Political Economy* Rousseau contrasts the state's perpetuity with the transitory nature of the family: the latter is designed and destined to "die off," while the former "was made to last foreve[r]" (242). See also 260.

condition of "natural" lawlessness akin to the point at which they began. In *Les Solitaires* this begins the moment of Sophie's disclosure, which sends Emile running for "obscurity under the trees" in a public garden, where he rambles, moans, and generally loses his mind: "I could no longer see anything, compare anything, deliberate, weigh, or judge anything" (892). After a period of dissolution and decay ("it was my own death for which I cried" [894]), Emile is ready for another rebirth ("I became, so to say, a new being" [899]), and thus he leaves his country in something resembling his natural state ("without valet, without money, without gear; but without desires and without cares" [911]).

In the course of his journey Emile is enslaved, first to Moorish pirates and then to the dey of Algeria. In this way the "new being" that he becomes incorporates the final images of the *Discourse on Inequality* in which "subjects no longer have any law but the master's will, nor the master any rule but his passions."[39] And Emile describes this time of servitude as "the time of my reign." This is because it allows him to realize the constancy, the inevitability, of his enslavement: "Subjected to human passions by my birth, whether their yoke is imposed on me by another or by myself, must it not always be borne, and who knows which of the two will be more bearable?" (917). Thus concluding that "there is no real servitude but that of nature," Emile compares his masters and their power to sometimes trivial, sometimes immovable, impediments: a "pebble," he suggests, or a "boulder," or again, a "grain of sand" (ibid.).

But Emile's newfound freedom is not quite primitive. Indeed, it requires that he wear "the barbarians' irons" and "submit to their passions without sharing them." In this sense the enchained Emile is not quite Epictetus: rather than a Stoic self-containment, his is a violently revitalizing subjugation. Because, of course, Emile is not the *Discourse on Inequality*'s impossible savage, and thus he can never (re)produce or sustain its naive immediacy: "Ah! in order not to dissolve into nothingness [*tomber dans l'anéantissement*] I needed to be animated by another's will [*volonté*] for want of my own" (ibid.). It is because of, not despite, the masters' domination that Emile's sense of self returns. He writes to his

---

[39] *Discourse on Inequality*, 191.

tutor: "Their deviance [*écarts*] provided me with lessons more lively than yours had been, and these vulgar masters gave me a course in philosophy even more useful than the one I received from you" (ibid.).

This *éducation sensible* teaches him anew about submission and domination. "I endured mistreatment," he muses, "but less, perhaps, than they would have endured among us." He has learned that the Moorish pirates "are not pitying, but they are just, and if one should not expect gentleness or clemency from them, neither should one fear caprice or cruelty" (918). It is only their slaves' "bad will" (*mauvaise volonté*) that his masters punish, never physical limitations or weakness. "The Negros would be happier in America if the European treated them with similar equity," Emile observes, rather than as mere "instruments of work" (ibid.). Having felt the tenuously mediated nature of all freedom, Emile now measures justice not with respect to the chains one might wear but with respect to the equanimity that their wearing affords. Both his will and his love of justice are reanimated, and through the practices of slavery: "My will, my understanding, my being, all that by which I was me and not some other, could assuredly never be sold" (ibid.).

This is a barbaric politics, to be sure, but it offers Emile freedom of a sort. He presents "proof" of this freedom in the final story in *Les Solitaires*, which recounts his response to the unreasonable demands of a "*prétendu maitre*," a slave overseer belonging to his "real" master, referred to in the text as "*le Maitre*" and then "*le patron*." After persuading the other slaves—through "a simple discourse simply delivered"—that their labor is vital to the master's "true interest," Emile stages a revolt that gives him an opportunity to represent the slaves' "just complaints" and "moderate demands" to their master (922–23). Impressed by Emile's apparent good sense, the master grants him power over all the slaves, including the former "pretend master." Emile reports that his success as overseer became legion and brought him to the attention of the Algerian ruler. One line later: "*Voilà* your Emile, slave to the Dey of Algeria." The text breaks off shortly after this proud report. In our last glimpse of him, Emile is rising in stature and his patron's estimation through the excellence of his slavish rule.

Although not the zealous fratricide whom Rousseau limns at the close of the *Discourse on Inequality*, Emile enslaved is an oddly reminiscent character. He has found freedom in submission, philosophy in bondage, and justice in hard labor: perhaps he is only a starkly drawn version of what the tutor had always imagined. And, indeed, *Les Solitaires* opens with Emile's announcement to his tutor that, in recounting his life story, "I believe I have nothing to say that can dishonor your work [*votre ouvrage*]" (882). So, too, Emile has (re)discovered the truth of natural servitude in the context of a barbaric politics, in the course of a journey that reverses the order of the one he undertook prior to his marriage. The tutor had mandated the earlier journey so that Emile could learn about the political society that he would enter upon marrying: "When you become the head of the family, you are becoming a member of the state, and do you know what it is to be a member of the state? Do you know what government, laws, and fatherland are? Do you know what the price is of your being permitted to live and for whom you ought to die?"[40]. Emile must know what it is to be a patriot before he knows what it is to be husband. (Again, Rousseau claims that there is "need for a natural base on which to form conventional ties," and thus it is "the good husband and the good father who makes the good citizen," but he reverses that priority relationship with conspicuous regularity.) It follows that expatriation is the consequence of the loss of his paternal power.

But this continues, rather than dissolves, Emile's political identity and the dynamics of his consent. On the one hand, it might appear that his enslavement follows the metaphoric logic of Rousseau's narrative: Emile's failures as father, husband, and lover reduce him to a condition of slavery. On the other hand, that condition turns out to be the "time of [his] rule," in part, because he comes to understand that submission to human passions is inevitable; given this, submissive desire becomes a feature of all freedom rather than an obstacle to it. This is also a time of Emile's rule because he puts his theory into practice, as the eager slave-ruler of the dey's slaves. And here we get a brief but arresting view of the coincidence of Rousseau's democracy and his slavery: "The rules by which I had to conduct myself in the new post [of slave overseer] flowed from principles that were hardly unknown to me. We had discussed them during our travels. And their application, although imperfect and quite small in scale in the situation I was

[40] *Emile*, 448.

in, was nevertheless steady and infallible in its effects. I will not fill you in on these minor details; that's not something of great concern between you and me" (923).

These political principles, which appear in Book V of *Emile*, repeat the basic claims of the *Social Contract*, including its derivation of the general will.[41] In thus bringing about a just political community, Emile has fulfilled his tutor's wildest dreams: the fact that this community and its justice cohere with slavery is but a "minor detail" about which they need not concern themselves. Stripped of his possessions, his country, and his Sophie, Emile, together with his *semblables*, has (re)learned the moral and political inevitability of domination and submission, and thus (re)gained his freedom and his identity. He now embodies what we first encountered with Sophie (and what Rousseau is, in general, more ready to acknowledge in its feminine form): one can be subjected and, in so being, rule, or one can simply be subjected. But it is never an alternative to avoid subjection altogether.

These are the object lessons given to both Emile and Sophie. Dolls, bodies, babies, bastards, and finally, the slave's chains: in each instance the imperatives of consensual nonconsensuality find material form and, in so doing, (re)constitute the natural world, as well as the *sensibilité* through which citizens apprehend it. In every instance save the last, sexual identity and experience directly hold and shape these materializations that organize, as they reflect, a political world of rulers and ruled that was always there. With respect to the last instance, the picture of Emile enslaved offered at the close of *Les Solitaires*, it might seem plausible to take from this ungendered script the conclusion that the problem of consent and freedom derives from nothing inherently sexual. Rousseau is revealing that, stripped down to its barest particulars, the paradox of consensual nonconsensuality originates in the paradox of conventional authority, and he (perhaps together with democrats everywhere) simply reads this into and through the identities of men and women. But there is that problem of origins again. Never mind that every step in Emile's circular journey is framed as a move away from or toward (and usually both) Sophie; never mind that *Les Solitaires* begins with the revelation that Sophie

[41] Ibid., 460.

now lives "in the *patrie* of just souls" and thus her death, like Julie's in *La Nouvelle Héloïse*, frames the political fantasies that will follow. There is no definitive differentiation of the like from the unalike, the *semblable* from the *différent*, the copy from the original, because Rousseau's object lessons constitute a metonymic chain that ties sex and politics together.

Life Stories

> Whether it is believed to be true or not, it
> makes little difference. I shall, if you please,
> have told fictions, but I shall still have
> explicated my method and I shall still be
> pursuing my ends.
>
> *Emile*

Textual Symptoms

In the hugely successful *Julie, ou La Nouvelle Héloïse*, Rousseau narrates a tale of moral autonomy that takes the form of a consensually nonconsensual romance similar to what we saw sketched in *Emile*. Both books feature female protagonists whose passion simultaneously endangers and preserves the social order, and both depict male moral maturation in the context of submission to that same, endangering and preservative passion. But unlike the story of Emile and Sophie, the story of Julie, her lover St. Preux, and her husband Wolmar unfolds through a ménage à trois that enacts the tension between romantic passion and conjugal duty. Or rather, Rousseau mobilizes that tension to conform to the dramatic imperatives of "corrupt peoples": the bifurcation of the moral end of his sexual politics onto two different characters, the lover who is ruled and the husband who rules, is critical to staging a successful literary *spectacle*.[1] Unlike the overtly didactic *Emile*, his epistolary novel serves as a cultural heuristic only to the extent it offers the seductions of character, plot, and narrative absorption. Rousseau thus sets out to tell a "real" story about ruling passions and the social transformations they engender, which is to say, a story with a beginning, a middle, and an end, as well as one that imagines its own factual origins. These factual "imaginings" begin with the novel's two prefaces, the second of which is staged as a

---

[1] The first preface to *Julie ou La Nouvelle Héloïse* begins: "Great cities must have theaters; and corrupt peoples, Novels. I have seen the morals of my times, and I

conversation between an author R. and a skeptical "man of letters" N., who pointedly asks if the letters are "real"; the imaginings continue throughout the novel in Rousseau's many editorial asides, some of which speculate on missing and "suppressed" letters.[2] The insistent ambivalence about its status as fiction underscores how the book functions as an object lesson, facilitating for its readers what the story itself represents, and what *Emile* prescribes: an *éducation sensible* that makes moral awareness inseparable from the ambiguously dominant and submissive experience of daily gender practice.

This ambiguity infuses the novel's portraits of husbands, wives, and lovers, what it means to assume those roles and fulfill those duties. But it also figures in the novel's representation of reading, a practice in which every character is passionately engaged: the narrative unfolds in their actions through and reactions to letters that titillate, promise, threaten, enchant, and implore. The relationships that constitute the novel's plot are thus represented in an exchange that undermines authorial absolutism, even as it insists upon a captive audience. In this way the narrative self-construction promised by the epistolary form is also called into doubt, or rather, its implied autonomy remains bound to a social and sexual dynamic of anticipation, recognition, and reward. From the flirtations of *Julie*'s early love letters to the epic moralism of its later expository digressions, the story's success hinges on its ability to produce literary sensations: a romantic *sensibilité* informs the readers in the novel, who, like readers of the novel, are not so much convinced by the power of narrative as they are subjected to it.

That this subjection has importantly gendered dimensions is noted by many, including, of course, Rousseau himself, who remarks in the first preface that the novel's "gothic tone is better suited to women than books of philosophy," while an "austere man" leafing through the early letters might understandably be moved to "throw the book down in anger [and] rail at the Editor."[3]

---

have published these letters." Rousseau, *Julie ou La Nouvelle Héloïse*, in *Oeuvres Complètes*, vol. 4, 5 (hereafter *Julie*).

[2] See *Oeuvres Complètes*, vol. 2, preface (5–6) and second preface (9–30). For readers' credulity apropos the book's factual bases, see Attridge, "The Reception of *La Nouvelle Héloïse*."

[3] First preface, 6.

In similar fashion Rousseau insists that he has given the book a "sufficiently clear title" to warn off "maidens" (*filles*) whose exposure to "a single page" would be their downfall: for the virginal (feminine), these "Letters of Two Lovers Who Live in a Small Town at the Foot of the Alps" produce a literary sensation that is perforce depraved.[4] And yet the picture Rousseau provides of his imagined readers in the second preface—a husband and wife reading this collection together, "finding in it a source of renewed courage to bear their common labors, and perhaps new perspectives to make them useful"[5]—invokes a model of transgendered impressionability whose benefits include the invigoration of virtue and the "rebirth" of nature's "true sentiments" in both their hearts: "How could they contemplate this tableau of a happy couple without wanting to imitate such an attractive model?"[6]

It seems that this imitative model aptly characterizes the self-understanding of at least some portion of Rousseau's readership: Robert Darnton's reconstruction of the "romantic sensitivity" of an eighteenth-century reading public draws on the literary testimony of both men and women to document the power and intensity of the novel's impressions.[7] And while Darnton compares the situation of his exemplary reader Jean Ranson to the modal rustic couple of the second preface, no evidence is provided which suggests that either Ranson's first or second wife joined him in actually reading the book. (But perhaps Ranson's unilateral application of Rousseauian principles to his own situation as suitor, husband, and, finally, father accurately realizes Rousseau's fantasy, which in the second preface transforms that ideally impressionable couple who pick up the book into "true Patriarchs" by the time they put it down.[8] There is ambiguity here: do they transform

[4] Ibid.

[5] Second preface, 23.

[6] Ibid.

[7] Darnton, "Readers Respond to Rousseau." So, too, an eighteenth-century readership might have encountered Rousseau's diagnostic pronouncements on novels in the *Encyclopédie*'s entry under "roman" (novel or romance), included in vol. 14 (1765). In this short essay, the Chevalier de Jaucourt quotes verbatim from St. Preux's letter to Julie, where Rousseau proposes that novel writers ought to depict "heavenly virtue" such that it remains accessible to corrupt humans and, in this way, "lead them imperceptibly [*insensiblement*] toward it from the bosom of vice" (*Julie*, 277).

[8] Second preface, 23.

into loyal supporters of patriarchy, or has Rousseau finessed his intended readers' gender identity? In either case, political power has been [re]masculinized, and through a process that depends on the sensuous excesses of romance.) So, too, Anna Attridge's review of contemporaneous responses to *Julie* reveals distinctions in tone and enthusiasm characterized more by class and cultural location than gender.[9] In short, while the content and the style of the novel as a genre have long been associated with a feminine readership,[10] it is a different matter whether or how this exemplary novel gendered the forms of reading it provoked and represented.

Undoubtedly what William Ray refers to as the "semiotic na-iveté" associated with women readers was instrumental to the novel's success: identifying the risks of narrative self-construction in women's natural (albeit paradoxical) tendencies toward passivity and excess served to minimize anxiety over the genre's general potential to destabilize.[11] Likewise, Ray's insistence that Rousseau's novel invites "multiple and incommensurate modes of reading" that differentiate between the semiotically naive and astute makes a good deal of sense.[12] But how to apply these claims to gendered readers is unclear: that affective submersion is gendered feminine while critical analysis is gendered masculine does not tell us much about the actual semiotic sophistication of male and female readers or about the representation of those readers within the text. Consider the examples of Emile, whose impressionability apropos the tutor's conjuring of Sophie rivals any chaste maiden's, and Sophie, who has practiced semiotics on her doll for a very long time before she meets Emile. In short, we need to consider that male readers must, on occasion, assume feminine poses, while female readers must occasionally assume masculine poses: the gendered dimension to Rousseau's interpretive designs is not monologic. When, in this light, we consider the heady excesses of St. Preux's letters—his demands to be punished, his recitations of rapturous domestic encounters at Clarens—and the firm but reasoned tone Julie takes when instructing her lover, for example, about dueling, the impression is of a cross-gendered cultural prac-

[9] Attridge, "The Reception of *La Nouvelle Héloïse*."
[10] See, for example, Watt, *The Rise of the Novel;* Armstrong, *Desire and Domestic Fiction;* McKeon, *The Origins of the English Novel.*
[11] Ray, "Reading Women," esp. 427. See also his "Rethinking Reading."
[12] Ray, "Rethinking Reading," 154.

tice of the sort which, as we have seen, consensual nonconsensuality always requires.

My interpretive approach to *Julie* insists that the ethical and political stakes of consensual nonconsensuality are not particular to genre. While differences in performative conventions matter greatly, my aim here is to retrace a structural constant that reappears throughout Rousseau's political, fictional, occasional, and autobiographical writings. In keeping with this project, I do not address in any detail some extremely interesting and not irrelevant questions, such as, For whom was *Julie* written? Who read it? How did they read it? To what ends? Rather, I pose these questions from within the novel's narrative frame: What are the relationships established in the exchange of letters? How do the correspondents read their letters, and to what ends? I present a symptomatic reading, one that focuses on the novel's narration of desire, authority, and moral development in order to explore further the perversities of Rousseauian consent. My use of symptom does not presume a psychoanalytic sensibility: rather, I introduce the term to indicate a pattern that cuts across thematic contexts. This pattern, which pertains to paradoxes of power and consent, emerges in *Julie*'s representation of how desire becomes intelligible. Thus I take up the novel's themes of romantic passion and conjugal duty (as well as their illicit contraries, romantic duty and conjugal passion) as opportunities to rethink Rousseau's politics and his sex.

It remains to be seen whether the ethico-political frame of *Julie*'s gender performances is unproblematically republican. While the story's (hetero)sexual sensibilities evoke the consensual nonconsensuality that I have identified as quintessentially republican, its representation of politics is decidedly authoritarian.[13] We might also recall here the "genuine Patriarchs" whom Rousseau hopes to produce from among an audience of simple (albeit literate) "peasants." In the end, it is difficult to fix precisely the relationship between *Julie*'s narrative representations and Rousseau's republicanism, given how the novel depicts a political community-cum-family that is coded patriarchal: in the context of Clarens, both

---

[13] The significance of this authoritarian structure is addressed in Shklar, *Men and Citizens*; Starobinski, *Transparency and Obstacle*; and Schwartz, *Sexual Politics*.

Julie and Wolmar are celebrated as Asian despots.[14] Moreover, the triangulation of ideal love and familial order through Julie's interactions with her lover and her husband strongly suggests the erotic and social codes of courtly love: just because of this "gothic" dimension, the story cannot claim to represent the social milieu in which it will circulate.

And perhaps the story is not making that claim. With its recurrent references to medieval and monarchical regimes (including, of course, in its title) perhaps *Julie ou La Nouvelle Héloïse* is better seen as a historical recapitulation of romantic love, a form of sociability and sentiment whose republican possibilities must be historically realized. In this sense the novel takes up the terms of erotic and sexual practice salient to the "corrupt people" of eighteenth-century Europe—the foppish courtiers, libertine aristocrats, *les petites-maîtresses* of high society, and those stubbornly *insensibles* bourgeois—to rework the dramatic repertoire of familial and sexual loyalty. If not precisely "genuine Patriarchs," perhaps sentimental ones can be engendered through this textual encounter: and, indeed, that is the libidinal and moral economy that Rousseau's republicanism requires.

Am I suggesting that the despotic rule through which Julie and Wolmar sustain their happy home is inconsistent with Rousseau's political vision? Not exactly; but while its depiction of loving obedience and beneficent rule is quite familiar, its context of rigid social hierarchy is not. The relationships that sustain Clarens resemble nothing so much as the demesne, where the absolutism of political rule is undergirded by the social and moral obligations of customary right. Rousseau's literary "tableau" is thus conjuring a bygone age to provoke a sentimentality rich with republican possibilities.[15] Here republican yearning is expressed symptomatically as idealized despotism, and it is St. Preux who narrates that idealization. A man for all times—a man without a proper name who, further, is never identified by name as either author or recipient of these

---

[14] *Julie*, 459.

[15] By contrast, both Martin B. Ellis (*Julie: A Synthesis of Rousseau's Thought*) and Lester Crocker ("*Julie* ou la Nouvelle Duplicité") argue that there is a close fit between the governance structure of Clarens and of Rousseau's ideal republic, although they offer diametrically opposed accounts of that fit.

letters[16]—St. Preux is the subject of this *éducation sensible*, and it is thus his fantasies we must probe.

The discursive symptomology I delineate and analyze in this chapter does not abandon issues of embodiment. On the contrary, in a context where romance takes the shape of a literary exchange, narrative's twofold imperative—for discursive and material articulation—becomes all the more pronounced. We thus should not be surprised when St. Preux, hiding in Julie's wardrobe prior to their nocturnal rendezvous, pauses to narrate an encounter with her corset ("which touches and enfolds . . . two slight curves in front . . . oh voluptuous *spectacle* . . . the whalebone has yielded to the form pressed into it . . . delightful imprints, let me kiss you a thousand times! . . . Ye gods! Ye gods! What will it be when . . ."[17]). Like Laclos's Valmont writing to his chaste mistress on the back of a prostitute, St. Preux's actions merely dramatize how successful narrative entails bodily inscription.[18] And if the epistolary antics of LaClos's libertine invite the reader to join in a smug, if scandalized, awareness of the potential disconnection between text and context, Rousseau's would-be scholar seems bent on closing that distance altogether. The immediacy of St. Preux's passion ("O desires! O fear! O cruel throbbings!") is always mediated through a narrative that gives it form and (thus) meaning, and ultimately, satifaction: "Someone is opening the door! . . . someone is entering! . . . it is she! It is she!"[19]

NOVEL CREATIONS

In broad design, the story is as follows: Julie d'Etange, a young noblewoman, and her tutor, St. Preux, are in love. Their relationship is thwarted by Julie's father, the Baron d'Etange, who has promised Julie in marriage to Wolmar, an old military friend to

---

[16] St. Preux is a pseudonym; all letters written to St. Preux are identified by their author (e.g., "From Julie," "From Bomston"), while all letters written by St. Preux are identified by their recipient (e.g., "To Julie," "To Mme D'Orbe").

[17] *Julie*, 147.

[18] See Laclos, *Les Liaisons Dangereuses*, 98–101. Ray uses this example to illustrate his claims about readers' semiotic sophistication; see "Rethinking Reading," 169.

[19] *Julie*, 147. Subsequent citations will be given in the text.

whom the baron owes his life. While Julie's mother is described as sympathetic to her daughter's predicament, we read that she is "lacking authority" and thus is unable to intercede effectively on her daughter's behalf. The first two (of six) sections of the novel establish the growing attachment between Julie and St. Preux and the changing nature of their interaction, as an initial playfulness gives way to more insistent demands. After their first kiss, Julie sends St. Preux away. During the course of their separation, St. Preux meets his future mentor and friend Edward Bomston, and Julie meets Wolmar. St. Preux returns when Julie's cousin and confidante Claire sends for him after Julie has fallen gravely ill. Their first sexual encounter follows quickly upon this reunion.

After some initial paroxysms of guilt and despair, Julie resumes a passionate and clandestine relationship with St. Preux. Claire, meanwhile, grows concerned that his indiscretion will cast suspicions on Julie, and she urges Julie to send him away. But Julie, with Bomston's help, tries to persuade her father to accept St. Preux, and in the process she confesses her feelings toward her lover. The baron responds with such outrage and violence that Julie ends up miscarrying the child no one knows she was carrying. Crushed by her father's declaration that he will never consent to her marriage to St. Preux, she asks Claire for help in sending her lover away again. The anguished St. Preux, unaware of what has transpired between Julie and her father, departs for an extended journey with Bomston. During his absence, Julie acquiesces to her father's demands and, after first obtaining St. Preux's consent, she marries Wolmar.

Julie de Wolmar takes up residence at Clarens and is transformed into a model wife and mother. She continues to write to and care about St. Preux, but she does so under cover of a loving friendship. Her relationship with Wolmar has changed her, she writes to St. Preux, and she is grateful for the opportunity to overcome her early mistakes. Together she and Wolmar persuade St. Preux to join them at Clarens, to witness and share in the grace of their lives. Once subjected to their domestic *spectacle*, St. Preux begins to reconcile himself to the changed nature of his relationship with Julie, and in a series of letters to Bomston he extols the virtues of Clarens's domestic economy and of Julie's and Wolmar's respective characters. Again he is sent away, this time to Italy to extricate Bomston from an unsuitable romance. After a final exchange of letters during which St. Preux rejects Julie's proposition that he marry the widowed Claire, he receives word that Julie has died as a result of an illness contracted while saving one of her children from drowning. In a deathbed revelation written to St. Preux, Julie reveals that she had never overcome her passion for him. Thus she dies willingly, even intentionally, with the knowledge that her virtue will never again be threatened by her desire.

Readers of the novel have shown a pronounced tendency, initiated by Rousseau himself, to see in it two distinct stories.[20] The first is a love story, told in terms of youthful excess, irrepressible passion, and individualistic, if not narcissistic, self-disclosure. The tone of these letters, most of which are illicitly written and surreptitiously exchanged, is expressive, and their style is revelatory. The love story moves through inner states (the presence or absence of Julie's desire, for example, or St. Preux's constancy, Claire's vivacity), and it thus "works" only insofar as readers sense—hear, see, feel—the characters' sentiments through their words. The second story is about the virtues of domesticity, and its style is exegetical. Most of the letters that constitute this second story are exchanged between characters at a distance from one another, and here the narrative becomes more informational and descriptive: pictures of life at Clarens are offered from the perspectives of St. Preux, Julie, and on one occasion, Wolmar, while their epistolary partners—for St. Preux it is Bomston, for Julie it is Claire—respond with questions that provoke further reflection and comment on the themes of marriage and domesticity.

This parsing of *Julie* emphasizes a thematic distinction between the charm and transports of erotic love, on the one hand, and the moral rectitude of conjugal piety, on the other. On this Rousseau's contemporaneous readers were as divided about the proper moral to draw from the novel as are readers today: Is Rousseau serving up a celebration of the harmonizing power of a passionless marriage, a cautionary tale about the costs of suppressed passion, or a testimony to the irreconcilability of individual happiness and the demands of community?[21] This determination depends to some

---

[20] See second preface, 17: "One would say that there are two different books which the same persons should not read."

[21] Both Fermon (*Domesticating Passions*) and Morgenstern (*Rousseau and the Politics of Ambiguity*) underscore the heuristic value of the Wolmar marriage; their

degree on where one's sympathies lie, with ideals of true love or of family. That the power of the former derives at least in part from its refusal to be constrained by custom or rational design means that the desiring couple will be imagined in relation to a social and familial order that opposes their union. In the novel this ordered opposition takes the form of Julie's father, but also the just and kind Wolmar: patriarchy, class, and the ethico-social bonds of military men together structure the worldly impediments to romance.

Likewise, because the force of true love is signified by an erotic excess, it requires the confirmation of a transgressive act, and Julie must be the first "maiden" whose corruption through these letters Rousseau foretells in the first and second prefaces. In similar fashion the skeptical critic N. of the second preface direly predicts that the "childish games" that precede the novel's "lessons of wisdom" will dissuade readers from continuing on to the end: "the evil scandalizes before the good can edify."[22] In these various ways, then, the reader is put on notice that the novel's thematic juxtaposition of erotic transport and social order will take shape through scandals and edifications: its multifold content—love and community, desire and economy—is already situated within an overarching structure of interwoven antagonisms and resolutions.

The two-story reading also emerges in response to a difference in rhetorical form: emotional declaratives of individual (youthful) expression versus reasoned assessments issued as a didactic exchange. Again, contemporaneous readers were divided on how to make sense of these different "voices." Some saw one, continuous authorial sensibility at play throughout the novel, while others reported irritation at what felt like abrupt shifts between exegetical and expressive styles.[23] Ray connects these shifts to a more general discursive design, suggesting that in the course of changing its "narrative register" the novel opens up opportunities for analysis and abstraction. In this way the change in convention, from romance to what Ray calls political allegory, parallels a change in reading protocols, from imitation to interpretation.[24] The "triage"

---

conclusions differ markedly from one another, and from my own, with respect to the political and social lesson(s) Rousseau intended for his readers.

[22] Ibid.

[23] See Attridge, "The Reception of *La Nouvelle Héloise*," 229–35.

[24] Ray, "Reading Women," 430–31.

performed on the reader discriminates between those who remain subject to the affective absorption prescribed in the second preface and those who are capable of analytic and critical detachment. On this account St. Preux emerges as an exemplary reader: although mesmerized by the various domestic *spectacles* of Clarens—Julie's garden Elysium, the festivities of the *vendange*—he goes further, revealing to Bomston his awareness of how these *spectacles* are staged, and to what ends.[25]

When taken together, these two-story analyses suggest a progressive scheme in which the narrative's content and its form reflect parallel moral and communicative maturation. The self-absorption of the novel's early sections gives way to the self-reflection of its later parts, as characters move from lovers to friends and enter a new familial order. But as I insisted in chapter one, there are problems with limiting Rousseau's narratives to linear, developmental designs. In *Julie* that design would progress from an original youthful folly, steeped in sensuousness and erotic delights, to the wisdom of an adult world built upon the mutuality of contentment and reasoned self-constraint. My concern is not principally that such an enlightened progression fits poorly with Rousseau's taste for devolutions, but that the two stories are profoundly interdependent, in terms of both their thematic content and their rhetorical form. The edification, in other words, is impossible without the scandal, and the theoretical abstraction assumes a prior narrative absorption. Rousseau appears to make just this point when, in the second preface, R. responds to N.'s accusations of inconsistency by claiming that "those who can profit from [the book] would not read it had it begun more solemnly."[26]

If the suggestion that its scandalous beginning serves as the novel's necessary lure brings to mind a narrative ploy akin to bait and switch, in the end it is difficult to reduce the novel to this design because, finally, the novel returns to where it began, with the self-revealing excesses of erotic desire. These final disclosures by Julie inevitably cast doubt on her previous representations: apparently the harmony and contentment of the Wolmar marriage, memorialized by every character who addresses the topic, is built upon

[25] Ibid., 434–35.
[26] Second preface, 17.

her unreconstructed passion for St. Preux. So, too, St. Preux's wise appraisals of Clarens as a model social and familial form never ignore Julie's continuing power over him: his celebratory assessment of domesticity results precisely from the absorbing image of his mistress playing house. And perhaps this ongoing, mutual absorption was always detectable in the voluptuous agitation that continues to animate Julie's prose, despite, or perhaps because of, her insistence that she is quite recovered from her youthful malaise.

This improbable coincidence of disease and cure looks very familiar: it is central to the ethical frame of Rousseau's (hetero)sexual ideal that a woman's success as a wife depends on her success as a mistress, and the husband's happiness depends on the lover's. Because *Julie*, unlike *Emile*, glosses the sociopolitical world in which these roles are embedded, the novel gives dramatic form to their very different performative demands. For the lover, it is complete submission to "a passion wrapped up in itself," while for the husband, it is attending to the duties of management and prudent rule. That both of these characters are needed to give *Julie* its plot threatens to expose the contradictions of a gender system in which social order is built upon sexual disorder. Chastity is guaranteed by its opposite, virtue builds upon vice, and modesty must secure for itself a continual audience: no longer a paradoxical challenge discreetly issued to Emile and Sophie, this (il)logic of republican romance structures the novel's intertwined stories of love and marriage.

To some degree, however, its central tropes of conversion and exemplification work to contain the contradictions. It is because Julie redeems herself as a "chaste spouse" and as St. Preux's "preacher" that readers accept her checkered past: "the worthy *mère de famille*," N. suggests, "causes us to forget the guilty mistress." And it is St. Preux's steady transformation into a confirmed patrician—one ready to play for his friend Bomston the same spoiling role as did the Baron d'Etange in his own life—that saves him from remaining, in the reader's indulgent or disdainful eyes, a maudlin sot. And yet, if for some reason Rousseau's N. is correct and readers do, in the course of the story, disregard "the guilty mistress," they are forcefully reminded of her at the story's end, *by* its end. St. Preux certainly never forgot her. For him, moral

113

maturation is premised on the "eloquence of disorder"[27] that fuels love stories and on the power of that eloquence to sustain illusion, including the illusion of a doubled Julie. If he is able to learn from Wolmar's wife and the world she organizes, it is because he remains enraptured by St. Preux's mistress and her worldly dominion. In this way the novel's drama of conversion disaggregates and orders what is, for Rousseau, experientially and politically intertwined: the sensuous and the reasoned, the ruler and ruled, nature and the law.

"Love is but an illusion; it fashions for itself, so to speak, another Universe."[28] This familiar observation, offered by R. in defense of the novel's early stylistic "imprecision," points to a familiar recursive logic and to the possibility that, in this instance, the illusion that love sustains is the orderly, productive, stable, and patriarchal universe fashioned over the course of the novel. Although tempting, it is probably not accurate to say that Rousseau reveals the illusory nature of this universe when his narrative returns us to Julie, who is once again d'Etange and once again espousing a rhetoric of passionate excess.[29] Such an appeal to an originary, and feminine, *dis*order would ignore how a recursive logic forecloses on all manner of stable beginning. The disciplined world of Clarens can thus never be only St. Preux's illusion; by giving form to his "ideals of perfection"—to the virtuous husbands, chaste wives, and loving families of his and Julie's social order—it also establishes the necessary conditions of their originary love. Following the logic that I sketched in the *Discourse on Inequality*, the novel shows how the worldly impediments to romance also make that romance possible, or even, if we are among those whom Rousseau hopes can "profit from it," make the romance inevitable.

GILDED PRIVATIONS

St. Preux is a teacher who must be taught. The irony is regularly flagged in Julie and Claire's mocking references to him as "the philosopher," for example, and the gentle condemnation his sta-

[27] Ibid., 15.

[28] Ibid.

[29] This final reference to "Julie d'Etange" is made by Claire in the novel's last letter; see *Julie*, 744.

tus as "pedant" regularly provokes. When he visits Clarens after Julie's marriage, she describes his improvement to Claire in terms that celebrate an educational devolution: "In general the love of truth has cured him of a systemic mind, so that he has become less brilliant and more reasonable, and one learns much more from him now that he is not so learned" (427).

These comments pertain to the instruction St. Preux has received in the course of his travels, the tempering, even humbling, effects that exposure to worldly variation and complexity afford. The familiar image recalls Rousseau's ideal of renaturalization, a stripping away of affectation and dogma to retrieve the more authentic, certainly the wiser, faculty beneath it all. But this notion of demystification, of life-learning as a return to common sense, does not follow obviously from our first impression of St. Preux's *éducation sensible*, where the subject of edification is a stripped-down passion, and tutelage requires interpersonal domination.

These are the themes introduced in the novel's opening letter where the schoolmaster, admitting that he is in love with his pupil, chides her for her inconsistency—overly familiar with him in the presence of others, distant when they are alone—and insists that she take control of the situation: "I see, Mademoiselle, only one way out of the quandary I am in; that the hand which plunges me into it pulls me out, that my punishment as well as my fault come from you, and that out of pity for me at least, you do me the favor of banishing me from your presence. Show my letter to your parents; have me refused entry to your house; dismiss me in whatever way you prefe[r]" (32). St. Preux's anxieties only multiply when Julie responds by displaying a consistent reserve. Now deprived of even that "innocent familiarity" she had previously shown him, the schoolmaster demands that she acknowledge his "fire," which "deserves to be punished but not scorned": "For pity's sake, do not leave me to myself; condescend at least to settle my fate; tell me your pleasure. Whatever you may command, I can but obey. . . . A hundred times a day I am tempted to throw myself at your feet, to bathe them with my tears, to obtain there my death or my pardon. . . . Satisfy a righteous vengeance. Am I not miserable enough to be reduced to begging for it myself? Punish me, you must" (36).

But when Julie finally acknowledges St. Preux's desire, it is by revealing her own. Not only does she refuse to punish him—for

115

offenses real or imagined—but she implores him to take charge, to realize that he is her "sole defender against yourself": "Can I believe you vile enough to abuse the fatal admission which my delirium wrings from me? No, I know you well: you will sustain me in my weakness, you will become my safeguard, you will protect my person against my own heart. Your virtues are the last refuge of my innocence" (40). Coincident with the admission of her feelings is an acknowledgment of her proper powerlessness, and it is thus only by persuading St. Preux to act with virtue that Julie has any hope of retaining her own, which is to say, of safeguarding her virginity.

In this apparent slave morality, surrender appeals because it shields from the responsibility of autonomous action. For Julie that responsibility pits her mind against her body, subjecting the integrity of her "person" to the power of her "heart." To protect herself she must cede control: "I would rather be your slave and live in innocence than purchase your dependency at the price of my dishonor" (ibid.). But this interpretation of Julie in flight from freedom forgets that women's consent is always enacted within the terms established by *pudeur*. Because good girls—be they maidens, be they wives—are always obliged to say no, the sincerity of their refusal turns on the absence of desire, and this, as we have seen, invites a decoding of bodily signs. Julie, by contrast, has left nothing to decipher, and when she removes all doubt about her desire, she loses the opportunity, if not the right, to register a refusal. In this sense St. Preux is her "sole defender" inasmuch as her safety depends ultimately on his actions, quite independent of her own.

My insistence on the indeterminacy of Julie's sexual agency may seem at odds with the enthusiasm of her confession, and even as she presents herself as prey—"drawn into the snares of a vile seducer"—we cannot help but read in her eloquence both desire and will. Certainly for readers "wrapped up" in her passion, the prospect of its nonconsensual consummation is positively unthinkable. And perhaps that is the point. Regardless, it is important to recognize that in crucial respects—namely, those that pertain to the social-sexual order that St. Preux and Julie represent—he is in control of this affair from its inception: because he can safely assume Julie's desire, he can fairly assume her consent, and what she stands to lose is not the integrity of her will but the mark of her honor. On this and not the consent she knows has already been vitiated, Julie stakes her claim for protection: "My honor makes bold to entrust itself to yours, you cannot preserve the one without the other; generous soul, ah! preserve them both and at least for love of yourself, deign to take pity on me" (ibid.).

St. Preux responds by consenting to rule virtuously—to be the stronger, we might say—but with a renewed excess of fantasy that gives pause:

> Although my reason is forever lost, although the agitation of my senses grows each instant, your person is henceforth for me the most charming, but the most sacred trust [*dépôt*] that ever honored a mortal. My flame and its object will together preserve an unalterable purity. I would shudder more to lay a hand upon your chaste form than to commit the most vile incest, and you are not more inviolably safe with your father than with your lover. Oh, if ever that happy lover forgets himself for one moment in your presence . . . Julie's lover could have an abject soul! No, when I cease to love virtue I will no longer love you; at my first craven action, I want you to love me no more. (42)

The terms of St. Preux's command are also those of his surrender: in both cases, he has lost his mind, his senses are inflamed, and it is the inseparability of his desire and its object that guarantees their mutual protection. And while in *Emile* we saw the love object appear only when and how the pupil needed her to be, here the pupil's attributes will take shape in accordance with the object's needs: it is unimaginable that Julie's lover would have an "abject soul," and so St. Preux must imagine himself to be a virtuous man. The plot unfolds through a structure of pity and self-love that we have seen before, one that links individual identity and (self-)rule to how one imagines others to be. It is Julie's attributes that will determine the quality of St. Preux's (self-)rule, and so long as he imagines her to be virtuous, then so, too, will be his rule.

Perhaps for this reason it makes sense that St. Preux chooses to imagine her as family. By fantasizing incest, he intensifies his desire for a virtuous abstinence. But he also risks multiplying his attachments to that "chaste form" whose inviolability depends, still, on his ardor: to the lover's passion he joins the father's protective zeal, thus rendering more "tender and true" the love that

117

unites them. The result is an imagined (im)balance of pleasures and pains ("To say it all in a few words, I abhor a criminal act more than I love Julie") that restrains the lover with appeals to the very desire that motivates him. This is the same strategy that motivates Julie when, at the end of the novel, she urges St. Preux to marry Claire so that they might all live together "without danger," by becoming "simply sisters and brothers to each other" (671). And while Julie plans to secure her familial fantasy juridically, through the institution of marriage, St. Preux has only the inconceivability of Julie's beloved pursuing such an aberrant transgression. In this, their earliest romantic encounter, he is already conjuring up crimes in order to sustain and protect his "natural" love.[30]

But the "voluntary abstinence" to which St. Preux commits himself always anticipates a reward. When, in the aftermath of his pledge of incestuous devotion, Julie displays an "indiscreet health," he complains bitterly that her avowed weakness was mere pretense to fend him off. He demands signs of a more genuine struggle—her former "touching pallor," he remarks, is now disfigured by a "blooming complexion"—or else he will return the "dangerous trust" (*dépôt*) that has heretofore kept her safe: "And of what avail to me is this eternal and voluntary abstinence from the sweetest thing in the world, if she who demands it is not grateful? Indeed, I am tired of suffering uselessly and of condemning myself to the hardest privations without being given credit for them" (48). Julie responds with the requested, reproachful severity: "In the same letter you complain that you have too much misery and that you do not have enough; consider the matter better and try to be consistent, in order to give your pretended griefs a less frivolous appearance." In explaining the perfection of their currently calm and chaste love, Julie repeats the warning issued by Emile's tutor: "The moment of possession is a crisis in love, and all change is dangerous to our own" (51). When, in his response, St. Preux shows himself contrite and reassured, it is unclear whether the reassurance arises from the evidence of her abiding love or from the promise of its sensual degeneration: "You gild

---

[30] On incest taboos as a product of political and juridical forms (i.e., nowhere existent in "nature"), see *Essay on Languages*, 406. This issue is addressed in more detail in chapter five.

with so much grace the privations you impose upon me that you nearly make them dear to me" (52).

These gilded privations anchor an exchange in which gratification depends on sacrifice and submission. St. Preux's persistent declarations of his obedience to Julie's absolutist rule are always couched in terms of a suffering to which he voluntarily submits, in anticipation of an eventual release. His pain, St. Preux observes, must be "the guarantee of its reward, for I know your soul too well to believe you capable of cruelty for its own sake" (70–71). In this he endures, even enjoys, the various tests to which Julie subjects him as so many steps on the way to his just deserts: "It is fair that you should know whether I am constant, patient, submissive—in a word, deserving of the blessings you are reserving for me" (71). He will submit to her privations—which is to say, he will refrain from acting on his desire—because this both intensifies and guarantees his future satisfaction.

But satisfied he must be, and thus we find that St. Preux, chafing against restraints that are self-imposed at another's behest, finally comes to his senses. No longer kneeling before Julie's throne but "roaring like an angry lioness," he announces that he has become incapable of refusing himself. No longer seeing himself through her eyes, he invites her to see herself through his, in a future where Julie's "beauty, even your beauty, will have its end" and perish like a flower "without having been picked." When an inner nature is roaring and an outer one is withering, right thinking is clearly on the side of immediate action: "You are losing yourself in your hopeless schemes," St. Preux insists, "enthusiasm for honesty takes away your reason, and your virtue is now only a delirium" (74). He ends the letter by introducing his own hopeless scheme: the nearby mountainside is as steep as the cliff at Leucadia, he writes, "and I am in despair." Imagining for Julie Sappho's last, despairing act of love, St. Preux lays bare the poetic consequences—her possession or his death—of Julie's once-gilded privations. Upon receipt of his letter Julie falls deathly ill; Claire arranges for St. Preux's immediate return, and shortly thereafter the two lovers make love.

Julie's version casts the seduction scene in terms that have less to do with fears of a withered future (or an ancient past) than with passionate feelings for the present. Writing to Claire, she claims that St. Preux must know how to love better than she, "because he knows how to conquer his passions better": "A hundred times my eyes witnessed his struggles and his victory. His eyes would sparkle with the fire of his desires. He would hurl toward me with the impetuousness of a blind passion; suddenly he would stop himself; an insurmountable barrier seemed to have surrounded me, and never would his impetuous but honest love have crossed it" (98). This pitiable "victory," note well, is St. Preux's refusal to ravish her, a refusal for which he is amply rewarded. As Julie explains to Claire, it was the force of this "dangerous *spectacle*" that finally over-powered her. By feeling what he felt, by sharing his torments, by thinking that she was merely "being compassionate" (*plaindre*), in short, by making St. Preux too much of a *semblable*, Julie comes undone: "Perhaps love alone would have spared me; O my Cousin, it is pity that ruined me" (96).

Let us consider this familiar juxtaposition of love and pity, here deployed to explain a sexual surrender in which virtue and vice hang in the balance. How can St. Preux's moral, which is to say social, rectitude survive this ravishing? How can Julie's honor? Re-call how the structure of Rousseau's pity prompts, in Marshall's phrase, "a comparison of the self with an other turned *semblable* in which one forgets oneself and imagines the point of view of the other."[31] This is the same logic of identification that has heretofore sustained St. Preux's (self-)deprivation. Similarly, the two pitying lovers "forget" their immediate interests, and what each sees "from the point of view of the other" is him- or herself. Just as St. Preux became Julie's knight-errant by seeing himself through her eyes, so Julie's pity moves her to be what her beloved needs, and much like St. Preux earlier "forgot" his carnal interest, so she now "forgets" her honor. That she will remember her honor, as he remembered his lust, is evident: those recollections signal the inevitable return to self-interest that moral and social awareness entails. But that in-terest is now mediated through an interdependent relationship in which satisfaction depends on another's control.

These accounts of courtship thoroughly confound the terms of consent: will and force, intention and subjection, cannot be disen-tangled in them. On the one hand, this illustrates the power of a *sensibilité* that fuses sentiment and its object, and it points again to the imaginary foundations of *amour propre:* our vanities, interests,

---

[31] Marshall, *The Surprising Effects of Sympathy*, 150.

and desires reflect the sense we make of worldly objects, and in making this sense, *amour propre* can be quite accommodating of the ambiguity, even the contradictions, of consensual nonconsensuality. Julie and St. Preux both rule and surrender in accordance with this logic of identification and desire. On the other hand, the sense being made in this story is of a heterosexual order, and as St. Preux's fury and near-suicidal despair make clear, it is driven by the imperative that men possess women. It is thus not just any *amour propre* that accommodates these ambiguities so readily, but a self-love structured through masculine and feminine identities.

From this perspective, heterosexuality as it appears in Rousseau's stories of moral and social maturation is best seen as an argument. Not simply an identity or a bodily situation, it is a structured demonstration of how domination and submission can cohere in the life of the moral agent, and how *amour propre* is truly satisfied only in relationships where one loses control. That at the very moment of masculine self-assertion St. Preux is striking a feminine pose—roaring like a lioness and threatening to repeat Sappho's leap—demonstrates the representational excess that disturbs these differences, and thus their ongoing fragility. Only the narrative itself keeps a rein on things, guaranteeing that at the end, after all the transgendered swooning and ruling, it is Julie who leaps. In this way the pity that brings them together and the love that holds them apart always work to reiterate a gendered dynamic of control in which sexed bodies are the limiting conditions for identifications of other and *semblable*.

CHALET MORALITY

> My liege, [o]n your knees before your Lady and mistress, your two hands in hers, and in the presence of her Chancellor, you will swear faith to her and loyalty on every occasion, which is not to say eternal love, a bond that one is never master of maintaining or breaking; but truth, sincerity, inviolable candor. You will not swear to be always submissive, but never to commit an act of treachery and at least to declare war before shaking off the yoke. This done, you shall have the accolade and be recognized the sole vassal and loyal Knight. (111)

In the aftermath of Julie and St. Preux's lovemaking their address takes on a decidedly political cast. The imagery is often

121

medieval, as in the preceding passage. So, too, one recognizes the promised "gothic tone" when Julie compares herself to Henry IV, Huguenot monarch of the sixteenth century, in forgiving St. Preux for an episode of drunken behavior and releasing him from his vow to renounce wine: "Your sovereign wishes to imitate the clemency of the best of Kings" (142). The antiquated and theatrical *mœurs* of courtly love are also evoked in St. Preux's repeated demands that Julie acknowledge and reward his prostrations. These overheated narrative performances do more than represent an adolescent love. They work in the service of Rousseau's heterosexual argument, and what we find couched in the language of sexual servitude are the hard lessons of republican sacrifice and reward.

On this score the lovers' interaction recalls the marital romance prescribed by Emile's tutor. Julie, like Sophie, seems to stake her own claims to rule through control of physical access. By threatening St. Preux with "lessons of the arbor" and "of the chalet," she withholds and promises passionate trysts as a condition of his ongoing devotion. That this sexual authority is exercised only toward the end of developing St. Preux's virtue follows naturally from Julie's near perfection: whether explaining to him the untenability of dueling and of the social codes on which it depends or discoursing on the motivational power of Pope's *Epistles*, she always uses St. Preux's riveted attention to good instruction. Typically he emerges from some training exercise—a foray into the world that deprives him of Julie's company—enamored of the sacrifice itself: "How strange is your empire! A power to make privations as sweet as pleasures, and to lend to what one does for you the same charms as one would find in self-gratification" (122). But precisely because in this moral economy self-gratification is not possible, Julie must reward the sacrifice, and thus after exclaiming on her powers more "divine than human" and pledging himself anew to the authority of her "celestial realm," his postscript brings them back to earth: "Would it not be possible to make a pilgrimage to the Chalet?"

In this way St. Preux's passion for Julie and his anticipation of its sensual gratification provide the impetus for his moral education. At one level this means that Julie introduces him to society through her own object lessons: whether he is helping with her good deeds in the local village or assessing Parisian women in the light of her charms, St. Preux masters the codes of rustic simplicity by seeing things through Julie and as she would have them be seen. After the confrontation with the Baron d'Etange that forces her, or rather compels her, to choose marriage to Wolmar, St. Preux's education simply enters its final stage. His ability to read her domesticity as the product of a saintly conversion testifies to his successful socialization, and when, near the end of the novel, he throws himself passionately into the task of preventing Bomston from making his own unsuitable marriage of love ("I will spare no means to prevent an unworthy and indecent alliance," he writes to Wolmar [624]), St. Preux is confirming his commitment to reproducing the same social order that has thwarted his own desires. Here the lessons to be learned—of sacrifice, duty, and virtue—constitute training in the social, productive, and reproductive practices that sustain a world figured as Clarens, the erotico-political world of *la patrie*.

But we must be cautious about reducing St. Preux's education to a developmental scheme in which he comes to a properly generalizable will by recognizing the superior claims of society. On that model, the raptures of adolescent love represent an ill-formed and unwieldy self-interest, while Julie and Wolmar's managerial romance represents community need, and the plot moves us steadily outward and upward, from the narcissistic indulgence of the first to the dispassionate virtue of the second. By contrast, the model of (re)constitution that I introduced in chapter one points to the continuity of theme and of object from moment to moment, or stage to stage, in Rousseau's various stories of progress and devolution. This is the logic of St. Preux's education in which dedication to the rules of social organization remains a function of his ongoing dedication to Julie. Far from renouncing her, it is precisely because he never loosens his grip on Julie that St. Preux acquits himself as a moral agent. I do not mean by this simply that he retains a lingering passion, some remaindered love that motivates good deeds and is itself transposable to other objects. I mean that he remains a man: the morality of republican sacrifice and reward is (re)inscribed into his servile desire.

This suggests that St. Preux's instruction is also in passion itself, and the lessons of the chalet are not bait, but the trap. At this level what is pivotal is his initiation into a sexual order that gives erotic form to the practices of consensual nonconsensuality. Here Julie openly assumes the role of teacher:

> Do you remember that once while reading your Plato's *Republic* we disputed this point of the moral difference between the sexes? I persist in the opinion I then held, and am unable to imagine a common model of perfection for two beings so different. Attack and defense, men's audacity and women's modesty, are not conventions, as the philosophers think, but natural institutions the causes of which can be rationally explained and from which are easily derived all other moral distinctions. (128)

Perhaps her unphilosophic approach to matters sexual explains her appeal to the vaguely oxymoronic "natural institutions" of masculinity and femininity, as well as her confidence in a nature subject to rational derivation. In any event these paradoxes are exceedingly familiar. So, too, we have seen before Julie's anxious certainty that these differences of attack and defense instantiate in bodily difference. "A taller stature, a stronger voice, and more prominent features do not seem to have any necessary connection to one's sex," she admits, "but these exterior modifications proclaim the intentions of the maker in the modifications of the mind" (ibid.). Now sex is presented as a primary feature of internal "modifications" that *must* out in the flesh. Anything else is unimaginable because anything else would make "wise men laugh and love flee [*fuir les amours*]."

Julie's task is to impress upon St. Preux the form these natural institutions must take. When, shortly after receiving this missive on masculine attack and feminine defense, he makes obvious and drunken overtures to her, she responds with an outraged imperiousness: "True love," she admonishes, "always modest, does not wrest its favors audaciously; it steals them timidly. Mystery, silence, fearful shame sharpen and conceal its sweet transports" (138). St. Preux responds by begging for a "just and severe" punishment, but he also registers, and enacts, some confusion: "If with a timid hand my ardent, trembling love sometimes made advances on your charms [*attenta quelquefois à tes charmes*], tell me, did its brutal temerity ever dare to profane them?" A reader, left to balance the criminal connotations of *attenter* with the sacrilege of *profaner,* might be understandably mystified. We have seen this problem before: When is ravaging consistent with, even constitutive of, the "chaste bond" that is true love, and when does it violate all that love could and should be? When Julie demands, indeed, commands, the right enactment of consensual nonconsensuality, she rehabilitates the normative dangers of a heterosexual romance by insisting on their importance to her own satisfaction and to the social order itself. The necessary conditions of this orderly love include a modesty undermined by Julie's commanding literary displays, a reticence shattered by her undisguised desire, and a shame made meaningless by her loss of virginity. All of this points to the paradox of Julie's situation, but it also points to the more general paradoxes of a romance whose natural form depends on the transgressive potential of sexual-social identities.

Rousseau's depictions of heterosexual practice are remarkably consistent. In both their broad themes of dominant and submissive role-taking and their particular tropes of errant knights and schoolboys, his stories tell a tale of sexual awakening that is simultaneously a moral and social initiation. In these stories, the coincident emergence of will and desire situates the initiates within a social order of rulers and ruled; their autonomy, which is to say, their practice of self-control, then consists in mastering the rules of that order. St. Preux's developmental trajectory follows precisely this path, as he moves from the chalet to Paris to Clarens, and gains an understanding of men and women, love and order, and the wisdom of paternal authority. In thus surrendering to Julie's choreography of masculine audacity and feminine submission, St. Preux surrenders to his own rule.

To be sure, this self-enslavement does not always depend on Julie's direct mediation: St. Preux's assessment of Parisian *mœurs*, of Clarens's political economy, and of Bomston's romantic entanglements all illustrate the independence with which he comes to exercise judgment and will. But it is precisely these autonomous displays that suggest he has fully bowed to the social and moral codes of masculinity, and that whether or not Julie is there to enforce it, he will remain a man. Claire expresses this twofold, sensuous and reflective, or worldly and internalized, aspect of his education when she informs Julie of her plan to enlist Bomston's help in effecting the lovers' separation. Claire explains how she overcame Bomston's reluctance to discuss the impossible situation openly with St. Preux:

You know your Epictetus so well, I said to him; here is the case if ever to put him to good use. Distinguish carefully between apparent and real good; that which is within us and that which is without. At a time when an ordeal is approaching from the outside, prove to him that one never receives any evil but from oneself, and that the sage, carrying it with him wherever he goes, also carries his happiness wherever he goes. I understood from his response that this touch of irony, which could not annoy him, was enough to provoke his zea[l]. (181–82)

And while this strategy, Claire admits, necessarily relies upon that "chattering philosophy" (*philosophie parlière*) disliked by both her and Julie, it succeeds in recruiting Bomston, that "*homme sensible* who thinks he is only a philosopher*," to help in the lovers' cause. But the implication that this stoic morality is an adequate surrogate for the lessons of the chalet is ironic indeed. Not only is Bomston quickly at work on a plan to circumvent the "vanity of a cruel father" by uniting the lovers in England—"that they might enlighten the world with their example"—but further, he is celebrating St. Preux's ongoing despair as a good philosophic omen: "Sublime reason is maintained only by the same power of soul that makes for great passions, and one serves philosophy worthily only with the same ardor that one feels for a mistress" (193). Thus when St. Preux returns to Clarens years later, less learned, more worldly, with a ruddier complexion and the "confidence of a righteous man," it only follows that his mistress remains well served: "Here is your Slave, Cousin," writes Claire. "I have made him mine during this past week, and he has borne his chains so contentedly that one can see he is just made for service" (435). Unlike Epictetus's, St. Preux's slave morality keeps him ever more firmly secure in his worldly attachments.

The conclusion that St. Preux's manly practices fail to, or better, refuse to, serve a stoic philosophy is in keeping with my larger claim about their political significance, that they give form to desires whose material satisfaction embeds him in structures of power and interdependence. This is not to deny the degree to which St. Preux, like Epictetus, "carries his happiness with him wherever he goes." But this is not because he has repudiated worldly goods; it is an effect of those "natural operations," pity and self-love, which remain central to any identification of interest, as well as to any desire. How St. Preux imagines Julie to be, in other words, is a critical component of their interaction and thus of his *éducation sensible*.

126

PICTURE PERFECT

St. Preux imagines Julie as a sovereign, an angel, a preacher, a holy flame—we are only too familiar with the gothic excess. But he also imagines her as a daughter, a wife, a mother, and a woman. I want to suggest that this second series, like the first, consists in metaphors of passionate and political excess through which his identity, as man and citizen, is being shaped. Purity, passion, solicitude, and devotion: each of these feminine ideals is given narrative form in the novel, and as its educational subject, St. Preux's task is to learn to grasp them, which means learning the social relations through which they are sustained. In this way his moral education is centrally concerned with imagining sexual difference: he is tied to the world of Clarens by a figural string of gender identities that bind his imagination to its models of sociability and power.

In the novel's opening letter, for example, where we find St. Preux's initiating act of submission, Julie is figured as an obedient and beloved daughter: her ultimate accession to her father's demands is thus to some extent anticipated in St. Preux's very love for her. So, too, Julie's honor, central to her charms and yet endangered by their sexual relationship, must be recuperated within the terms of filial and marital devotion. Her lengthy excursus on the sanctity of the marriage vow, written to St. Preux shortly after her wedding, ends with her quoting back to him portions of a letter he had written at the very beginning of their relationship. "I have in memory a passage from an Author you will not impugn," she writes: " 'Love,' he says, 'is deprived of its greatest charm when honesty abandons it. To feel its full value, the heart must delight in it and raise us up by raising up the loved one. Take away the idea of perfection, you take away enthusiasm; take away esteem and love is no longer anything'" (363).

The citation is from a letter in which St. Preux explains to Julie why he will not accept payment for his tutoring services. In the course of this explanation he offers his thoughts on Abelard and Heloise (in the novel's only reference to that eponymous figure). He ventures that while Heloise was surely to be "pitied," Abelard was nothing but "a wretch deserving of his fate" (85). The problem here is not merely or mostly Heloise's seduction and pregnancy; it is that their love affair must be figured as a violation of paternal dominion inasmuch as it was Abelard's employment as her tutor that secured his access. "What more precious possession can a father have than his only daughter?" St. Preux wonders; when, then, a man who "sells his services" makes love to that daughter, it will perforce "offend in his most vulnerable part the man to whom he owes fidelity." Such a tutor is a "traitor" whom "the laws quite justly condemn to death" (ibid.). Such is Abelard, whose passion apparently outstripped his virtue, and thus his love. St. Preux closes his condemnation of Abelard with the passage later quoted by Julie on "love deprived of its greatest charm."

The figures of Heloise and Abelard, well known to an eighteenth-century literary public, represent a tragic passion and an erotic deferral, but also a worldly retreat, a withdrawal from family and society, into philosophy, theology, and text. And if Heloise, perhaps because she protested this material renunciation, remains "pitiable," Abelard's unmanly refusal of both paternal *mœurs* and their sensuous demands suggests that he got his just deserts: the castrated figure appears as a sharp reminder of what a philosophic passion, unbeholden to worldly order, portends. And just how well can Abelard serve philosophy, given how poorly he served his mistress? But let's notice that it is not Abelard's love, or lovemaking, or not those alone, that St. Preux finds dishonorable and unworthy of pity; it is his repudiation of the sexual-social order in which his love and lovemaking have meaning. First when he accepts employment from the man whose "possession" he would violate, and again when he renounces his marriage in favor of a monkish and philosophic life, Abelard shows himself to be neither a man of action and honor nor a man of duty and virtue; little wonder that he ends up hardly a man at all.

St. Preux wants to believe that in refusing a stipend from the d'Etange family he has freed himself, perhaps even Julie, from the restraints of familial and economic convention. Contrasting their situation to the medieval Theologican's, St. Preux insists that they remain "in the prime of their freedom" and thus bound only by love's "innocent chains" (70). But now, years later, when Julie reiterates his insistence on "ideas of perfection" after an extended digression on the social, political, legal, moral, and aesthetic functions of marriage—which, she cautions St. Preux, that insidious "philosophy of words" (*philosophie en paroles*) constantly challenges—he immediately, if painfully, concedes his error. Casting her marriage as a "feat of courage" that "makes you ever more like yourself," he confirms the necessity and effectivity of ideal forms: "You are never more my Julie than at the moment you renounce me. Alas! It is by losing you that I have found you once more" (301).

If these ideal forms belong ultimately to an inner realm of reverie and imagination, they take shape there in accordance with worldly designs. Thus it is Julie's marriage to Wolmar and her housekeeping at Clarens that fulfill St. Preux's idea of feminine perfection, and that ideal is confirmed only when he is reunited with her. The letters to Bomston, written during his stay at Clarens, attest to St. Preux's ongoing figuration of sexual bliss, albeit now in the context of extended meditations on household organization. "In truth," he admits to Bomston after a particularly long discussion of how the servants are managed, "it all makes for such a ravishing *tableau* that one can love looking at it [*le contempler*] without any other interest than the pleasure it gives" (470). The continuous *spectacle* offered by the well-governed home—from Julie's wondrously contrived garden retreat Elysium, to the games and dances organized under the Wolmars' watchful gaze—impresses upon St. Preux the pleasures of paternal rule. In so doing it returns him to his original sensuous design, to be subject to his mistress's will.

But now that will is generalized to encompass the whole of Clarens. St. Preux records the following scene, initiated by Julie's plaintive remark that she envies sovereigns "the pleasure of making themselves beloved":

> "Envy nothing," her husband said in a tone of voice he should have left to me; "we have all long been your subjects." At this word, her needlework fell from her hands; she turned her head and cast on her worthy husband such a touching look, so tender, that I myself thrilled at it. She said nothing; what could she have said to equal that look? Our eyes also met. I could feel from the way her husband clasped my hand that we were all three caught up in the same emotion, and that the sweet influence of that expansive soul was acting around her, and triumphing over insensibility itself. (559)

The sensuous excess shared by St. Preux, his mistress, and her husband enamors them all of a conjugal order where commingled desire and submission subtend the logic of contractual obligation and right. That emotional *sensibilité* in which they are all "caught up" circumvents the performative impossibility of promising to love, which, like promising to honor, cherish, and obey, pretends to subject to rational design—to convention—what remains forever contingent upon sensuous and sensible experience. In this way Julie recuperates the marital, hence contractual, relationship for both her husband and her lover, by sustaining their shared fantasy of coincident subjection and control. Overcoming "insensibility itself," she guarantees that a pathos of identity and desire will tie them both to the sexual-social order.

Picturing Julie as a wife is thus crucial to St. Preux's *éducation sensible*, an exercise that always entails moving between "ideas of perfection" and their worldly form. The complexities of this twofold movement, thematic throughout the novel, are synoptically conveyed in St. Preux's reaction to a portrait Julie sends him after he has begun traveling with Bomston. An initial letter from her announces the imminent arrival of an unidentified "amulet":

> There is a curious manner for making it work. It must be gazed upon every morning for a quarter of an hour until one feels penetrated by a certain tenderness. Then one applies it to the eyes, to the mouth, and to the heart; that acts, they say, as a perservative during the day against the bad air of the land of gallantry. A most singular electric virtue is also attributed to this sort of talisman, but it works only between faithful lovers. It is to communicate to the one the pressure of the other's kisses at more than a hundred leagues' distance. (264)

St. Preux's letter documenting its arrival lends an air of immediacy to the effect her portrait produces. As he shuts himself in his room with the package, to grasp its contents for the first time ("Julie! . . . O my Julie! . . . the veil is rent . . ."), the verb tense changes from the past to the present, and the narrative itself becomes coincident with his submissive devotion: "I behold your divine charms! My lips and heart pay them their first homage, my knees bend . . ." (279). Like his earlier pedant self, crouched in Julie's wardrobe and enchanted by the *spectacle* of her corset, so this "idolatrous Lover" is overwhelmed by representation, and again his narration embodies his desire: "Do you not feel your eyes, your cheeks, your mouth, your breast, pressed, crushed, overwhelmed with my ardent kisses? Do you not feel your whole being inflamed with the fire of my burning lips!" Although the ecstatic distance that separates the question mark of the first sentence from the exclamation point of the second suggests a satisfying (self-)representation, the narrative ends by interrupting this possibility: "Heaven, what do I hear? Someone is coming. . . . Ah let us secure, hide my treasure. . . . an intruder! . . . cursed be the cruel person who comes to disturb such sweet transports!" (280).

No sooner has Julie responded with enthusiasm to the apparent "truth" of the "Talisman" than St. Preux sends her a second reaction: now moved beyond his initial transports, he notices the portrait's many flaws. The hairline is placed too far from the temples, the coloring appears artificial, the artist has missed "two or three small veins under the skin," as well as that "almost imperceptible spot" under the right eye and another "on the left side of the neck," and the breast is entirely too "disordered" (291–92). So he has the portrait altered. The proposed alterations are first tried on a copy, St. Preux explains, and only after he and the painter he has contracted "are quite sure of their effect" do they transfer them to the original. If only they could show her "soul alongside your face, and depict at once your modesty and your charms!" (293).

Here the movement between his "idea of perfection" and its worldly form is an unsteady negotiation. The authentication of spots and veins; the addition of drapery to make more visible her naked form ("the better to see all of you that I clothe you so carefully"); a miraculous reconciliation of the sacred and the profane: when he imagines Julie, St. Preux (re-)creates the world. The artifice necessary to Rousseau's sexual design implicates its subjects, not only in their vulnerability to self-absorbing illusions but as rhetoricians of that very design, and when St. Preux anatomizes his romantic fetish, he becomes its re-creator. That he is perfecting an illusion in order to re-create a more authentic original underscores, again, the inseparability of ideological and material form: this is not a function of a desire that is somehow counterfeit but of the rhetorical reconstitution desire always entails.

SELF-PERFECTING NARRATIVES

The narrative imperatives that structure *Julie*'s plot challenge any simplistic dichotomy of feminine absorption and masculine detachment: as both a reader and a writer of cultural scripts, St.

Preux is learning to fashion the social-sexual identity that overpowers him and in so doing, he becomes simultaneously its master theoretician and its slavish imitator. St. Preux serves as a model of the novel's own discursive logic, inasmuch as the genre's promise of self-determination is always made in the context of the social relations it represents: virtuous wives, modest mistresses, controlling fathers, and good-hearted peasants together constitute a world that sustains the moral and discursive possibilities of St. Preux's autonomy. By figuring his sexual surrender as a function of his narrative self-construction, *Julie* reiterates the logic of consensual nonconsensuality through its own cultural practice.

In both its romantic and its representational excess, then, the novel plays an important role in organizing the republican *sensibilité* of a "corrupt people," which is to say, of Rousseau's reading public. Stephanie Jed's argument linking fifteenth-century republicanism to the reception of Scholastic texts offers a helpful counterpart to my claim: "Florentine humanists," she writes, "constructed their political identity from their textual relations with the Roman authors."[32] By showing how the "chaste thinking" that structures civic humanist thought assumes its rhetorical form in interpretations of Lucretia's rape and suicide, Jed shows how modes of reading and writing are deeply implicated in the (re)-constitution of political and sexual sensibilities. In the case of Rousseau's readership, the textual relations in question are not primarily with Scholasticism but with genres of self-narration, those "contemplative readings" to which Rousseau credits a more withdrawn, thus less frivolous, lifestyle among English men and women.[33] Along with the epistolary novel this includes autobiography, which in Rousseau's hands continues the project of giving rhetorical form to his "ideas of [sexual and social] perfection." Turning now to the *Confessions,* we will find a literary practice reminiscent of *Julie*'s: in his self-narration, as in his fictional designs, Rousseau sketches autonomy and self-subjection together, in depicting an *éducation sensible* through which ethico-erotic identities emerge.

Intus et in Cute ("Inwardly and in the Skin"): already with its epigraph the *Confessions* points to the mutuality of self-narration

[32] Jed, *Chaste Thinking,* 52.
[33] See *Letter to d'Alembert,* 75.

and bodily signification. The original fragment from Persius's *Satire III*—"I have known you inwardly and in the skin" (*ego te intus et in cute novi*)—lends a grammatical presence to the narrative's interactive imperatives: what is framed as self-revelation requires bodily inscription, where meanings that matter are read by others.[34] Again the rhetorical form of self-knowledge proves to be profoundly dialogic. It will take a literary public to make sense of Rousseau, and thus the book's opening paragraphs hail its readers, the "*semblables*" called to assembly in a series of hortatory exclamations (*qu'ils écoutent, qu'ils gémissent, qu'ils rougissent*, etc.) that begins with the end—a call for the "trumpet of last judgment" (*Que la trompette du jugement dernier sonne*) when Rousseau will offer up these stories as testimony. Having lost his body, he will still have his book, where the "sovereign judge" can read "all that I did, all that I thought, all that I was."[35]

So it was in the beginning: a few paragraphs later we read that reading is the first thing Rousseau remembers about himself. "I felt before I thought; this is the common lot of man. It affected me more than another. I don't know what I was before the age of five or six; I don't know how I learned to read; I only remember my first readings and their effect on me; it is from that time that I date an uninterrupted self-consciousness."[36]

These first books were novels that had belonged to his mother, which he and his father read together. Through them Rousseau became adept at self-expression, as well as intimately familiar with the passions: "I had no idea about things, but I had known every feeling." After exhausting the novels, he and his father moved on to some "good books": by Bousset, for example, and Ovid, La Bruyère, and especially Plutarch, who proved to be his "favorite." Al-

---

[34] See Persius, "Satire III." In his copius and indispensable notes, Gildersleeve suggests "inside and out" as a rough equivalent of *intus et in cute*. The satire concerns an indolent student whose friend exhorts him to take seriously the pursuit of knowledge. The first half of the satire contrasts bodily indulgence with philosophic study—for example, the slothful student too hung over to hold a pen—while the second half assimilates physical well-being to knowledge-seeking, by developing the metaphor of ignorance as disease. The use of body imagery in this piece, and in Persius's writings in general, is strongly reminiscent of Rousseau's own rhetorical strategies.

[35] *Confessions*, 5.

[36] *Confessions*, 8. Subsequent citations will be given in the text.

though he writes that these new pleasures cured him "a bit" of his passion for novels, his descriptions of fiercely identifying with ancient characters continue the figural excesses of romance.[37] Further, he claims that these literary engagements formed his "free and republican spirit, that indomitable and proud character, impatient with the yoke of servitude." Rousseau thus links his own political identity to incessant rereadings of Plutarch ("*le plaisir que je prenois à le relire sans cesse*") and an incessant preoccupation with antiquity ("*sans cesse occupé de Rome et d'Athénes*") (9). But it should not be surprising to see independence—of mind, character, and country—born of textual absorption and in need of ceaseless narration: this is precisely the strategy used to engender St. Preux's autonomy.

To approach the *Confessions* as a more or less accurate and more or less comprehensive work of self-exposure is to disregard, then, how it foregrounds the experience of reading. One risks overlooking how the book addresses problems of (self-)interpretation in a manner wholly consistent with his other writings, namely, through the structure of a moral and political *sensibilité*. But Rousseau becomes a man just like St. Preux and Emile do, by defining himself and his social world through relations of consensual nonconsensuality. As with those explicitly fictional characters, Rousseau's ethico-erotic development depends upon a publicity that he refuses: authorizing his authenticity through that most public of private acts, the memoir, underscores the necessity of cultural articulation. Thus when we see in Rousseau's private divulgences a continuity with political and social dilemmas, it is not necessary to resolve this as a matter of causal priority—is he externalizing his own psychic dramas or internalizing the sociopolitical milieu of ancien régime inauthenticity and (pre)revolutionary possibility?—because the narrative structure points consistently to a mutual reconstitution of self and world.

---

[37] In a 1762 letter to Malesherbes, Rousseau writes of these early formative experiences: "At six years of age Plutarch fell into my hands, at eight I knew him by heart; I had read all the novels, they made me shed buckets of tears, before the age at which the heart takes interest in novels. Since that time there formed in my own heart a heroic and romantic taste which has only increased up until now, and which succeeds in making me disgusted with everything, except what resembles my *folies*"; *Oeuvres Complètes*, vol. 1, 1134.

It is tempting, after reading the account of Rousseau's own blend of sexuality and domination, to agree with Starobinski that "it took Freud to 'think' Rousseau's feelings."[38] Starobinski also observes, however, that the fertile ground of psychoanalysis is less interesting than Rousseau's own designations, and what he designs is a sensuous philosophy that links sexual identity to a political awareness of domination and self-determination. This is starkly sketched in the stories of his stay at Bossey, where he and his cousin spent two years under the care of Mademoiselle and Monsieur Lambercier. To this time Rousseau attributes the first appearances of his sexuality, his commitment to justice, and his vanity. The critical event with Mlle Lambercier is well known: she administers a beating in response to some childish transgression, during which Rousseau discovers "in the pain, even the shame, a blend of sensuality that left me more desirous than fearful" of enduring it again (15). Only his greater desire to please the young woman keeps him from soliciting punishment. So when the next beating occurs, warranted but unwilled, he is able to enjoy it in good faith: "The next occasion, which I was postponing without dreading, arrived through no fault of mine, which is to say, without it being deliberate [*de ma volonté*], and thus I profited from it with, I must say, a clear conscience" (ibid.).

This first arousal of will, recognized as such in an act of self-denial and then rewarded for this with its ultimate satisfaction, ushers Rousseau into the sexual order: he reports that Mlle Lambercier quickly decided to suspend these punishments after "no doubt" perceiving "some sign" that they were not having *her* desired effect. Two days later, he and his cousin are moved out of her bedroom, where they had been sleeping, and given their own. "Henceforth," Rousseau writes, "I had the honor, which I would have happily passed over, of being treated like a big boy" (ibid).

In presenting this first experience of arousal as what "decided my tastes, my desires, my passions, myself, for the rest of my life"— and then continuing with details of his repeated frustrations on this score (three times in as many paragraphs he tells us that he has never told his various beloveds about his erotic preferences,

---

[38] Starobinski, *Transparency and Obstruction*, 115. Starobinski is here borrowing from Eric Weil, who remarked that "it took Kant to think Rousseau's thoughts"; see Weil, "Jean-Jacques Rousseau et sa Politique," 11.

bemoaning that only in his "imagination" did he "make use of women in my fashion, like so many Desmoiselles Lambercier")— Rousseau has made "the first and most difficult step into the obscure and murky labyrinth of my confessions." Readers can now rest assured, he suggests, that what follows will be the truth: his perversity vouchsafes his integrity. But before going further, "without leaving the subject of which I've been speaking," he continues, "one will see it leave a very different impression" (18). With this he begins a second beating story, one in which his uncle is called to Bossey after Rousseau refuses to admit to breaking Mlle Lambercier's comb. The subsequent punishment by his uncle reduces Rousseau to a "hideous condition," but he does not bend. Eventually "even force had to yield to the diabolical obstinacy of a child," and Rousseau emerges from this "cruel ordeal shattered but triumphant," clinging to his cousin as they shout out in unison, "*Carnifex, Carnifex, Carnifex*" (19–20).[39]

Conceding that all appearances were against him, Rousseau must address the issue again fifty years after the fact: "*Hébien*, I declare before Heaven that I was innocent, that I neither broke nor touched the comb, that I did not go near the stove, and that I didn't even think of doing so." Apparently the outrage of the falsely accused lasts as long as the ardor of the justly castigated: "I feel in writing this that my pulse is quickening once more; these moments will always be with me if I live to be a thousand. This first sentiment of violence and injustice has remained so deeply engraved upon my heart that all ideas that remind me of it take me back to my first emotion" (20).

As with his erotic desire, his passion for justice sustains relations of imagined pleasures and pains in which power, triumph, and submission shape the most private, and the most public, identities. And the marks of these inescapably worldly encounters—with injustice, with sex—are inscribed upon his body: in the "sign" that Mlle Lambercier's punishment is misfiring, in the "bodily pain" (*douleur de corps*) and the "hideous condition" that Uncle Bernard's beatings produce. In these signs we read all the difference between the severe pleasures of righteous justice and the unbearable excess of a forced confession, of a nonconsensual consensual-

---

[39] The Latin *carnifex* denotes both the Roman office of executioner and, more colloquially, a vicious scoundrel.

ity, one might say. But it is all in the reading. These are the two incidents Rousseau chooses to illustrate "the first traces of my sensible being" (*être sensible*), and he recognizes they are of a piece: "Who would believe that one of the most vigorous elements of my soul was steeped in the same source from where the lasciviousness and weakness have flowed in my blood?" (18).

Together these incidents mark Rousseau's entry into the "big boys'" world, an entry akin to leaving the state of nature: "There ended the serenity of my childish life. From that moment I ceased to enjoy pure happiness, and I feel even now that the memory of the charms of my childhood stopped there. We stayed at Bossey a few months longer. We lived there like we are told the first man lived in an earthly paradise, but we no longer enjoyed it. It was in appearance the same situation, and in reality a totally different manner of being" (20). The loss he describes is total: the countryside appears desolate, innocent amusements take an "ugly turn," and he and his cousin no longer "cultivate our little gardens" (21). In all the time since he left Bossey, Rousseau continues, he is only now able to recollect in any detail that paradise lost. Indeed, after a paragraph devoted to chronicling the end of childhood, we read one in which Rousseau points to a flood of happy memories that can bring it back: minute descriptions of the Lambercier house, for example, its study and garden. "I well know that the reader has no great need to know all that," he writes, "but me, I need to tell him about it." And why not recount a few instances which, in the recollecting, bring him such pleasure? "Surely five or six. . . . Let's make a deal," Rousseau interrupts, turning directly to the reader with a second-person address: he will trade us five for one, "provided that I'm allowed to take as long as possible in telling it, to prolong my pleasure" (22).

This third and final Bossey story recounts the plotting and execution of a scheme to siphon water intended for Monsieur Lambercier's walnut tree in order to irrigate Rousseau's own willow. Having resolved it "a finer thing to plant a tree on a terrace than a flag in the breach," Rousseau and his cousin undertake this engineering feat in order to "win that glory" and "share it with no one" (ibid.). Their success silences even Monsieur Lambercier, who destroys the usurping tree but cannot bring himself to punish the clever boys. Thus Rousseau experienced, he writes, his first "first well-defined attack of vanity," much beyond the simple bouts of pride he felt when playing Brutus or Aristides: with this act of derring-do he reached "the height of glory: at ten years of age I understood it better than Caesar did at thirty" (24).

The trajectory out of Eden is familiar: sexual awareness, the perception of injustice, prideful self-distinction. And like other banishments from nature, these first experiences of desire and will are presented by Rousseau in terms of a social-sexual *spectacle*, one featuring severe maidens, *carnifex*, and Caesar: republican patriots and villains in which he has inscribed his self-awareness. A figural string of gender metaphors ties Rousseau to his own *éducation sensible*, through lessons he both writes and receives. We could retrace these same stories as they repeatedly appear in the *Confessions*: Rousseau's incessant narration of his efforts to assume the position of the willing submissive, of how these desires conform perfectly to his pure and honest soul, and of how they give form to his independence and self-fashioning. But (to echo Rousseau) let's make a deal: I will tell just two of these stories, and briefly.

The first concerns Louise Éléonore de Warens, whom Rousseau describes as playing a pivotal role early in his life as a spiritual, social, and emotional tutor. Mme de Warens was instrumental in his early conversion to Catholicism; she instructed him in dancing, music, and other arts of genteel society; he lost his virginity to her; and she provided a home and refuge for him over the course of twelve years. First at Annency, subsequently at Chambéry and Les Charmettes, life with Warens is presented as one lived close to nature. He compares her home to the Edenic Bossey, her solicitude to a mother's (much has been made of his practice of referring to her as *Maman*), and his own devotion to St. Preux's: newly arrived at Warens's home after his sojourn in Turin, "I saw my little bundle carried to the room where I would stay much like St. Preux saw his carriage being put away at Mme de Wolmar's" (104).

In the same measure that Sophie is a composite creation, a generalized abstraction whose fictive status Rousseau constantly underlines, so Warens is a particularized individual, one whose presentation in the *Confessions* is marked by the contradictions and complexities one might expect of a genuine personality. A woman of refinement, grace, kindness, and fierce religious devotion, she is also described as generous with her sexual attentions, prone to wander in conversation, and an easy mark for "charlatans and quacks." She had both a "sensitive character," Rousseau insists, "and a cold temperament" (*un caractère sensible et un temperament froid*), and while she was a "good Catholic" whom he compares to the saintly Mme de Chantal, she also worked out a religious system that "destroyed" the doctrines of original sin and redemption.[40] On Rousseau's telling, she makes the celebrated *frondeuse* Mme de Longueville look like a mere "busybody" (*tracassière*): in Longueville's place, Warens "would have ruled the State" (51).

But as Rousseau recounts the stories of their relationship, it becomes clear that it lacks a critical dimension. To inculcate a durable passion requires risk, and for all his devotion, Rousseau never experiences with Warens the requisite challenge and uncertainty, which is to say, the drama of domination and subordination, that outs the will. Doubt about her capacity to serve as his mistress surfaces at the very beginning of their relationship: "Supposing that what I felt for her was really love—which will appear at least doubtful to anyone who follows the story of our intimacies—how could that passion have been accompanied from its birth by the sentiments it inspires the least; peace of heart, calmness, serenity, security, confidence?" (52).

This serenity signifies both the power and the limitation of their relationship. The "sweet sense of well-being" afforded by her company, where thought and speech are "the same thing," where he felt "neither transports nor desires" but a "ravishing calm, feeling joy without knowing about what": these are depictions of an *amour de soi* untroubled by the potential challenge of other selves (205). But so, too, this suggests a "sentiment of existence" that denies the very self who can imagine difference: "Feeling that we were not only necessary but sufficient to one another, we grew accustomed to thinking of nothing outside ourselves, completely to confine our happiness and all our desires to this mutual possession, perhaps unique among humankind, which was not, as I have said, that of love; but a possession more essential, which without depending on the senses, on sex, on age, on appearance [*figure*], depended on everything by which one is oneself, and which one can lose only by ceasing to be" (222). Like all returns to nature,

[40] *Confessions*, 229. The widowed Jeanne de Chantal was the founder (in 1610) of the Visitation Order at Annecy and she was canonized in 1767. Rousseau compares Warens to her at 51. For the discussion of Warens's religious cosmology, see 228–30.

this "essential possession" of another denies the pity and self-love through which pleasure as well as pain, and judgment as well as vanity, come to be. Thus Rousseau finds himself growing restless, "incessantly drifting from one thing to another" and increasingly drawn to study and the latest news from "the Republic of Letters" (218). Thus the figural string pulls him away from *Maman*: "I had a tender mother, a dear friend, but I needed a mistress" (219).

That at this point their relationship is sexual, and had been for some time, has little bearing on the matter. Rousseau likens their first encounter to incest; this did not prevent him from "tasting pleasure," but it introduced an "invincible sadness that poisoned the charm" (197). As for Warens, he describes her as "tranquil and caressing" throughout: "as she was hardly sensual and had not sought pleasure [*volupté*], she did not experience delights in it and so never had the regrets that go with them" (ibid.). Indeed, on his telling the lovemaking was a continuation of her custodial care, effortlessly incorporated into their repertoire of familial and divine devotions. When early in the story of their relationship Rousseau writes, "I saw in her a tender mother, a beloved sister, a delightful friend, and nothing else" (109), we know he will be moving on. And years later, after trying to imagine the necessary mistress in Warens's place—"fashioning her in a thousand ways so as to fool myself"—Rousseau does (219). When soon thereafter he attempts to return, unable, in a moment of despair, to "resist such tender memories" as he carries of Warens, the reality proves disillusioning: "I had come to rediscover a past that no longer was and that could not be reborn" (270).

My final story from the *Confessions* concerns a past that is continuously reborn. It is set in the period following Rousseau's departure from Bossey, after his first tastes of injustice, submissive titillation, and vanity. "I was already a righter of wrongs," he writes. "To be a proper knight-errant [*Paladin*] I needed only a Lady; I acquired two" (26). The doubled ladies, Mlles de Vulson and Goton, embody feminine differences much as St. Preux and Wolmar represent masculine alternatives. These are the differences that, as Rousseau explains in introducing the two damsels, have always punctuated his experience and expression of passion: "I have known two very distinct sorts of love, very real, and which have almost nothing in common except that they are alike very ardent [*vifs*] and in every way different from a tender friendship. The whole course of my life has been divided between these two loves of such diverse natures, and I have even had them both at the same time" (27).

The nature of his love for Vulson, an artful flirt of twenty-two, was that of the social *galant*. He writes that he "publicly and tyrannically" monopolized her, throwing himself into the dramas of jealousy and wit that unfolded around them, and he was reassured and enlivened by "the applause, the encouragement, the laughter" with which these dramas were met. In imagining a private exchange, however, Rousseau believes it would have left him "constrained, cold, perhaps bored" (28). He insists that his tenderness for her was real, that he missed her and thought of her often when they were separated, but "her caresses touched my heart, not my senses": "I gave myself to her with all my heart, or rather, with my head, for it was only there that I was in love, even though I was madly so, and even though my delirium, agitations, and furies provided scenes to provoke side-splitting laughter [*à pâmer de rire*]" (27). The wholly imaginary love provides wholly imagined pleasures—"my imagination asked only for what she granted me in fact"—and what he imagines is exactly the contrary of St. Preux: "I loved her like a brother, but I was jealous of her like a lover" (28).

With Goton, by contrast, Rousseau was deeply *sensible*: "All my senses were agitated." Obligingly playing the severe schoolmistress to his errant pupil, she "permitted herself the greatest liberties with me, without ever allowing me to take any with her" (27). Her "mixture of audacity and reserve" served perfectly the demands of a private passion. Instead of the applause and adulation accorded him with Vulson, Goton's "treatment" was a "favor to be asked for on bended knee" (28). He was "familiar" with Vulson without "great familiarities," but he believes that had he stayed any longer with Goton, "I would not have lived: the palpitations of my heart would have choked me." In short, it is his body that bears the marks of her, or rather his, desire: Goton blinds him, disrupts his sense, chokes him. When their secret is discovered—or was "less well kept by my little schoolmistress than by me"—they are quickly separated.

The differences between the two relations—one public, the other private, one heartfelt, the other erotically charged—cannot be parsed in terms of their respective authenticity, impact, or even importance as markers of Rousseau's romantic *sensibilité*. On the contrary, they together recapitulate the theatrical, socially mediated forms of sexual identity that thread through his work. That these social-sexual forms are depicted on Rousseau's eleven-year-old self says less about their origins or accuracy than it does about the power of a recursive logic to assimilate multiple stories to its reiterated design of ethico-erotic practice. "I wouldn't have wanted to anger Mlle de Vulson for anything in the world," Rousseau writes in concluding his comparison, "but if Mlle Goton had ordered me to throw myself into flames, I believe that I would have obeyed her in an instant" (29). This critical difference—"to the one I was compliant, and to the other, obedient"—echoes the distinction Rousseau makes in the *Discourse on Political Economy* when he discusses how to secure citizens' loyalty:

> The government will have a difficult time making itself obeyed if it limits itself to obedience. If it is good to know how to use men as they are, it is better still to turn them into what one needs them to be. The most absolute authority is that which penetrates to the interior of man and is exerted no less on his will than on his actions. It is certain that in the long run people are what the government makes them. Warriors, citizens, men, when it wants; rabble and scoundrels when it so pleases.[41]

Genuine obedience depends on more than a compliant attitude, more than deep affection, more than a flattered vanity: it depends on a submission so complete that it embodies the very act of willing. This is St. Preux's experience with Julie ("Your empire is the most absolute I know," writes Claire, "it extends as far as others' wills")[42], and it is what Rousseau describes with Goton. That in these stories what is being willed through submissive acts is an erotic satisfaction confirms Rousseau's observation in the *Discourse on Political Economy*: the stakes in political community and rule include sexual identity. Indeed, what his republic "needs people to be" are the lovers and husbands, and mistresses and wives, who populate his cultural imagination. And if this sexualization of power and interdependence doesn't render every subsequent act of political submission an erotic delight, still it impresses the re-

---

[41] *Political Economy*, 251.
[42] *Julie*, 409.

publican ideal of consensual nonconsensuality onto that most un-reflective level of awareness, a romantic *sensibilité*.

I suggested in chapter one that the gender identities necessary to this romance are forged through the political, juridical, and familial institutions whose conventionality Rousseau occludes in a narrative of unnatural devolution. The occlusion continues in the fictional and autobiographical writings that lend to these identities an interiorized form and origin: the psyche, envisioned either as the precarious result of childhood's formative experiences or as the site of an unbridled and ahistorical creativity. Circulating through public acts of self-narration, these invitations inside—to see "private" letters, personal perversions, moments of triumph and shame—implicate their readers as voyeurs and *semblables* whose very acts of witness and empathy give meaning to that inside. But the familiarity of what we find there—an autonomous self, sustained as such in negotiating the tension between submission and self-completion—returns us to the outside, where this tension takes a political shape. In giving content and form to consensual nonconsensuality, Rousseau's depictions of the republic are continuous with his depictions of the romantic dyad. As I will argue in the following chapter, his republican practices are intelligible precisely because they are inscribed in the bodily terms of (hetero)sexuality. Even as Rousseau's readers are forced out of Julie's closet and into the village square, he continues to write to and through a romantic *sensibilité* that allows them to know each other—his own illustrations repeatedly confirm it—*intus et in cute*.

143

Loving the Body Politic

> The transports of tender hearts appear utterly
> fanciful to anyone who has not felt them.
> And the love of country, a hundred times more
> ardent and delicious than that of a mistress,
> likewise cannot be conceived except by being felt.
>
> *Discourse on Political Economy*

WORDPLAY

The "essence of the political body," Rousseau writes, "is in the harmony of obedience and liberty, and the words *subject* and *sovereign* are identical correlatives whose meanings combine in the single word Citizen."[1] How is this possible? The notoriously cryptic answer given in the *Social Contract* is: through the general will. Inalienable, unerring, and indivisible, the general will guarantees the perfect correlation of republicans' subjection and their sovereignty. Is this a faculty of the individual? Yes: "Why is the general will always right and why do all constantly will the happiness of each of them if not because there is no one who doesn't apply this word *each* to himself and who doesn't think of himself when he votes for all?" (373). Is this a collective faculty? Yes: "The will is general or it is not; it is the will of the body of the people or of only a part" (369). Is it a tool of self-interest? Yes: "Equality of right and the notion of justice that it produces derive from the preference that each person gives to himself and consequently, from the nature of man" (373). Is it a tool of self-sacrifice? Yes: "Each individual can, as a man, have a particular will contrary or dissimilar to the general will that he has as a citizen," and "If it is not impossible that a particular will accords on some point with the general will, it is impossible at least that this accord be constant

[1] *Social Contract*, 427. Subsequent references to this work will be given in the body of the text.

144

and durable, for the particular will by its nature tends toward [partial] preferences, and the general will, toward equality" (360, 368).

The resolution of only apparent contradictions is central to the *Social Contract*, which famously opens with Rousseau's declaration that "man is born free and everywhere he is in chains": "How did this change take place? I do not know; what can render it legitimate? I believe I can resolve that question" (351). From the beginning, readers are advised that "resolving that question" entails precision in the use of terms and the presentation of concepts. Rousseau repeatedly alerts his readers to concepts that need clarification, genealogies that must be observed, propositions that are "poorly stated" (*mal posées*), and words that need careful definition. These latter include force, right, freedom, slavery, equality, law, tyranny, tyrant, citizen, finance, and representation: each is singled out as equivocal or misused, a term to be cleansed of ambiguities, redundancies, and everyday corruptions. Most insistently, Rousseau advises that the many names used to refer to the *body politic* must be distinguished "in all their precision": *city, republic, state, sovereign, power, people, citizens, subjects* (361–62). Only when these words are understood and applied with specificity can one avoid the mystification that unsettled significations produce.

And the central object of this semantic solicitude is a metaphor: "A public person formed by the union of all the other persons" (361). Only the "moral person" that is the collectivity can express a will that is truly general, and only that person can authorize the force necessary to enact its designs (ibid.).[2] In this way, legislative and executive power—the power of the voting citizens and the power of the government—are derived from bodily properties, and it is the latter that does, "in a way, for the public person what the union of soul and body does for a man" (396). The active and passive postures of the body politic (called sovereign and state, respectively) and the active and passive postures of its members (called citizen and subject, respectively) are thus reconciled by an "intermediary body" (government) charged with communicative, disciplinary, and preservative functions that hold together all these different, and identical, parts. No wonder that Rousseau repeatedly invokes the need for conceptual and semantic care: while his forays into the language of mathematical proportion imply the

[2] See 369n.

eloquence of algorithmic calculation, he is acutely aware that "geometric precision has no place in moral quantities," and in the end, it is a slippery, worldly referent—the bodies of the citizen-subjects—that will be invoked every time.[3] For this reason, the rhetoric of precision that drives the *Social Contract* is always harnessed to the imaginative goal of a pitiable and sensuous identification. Activity and passivity, individuality and collectivity, interest and duty: throughout the text, these distinctive postures come together and they come apart through depictions of the body politic and how it feels.

This is, to be sure, a game of words: the natality, mortality, voice, and health of a republic are all made possible through transposed and inverted meanings. That these transpositions and inversions are themselves sustained through a logic of literality accords with Rousseau's general narrative structure, which insistently affirms differences in the process of accommodating their transgression. In previous chapters I have retraced that narrative structure through stories that give form to sexual difference and transgression. In this chapter I turn to writings in which Rousseau offers explicit—literal, definitive—accounts of political differences and transgressions. These writings reveal a language of *sensibilité* whose bodily appeals are quite familiar. In this language, the resolution of contradiction—how multiplicity thrives within unity, how sacrifice produces fulfillment, how freedom demands subjection—is achieved as a passionate imperative: love and pity, pain and pleasure, become intelligible through invocations of the corporeal.

But these romantic articulations should not be parsed as simple oppositions to some other, rational design. As already suggested, a plea for conceptual clarity can be made in the service of sustaining a coherent metaphor, and the analytic discipline Rousseau imposes on readers of the *Social Contract* is less to preclude conceptual slippage than to orchestrate it. Further, the narrative posture of citizenship combines what, in discussing St. Preux's moral education, I introduced as distinct terms—affective absorption and critical detachment: each relies upon the other, and both upon a passionate bent that ties one to, and holds one at a distance from

---

[3] Ibid., 398. For examples of an arithemetical language of calculation, see *Social Contract*, 271, 397.

semblables. In short, meanings move, and Rousseau's periodic exertions to make them stand still do not deny that fact. Indeed, these exertions aim to (re)constitute the field of play.

When, then, we read of citizenship and governance in terms of familial and erotic experience, it is not quite right to conclude that this is metaphoric mystification obscuring some other, more literal possibility, any more than it is metaphoric mystification to read power and rule into romance. Both the polity and the romance are figured conventions whose difference, like their similarity, is a question of imaginative possibilities. Does this mean that political life is the same as erotic life? Are the ties that bind families identical to the ties that bind citizens? The unquestionably prudent approach taken by most interpreters who address these matters is to track the worldly differences: families, states, lovers, sons, and citizens denote entities and relations whose particularities must be carefully delineated. But in Rousseau's republican romance, these very old questions are (re)constituted within a narrative structure organized by paradox and transgression. He will insist upon the difference, for example, between the child's attachment to his father and the citizen's attachment to the republic, and then proceed to collapse that difference through evocations of the state's parental body and a citizen's filial love; or he will underscore the tension between individual attachments and the demands of the community, but he will continue to depict each in the language of the other.

In the end, the conceptual precision that holds sexual and republican identities apart works in a manner similar to the differentiation of the *body politic*'s many names: in both cases, the aim is to make distinctions between what is, experientially and referentially, coincident, not in order to deny that coincidence but to make its otherwise paradoxical and inconsistent dimensions imaginable. And while it might thus appear that these linguistic transpositions represent a parasitic relationship—the justification for state power is feeding off the irrationality of erotic passion, while the justification for sexual submission invokes the prerequisites for political order—these assumed priority relations are not borne out in Rousseau's writings: he narrates politics in the language of sex, sex in the language of politics, and both in a language of *sensibilité* that must be felt to be conceived. On this account, the merely

147

metaphoric is always also constitutive, and when Rousseau lays bare the discursive chains through which a body politic is made, it is to reiterate, not to denounce, that body's representational excess.

PERSONATIONS

The figure of the general will first appears in an article Rousseau wrote for the *Encyclopédie*. Published seven years before the *Social Contract*, the *Discourse on Political Economy* introduces many of the themes developed in that later text, but without invoking its contractual language or logic. *Political Economy*'s one allusion on this score ("it should be remembered that the foundation of the social pact is property"[4]) appears in a discussion of taxes, where Rousseau asserts that taxation is legitimate insofar as it is a function of the general will. But this is a matter of rationalizing policy: the question of political origins, to which the contract is Rousseau's later response, is never posed directly in *Political Economy*.[5] Sovereignty and (thus) legitimate legislative power are the foundational presuppositions of his account of political economy:

> Again I ask my readers to distinguish carefully between *public economy*, about which I have to speak and which I call *government*, [and] the supreme authority which I call *sovereignty*, a distinction which consists in the one having the right of legislation, and obligating, in certain cases, the very body of the nation, while the other has only executive power and can only obligate particular individuals. See POLITICS and SOVEREIGNTY. (244)

Rousseau thus delimits the scope of his inquiry to governance: no originary tales need be told in an essay whose focus is the maintenance and good management of the state and whose object of concern is how best to obligate particular individuals, not how best

[4] *Political Economy*, 269. Subsequent references to this work will be given in the body of the text.

[5] For an alternative perspective on this point, see Vaughan's introduction to *Political Economy* in *Political Writings of Jean-Jacques Rousseau*, vol. 1, 228–36. Vaughan suggests that while the notion of the contract is "hurriedly slurred over" (230) in this essay, the logic and normative implications of Rousseau's "mature" (meaning contractual) political thought are present in all their essentials.

to (re)constitute wholes. Up until this point, over the first several pages, he has been expounding on the difference between paternal and political organization and between the ruling sensibilities characteristic of each domain. But these are not, we now read, matters that pertain to sovereignty in any way: supreme power, collective action, and the bodily obligations of the nation have never been the object of his concern. So perhaps the essay's initiating distinctions between familial and political identity do not apply to foundational matters: how best to portray sovereign performances remains an open, and displaced, question.

This representational uncertainty is flagged in the first line of the essay, which introduces its subject matter by tracing the derivation of the word *oeconomy* from its Greek origins, "*oikos, house,* and *nomos, law*" (241).[6] Rousseau observes how the term has moved, from an initial signification of "wise and legitimate government of the home, for the common good of all the family" to its application to "the large family that is the state." "Only the one [*general* or *political economy*] is the subject of this article," he explains, directing readers interested in the other—*domestic* or *particular economy*—to the proper encyclopedic entry ("see FATHER OF THE FAMILY"). If his subsequent elaboration of the differences between paternal and political rule illustrates the dangers of *oeconomy*'s graphic origins, it also plays on their productive possibilities. "Even if there were as close a relation between the state and the family as some authors maintain," he begins, "it would not follow from this that the rules of conduct proper to one of these two societies would be suitable for the other." Differences in size and visibility, as well as in the respective governors' strength, skill, and motivation, all attest to the dissimilarity between wise management of the state and of the home. But on every point, Rousseau frames the comparison in terms of "the large family" versus the small. The difference seems to be one of scale, not kind: "In a word," he writes, "the little family is destined to die off," while "the large [is] made to last forever in the same condition."

The possibility that Rousseau is merely ironizing "some authors" who see similarities where he, in fact, sees none is complicated in

---

Vaughan also detects contractual allusions in two additional passages (see *Political Economy,* 248, 256).

[6] The terms are printed in Roman and Attic Greek characters in the *Encyclopédie.*

the following paragraph when he turns directly to the question of rulers. There the language of large and small families disappears entirely in a discussion of how best to characterize the "leaders" of the two societies, one of which requires the father's absolute, if temporary, control, while the other requires the magistrate's strict adherence to "public reason, which is the law" (243). He admits that the "functions" of both leaders "should tend toward the same goal," but confounding the two might lead us to arrive at "false ideas of the fundamental laws of society": nature, love, and what is written on the heart guide the father, but none of these can in any way authorize the magistrate. If it did the result would be not an ardently felt republicanism but a monarchical sensibility: "I thought these few lines would suffice to destroy the odious system that Sir Filmer has tried to establish in his work entitled *Patriarcha*," Rousseau concludes (244). Here again is that insistently displaced issue of sovereignty: fundamental political laws are at stake in questions of linguistic representation because metaphors figure relations of power.

The monarchical threat embedded in the metaphor of the family is presented more pointedly in a draft of this passage, which appears in the first version of the *Social Contract*. In that text the assertion that magistrates must follow "public reason, which is the law" is followed by: "Thus nature has made a multitude of good Fathers of the family; but I don't know if human wisdom has ever made a good King."[7] (In *Political Economy* this last line becomes: "It is doubtful if, since the creation of the world, human wisdom has ever made ten men capable of governing their *semblables*" [244].) Fending off "false ideas" about politics requires the careful use of language, and when Rousseau drops the familial trope, it is to fend off the possibility of kingly rule. He thus abandons an unjust metaphor (the "large family") in favor of one better suited to republican ends: a public body that "reasons" and, in the process, produces law.

So what initially appeared to be a determined precision—here is the word and its etymology, here is the definition, here is where

---

[7] Rousseau, *Du Contrat Social (1ᵉ version)*, in *Oeuvres Complètes*, vol. 3, 300. For a discussion of the textual linkages between this (incomplete) version of the *Social Contract* and *Political Economy*, see the introductory discussions in *Oeuvres Complètes*, vol. 3, lxxiv–lxxv.

to go to pursue a related but distinct subject—in fact serves as preface to a digressive reflection that deploys, as it seeks to contain, the referential ambiguity preserved within the word. The same slide from precision into metaphoric excess occurs when Rousseau reframes his subject in terms of legislative and executive power. After imploring ("again") his readers to "distinguish carefully" between *sovereignty*, which is not his concern, and *government*, which is, and again directing readers interested in the unaddressed topic to consult the proper encyclopedic entries ("see POLITICS and SOVEREIGNTY"), he begs our leave to pursue "a common comparison, in many respects inexact, but useful for making myself better understood" (ibid.). And then he launches into an extended digression on the body politic, which begins by announcing its metaphoric design (the body politic "can be considered like an organized and living body, similar to that of a man") and ends by ignoring it ("the body politic is thus also a moral being which has a will" [245]). Again his semantic exactitude sets the stage for figural transports, and when Rousseau turns, finally, to discuss the principles of right rule, he will make steady use of a rhetoric of corporeal, as well as familial, experience.

In the *Social Contract* Rousseau compares theorists who depict sovereignty through bodily imagery to "Japanese charlatans" who "cut up a child before the eyes of spectators, then throwing all the parts in the air one after another, make the child fall back down alive and completely reassembled."[8] Having carefully set sovereignty to the side in *Political Economy*, Rousseau does not hesitate to conjure up a body politic in exquisite anatomical detail: the brain, nerves, organs, mouth, stomach, blood, and limbs all correspond to different persons and resources that, together make up a "*self* common to the whole [*le moi commun de tout*], the reciprocal *sensibilité*, and the internal coordination of all the parts" (244–45). This fantasy of a common flesh makes governmental misrule inconceivable: "There is no reason to believe that one can injure or cut off an arm without the pain being transmitted to the head; and it is no more believable that the general will would authorize a member of the state, whoever he might be, to hurt or destroy another, than that the fingers of a man in his right mind would go and put out his eyes" (256).

[8] *Social Contract*, 371.

Just as the fingers of a sane man can move only in accordance with his will, so the limbs of the body politic (the citizens) can act only in accordance with its brain (the sovereign). A deeply etched sense of this corporeal unity is more persuasive than virtue, wisdom, or reason in sustaining the citizens' loyalty because identification with and through the body politic means that individual pleasures and pains will always be imagined as generalized sensations. Thus, when Robert Derathé insists that Rousseau's use of body imagery is not evidence of an "organicist conception of society" (he notices that the text also refers to the body politic as a "machine"), it is somewhat beside the point: Rousseau's reference to what Derathé contends is an "artificial man or body" (indeed: what other kind could it be?) constitutes a narrative performance the representational value of which lies in what it makes readers think and feel.[9] Here again, the question of how to interpret Rousseau's political vision turns on a foundationalist commitment. But I want to insist that the issue is not whether the community is "really" natural or artificial, or whether citizens are "really" individually or collectively inclined. The issue is how these possibilities are imagined and practiced: as "identical correlatives" or strict oppositions. This means that political possibilities are always tied to rhetorical designs.

When Rousseau depicts his corporeal state, it is less to denote an organic or mechanistic vision of society than to promote a "reciprocal *sensibilité*" through which political identification and the identification of self-interest are made coincident, and *amour propre* is (re)constituted through the "moral body" that is the state:

> Suppose someone tells me that whoever has men to govern should not look beyond their nature for a perfection of which they are not capable; that he should not wish to destroy the passions within them, and that the execution of such a plan would be no more desirable than it is possible. I will agree all the more with this, as a man without any passions would certainly be a very bad citizen; but it must also be agreed that if one cannot teach men to love nothing, it is not impossible to teach them to love one object more than another, and to love what is truly beautiful rather than what is deformed. If, for example, one trains them early enough never to consider their own persons but

[9] See introductory discussion to *Political Economy*, in *Oeuvres Complètes*, vol. 3, lxxiv.

through their relations with the body of the State, and not to perceive their own existence, so to speak, but as a part of that state, they may finally come to identify themselves in some way with the greater whole, to feel themselves members of *la patrie*, to love it with that exquisite sentiment that every isolated man feels only for himself. (259)

Passions and the imaginative identifications through which they are provoked are as critical to political identity as they are to sexual identity; here it is the passion aroused by, and on, the state's moral body that guarantees the proper moral effects. As in the lover's relationship with his mistress, the citizen will come to see the state as both the object of his desire and the guarantor of its satisfaction (recall St. Preux's exclamation to Julie: "How strange is your empire! A power to make privations as sweet as pleasures, and to lend to what one does for you the same charms as one would find in self-gratification").[10] In this dynamic of pitiable identification and loving surrender, there are no clear distinctions to be made between interest and duty, between what "every isolated man feels only for himself" and what *la patrie* demands from him. A passionate man is a good citizen, and one trained through object lessons that tie his passions to the pleasures of (self-)rule is the best of all.

In *Political Economy* we find that the imaginative and experiential foundation of citizenship is identical to that of masculinity, and both are narratively constituted through a romance. "The greatest support for public authority is in the heart of the citizens," Rousseau writes, and "history shows us in a thousand ways that the authority [the people] grant to those they love and by whom they are loved is a hundred times more absolute than all the tyranny of usurpers" (252, 254). And again: "Love for *la patrie* is the most effective, for as I have already said, every man is virtuous when his particular will conforms in everything with the general will, and we willingly want what is wanted by those we love" (254). To willingly want what is wanted by others is to embrace a consensual nonconsensuality and thus to enter into a relationship that replicates the dynamics of the (hetero)sexual romance. It is a close fit: in both cases, sexual and political, the distinction between desiring and obeying is obscured by a *sensibilité* that imagines bodily

[10] *Julie*, 122.

satisfaction through some other's will. And in both cases, sovereignty and subjection are "identical correlatives": "If you want the laws obeyed, make them beloved, and to get one to do what he should, it is enough that he think [*songer*] that he must do it" (251–52).

Making the law beloved, that materialized will of the body politic that is always one's own and some other's desire, is precisely the art of politics—the "inconceivable art" of "subjecting men in order to make them free"—and it is this practice that constitutes a *general* or *political economy* (248). Until the essay's final section, when Rousseau turns directly to the question of state income and expenditure ("Forget the ledgers and papers," he advises, "and put the finances in faithful hands; this is the only way that they will be faithfully administered" [266]), his attention stays trained on the business of sustaining a public love. And we know from the *Letter to d'Alembert* that "however love is depicted for us, it seduces or it is not love."[11] Thus *Political Economy* is punctuated with warnings about dangerous *spectacles*—clever orators who confound with their "eloquence," politicians who "bedazzle" the citizens' eyes— even as it stages its own. But, again, this is the art of governance: "While the government is not the master of the law, it's quite a bit to be its guarantor and to have a thousand ways of making it loved. The talent for ruling consists in none other than this" (250).

Those "thousand ways" of making the body politic beloved, as well as the law that is its will, include the spectacular and imaginative strategies through which romances are made. And the talents for this are all feminized, inscribed on a body that is the sign of a loving mother, submissive wife, and masterful mistress: identical correlatives whose meanings combine in the word *woman*.

MATERNAL LEARNING

Rousseau's answer to the question, How is the general will to be realized? is "in a word, make virtue reign" (252). He elaborates on this scheme by addressing, in turn, the state's need to protect the citizens' lives, to guarantee their economic security, and to oversee their education. Together these three functions duplicate the du-

---

[11] *Letter to d'Alembert*, 51.

ties of the father toward his children, sketched in the essay's opening discussion. Of course, we have already been advised that the
functions of both domestic and public governance "should tend
toward the same goals." It is the rationale and motivation for their
actions that are markedly different: the father writ large on the
nation would act just like a king. But in the course of explicating
republican state practices, Rousseau returns to the language of
familial care, and in so doing the body politic assumes a maternal
form. *La patrie*, Rousseau writes, must "show itself as the common
mother of all the citizens," or again, as "the tender mother who
nourishes them all" (258, 260). Rousseau's figuration is persistent,
and blithely undeterred by the graphic traces that bear witness to
its representational excess: the fatherland (*la patrie*) as mother.

So how literal can this be? To what could this mother-state refer?
Surely the generalizing of a maternal will can only destroy or "de-
nature" it, and thus destroy or endanger the integrity of a family
whose essence is particular interests and devotions. The paradigmatic case here is offered in *Emile*, where the model *citoyenne*
is represented in the figure of the Spartan mother described by
Plutarch, who praised the gods for victory despite the death of her
five sons.[12] For the loyal citizen, maternal commitment represents
the profoundly particular attachments that must be overcome.
When Rousseau then uses the vocabulary of gendered familial devotions to portray political loyalty in *Political Economy*, it seems contrary to the terms' original meaning. But the maternalizing of the
general will is not, I want to suggest, a simple confusion of categories and roles: as a site of sexual learning and control, the body
politic is itself a force in how those categories and roles come to
be understood and lived. What I've described in chapter one as a
recursive logic applies here to the essay's referential design: just
as Rousseau's narrative ends are embedded in his beginnings, so
his feminized state is always insinuated in his depictions of sexual
identity and practice. Tackling the issue from this perspective, we
need to consider how the imperatives of republican politicization
figure in Rousseau's account of maternal identity. To act like a
woman, we will find, is to enact a political design.

Consider, for example, Rousseau's attack in *Emile* on the moral
travesty that is wet-nursing. The trend toward delegating nurtur-

---

[12] *Emile*, 249.

ance to a paid professional is, on his telling, directly implicated in processes of political and social decay: "This practice, added to the other causes of depopulation, presages the impending fate of Europe; the sciences, the arts, the philosophy and the morals that this practice engenders will not be long in making a desert of it; it will be peopled with ferocious beasts; the change of inhabitants will not be great."[13]

Nonmaternal breast-feeding is part and parcel of social practices, values, and institutions whose degenerative effects are coincidentally politically barbarous and sexually barren. Here we must put the possibility of natural scientific (mis)understandings to the side: Rousseau's fears about depopulation are expressed in terms of the unnurturing mothers' moral and social preoccupation with their own pleasures. These women begin by "devot[ing] themselves daily to the entertainments of the city"; but very soon, "not satisfied with having given up nursing their children, women give up wanting to have them."[14] So when Rousseau envisages a form of biopolitics on the body of the nursing mother—the size, health, and fertility of the body politic as evidenced by its (suckled) population—he is (still) pursuing a politics whose axes of struggle are men's and women's wills.[15] Thus, while the state needs women to be prolific reproducers, it also and as insistently needs women to be attached to the family, and the form these attachments take—heterosexual desire and maternal devotion—remain ongoing political concerns.

The inconstant foundations of these attachments and the need for their continuous rhetorical fortification are evidenced by Rousseau's multilayered account of the family. In a discussion of Locke, for example, he denies that conjugal and parental attach-

---

[13] Ibid., 145. Note the ambiguity in this passage, where Europe's fate (i.e., to be "peopled with ferocious beasts") can mean either that its population will decrease or that it will be filled with selfish individuals. Thus a mother's failure to nurse evokes the image of a diminishing civilization, in terms of both virtue and absolute numbers. See *Discourse on Inequality,* 202, for further discussion of the "brutal tastes" and "corrupt imagination" that lead to birth control and "secret abortions."

[14] *Emile,* 44.

[15] Rousseau's depiction of a "population" whose hygiene, nutrition, exercise, and reproductive practices are all of direct political interest seems exemplary of Michel Foucault's notion of "biopower"; see *History of Sexuality,* vol. 1, 140–44. At

ment are present in the state of nature: precisely because the frequency and number of pregnancies are low, females maintain a natural independence.[16] Where the "habit of cohabitation" has not yet set in, Rousseau opines, both the occasion for and the interest in intercourse is minimal; thus the natural woman is independent because she is infrequently incapacitated, and she is infrequently incapacitated because she is independent of men. In this same discussion Rousseau explicitly rejects the notion of an innate maternal instinct. In the state of nature, he writes, females fed their young because it was in their interests to do so, presumably, for bodily comfort. Only after repeat performances do they develop any attachment to their children: "The mother at first nursed her Children for her own need; as the habit endeared them to her, she later nourished them for their own need; as soon as they had the strength to look for their own sustenance, they did not hesitate to leave the mother herself."[17] The inescapable conclusion is that Rousseau imagines a natural feminine indifference—toward babies and men—the overcoming of which is vital to his sexual and political vision.

For some interpreters, this depiction of an original, ungendered independence exposes a contradiction typical of Rousseau's sexual politics: the "evidence" that nature favors human freedom is disregarded in the case of women.[18] For others this depiction signifies a limit to his biologism, and thus it confirms that his sexual politics are shaped by normative rather than naturalistic concerns.[19] These undoubtedly correct observations suggest a priority relation that I will ignore—beliefs about nature are either the inspiration for Rousseau's political prescriptions or they are mere pretext—in order to consider how his image of nature is itself symptomatic of his political desires. In other words, I am

the same time, Rousseau's preoccupation with sovereignty, and thus with the family as a model for and site of relations of power and its legitimation, challenges the political narrative through which Foucault chronicles the emergence of biopower; see "Governmentality," in *The Foucault Effect*, 99–101.

[16] *Discourse on Inequality*, 216–18.

[17] Ibid., 147.

[18] Okin, *Women in Western Political Thought*, 109–11. Kofman also underscores the inconsistencies in Rousseau's use of nature; see her "Rousseau's Phallocratic Ends."

[19] See, for example, Weiss, *Gendered Community*, 37–52.

proposing that his naturally independent and indifferent female represents a politics whose purposes are realized through a heterosexual design. My interpretive challenge is thus not to determine whether Rousseau's maternal vision arises from his understanding of nature or from his republican convictions, but to clarify how each gives form to the other, on and through the figuration of women's bodies. From this perspective, good governance becomes coincident with the *éducation sensible* that orders bodily practices, and in a woman's passion for men and for babies we see republican principles in action. The savage female, by contrast, represents the unpitiable (im)possibility of a life without politics.

My claim that heterosexual relations of attachment, nurturance, and identity constitute a form of political practice parallels Londa Schiebinger's analysis of eighteenth-century natural scientific discourse.[20] She argues that the adoption of Linnaeus's nomenclature for the highest class of vertebrate (*Mammalia*) can be traced to its political and cultural context, where contestations over citizenship and labor played out in part through contestations over women's domestic and conjugal roles. Her conclusion, that the ratification of *Mammalia* "helped legitimize the sexual division of labor in European society," underscores how the changing structure of child care and home, and the changing structure of politics and economy, are mutually effecting.[21] So, too, it points to language as a site of social contestation: Schiebinger identifies in scientific terminology the graphic traces of a historical process whose political and sexual instabilities that terminology helped to adjudicate. I am suggesting that Rousseau's figural language performs a similar role, serving less as a reflection of worldly referents than as a site of their production. That these productions are both individual and national, applicable to women's bodies and to the body of the state, is a function of their discursive design: "Let mothers deign to nurse their children, morals will reform themselves, nature's sentiments will be awakened in every heart, the state will be repeopled. This point, this point alone, will bring everything back together."[22]

[20] See Schiebinger, "Why Mammals Are Called Mammals."
[21] Ibid., 409.
[22] *Emile*, 46.

Rousseau's insistence in *Emile* that this "one point" is central to republican virtue suggests, again, the importance of women's disciplined conduct to his republicanism. But so, too, it inscribes on women's bodies a dynamic of care and control that figures the body politic. Consider the parallel formations in *Emile* and *Political Economy*. "Do you want to bring everyone back to his first duties?" Rousseau writes in *Emile*. "Begin with mothers."[23] *Political Economy* echoes this exhortation with "Do we want people to be virtuous? Let us begin by making them love their country."[24] At stake in both cases is the citizen-child's attachment to the source of his protection and nurturing, and, through her, his identification with other citizen-siblings. Where maternal love wanes, the tutor insists, family members "hardly know one another."[25] Where patriotism fades, Rousseau advises the statesman, "country means no more to [the citizens] than it does to foreigners."[26] The duties between mother and child, *Emile* continues, "are reciprocal, and if they are ill-fulfilled on one side, they will be neglected on the other."[27] The commitments of society, *Political Economy* repeats, "are reciprocal in nature, [and thus] no one owes anything to someone who claims to owe nothing to anybody."[28] And as the textual return to the breast makes clear, this reciprocal *sensibilité* must be felt: the body provides the sensuous confirmation of maternal devotion, and "where I find a mother's care do not I owe a son's attachment?"[29]

In the public as in the domestic realm, these attachments are generated and sustained through the staging of a maternal *spectacle*:

> If children are raised in common in the bosom [*sein*] of equality, if they are imbued with the laws of the state and the maxims of the general will, if they are taught to respect them above all other things, if they are surrounded by examples and objects that speak to them ceaselessly of the tender mother who nourishes them, of the love she

[23] Ibid.
[24] *Political Economy*, 122.
[25] *Emile*, 46.
[26] *Political Economy*, 122.
[27] *Emile*, 46.
[28] *Political Economy*, 117.
[29] *Emile*, 45.

has for them, of the inestimable goods they received from her, and of what they owe her in return, let us not doubt that they will learn in this way to cherish one another like brothers, to want only what society wants, to substitute the actions of men and citizens for the sterile and vain babbling of sophists, and to become one day the defenders and the fathers of *la patrie* whose children they have been for so long. (261)

Inscribed on the heart with our earliest worldly encounters, the felt truths of maternal solicitude contain and continue republican unity. Pity and self-interest, the dynamics of identity and differ-ence, move through an imagined body politic fashioned on the body of the mother.[30] "Every true republican," Rousseau writes in *Government of Poland*, "sucks in with his mother's milk a love of *la patrie*, which is to say, of the laws and of liberty; this love makes up his whole existence, he sees only *la patrie*, he lives only for her."[31] Here the figural excess corresponds to an attachment beyond re-flection or analysis; or rather, it sustains a pitying identification that sees another's body—the state's, the mother's—as cause and culmination of one's deepest desires. And in this way, life lived in the bosom of the republican state offers protection from dema-gogic seductions: the "sterile babble of sophists" is no match for the comforts of the mother tongue.[32]

Attending to Rousseau's rhetorical design as a site of political and sexual (self-)constitution suggests a resolution of the apparent contradiction between familial and political experience, first out-lined by Susan Okin. This contradiction consists in the conflicting loyalties of citizens who are socialized in a nuclear (patriarchal) family, "which requires its members to have a very strong loyalty to its needs and wishes, which may very well conflict with the good

[30] Berman also argues for the significance of Rousseau's maternal imagery; see *Politics of Authenticity*, 203–4. It is unclear what subject position Berman occupies when he concludes from this that Rousseau's state is a source of nurturance and love; given that he seems to present the meanings of this imagery as self-evident, his position might be that of the imagining citizen.

[31] Rousseau, *Considerations sur le Gouvernement de Pologne*, in *Oeuvres Complètes*, vol. 3, 966 (hereafter *Government of Poland*).

[32] Recall Rousseau's admission in *Emile* apropos the tutor's introduction to an imagined Sophie: "It is unimportant whether the object I depict for him is imagi-nary; it suffices that it make him disgusted with those that would tempt him; it suffices that he everywhere find comparisons which make him prefer his chimera to the real objects that strike his eye" (329).

of the greater society."[33] The problem intensifies when one considers these inconsistencies in light of Rousseau's claim that one can be raised to be either a man or a citizen, but never both. Okin finds the "climax" to this paradox in Rousseau's attack in *Emile* on Plato's abolition of the family. According to Rousseau this leads to

> [t]hat subversion of the sweetest sentiments of nature, sacrificed to an artificial sentiment that can only be maintained by them—as though there were no need for a natural base on which to form conventional ties; as though the love of one's nearest were not the principle of the love one owes the state; as though it were not by means of the small fatherland that is the family that the heart attaches itself to the large one; as though it were not the good son, the good husband, and the good father who makes the good citizen![34]

Okin observes that this argument must remain "highly puzzling" in light of "Rousseau's belief that human nature had to be deformed in order to make men into citizens."[35] But if one assesses Rousseau's patriarchal family as a political and rhetorical construction, rather than as a natural grouping whose discrete interests emerge prior to politics, then the issue of its complementarity with the republican state appears less puzzling. The experiences of dependence, otherness, freedom, and submission that the family represents give form to the experience of republican citizenship. The issue is not, then, that the family encourages "affections for and loyalties to just a few people," but that it gives form to sexual identities whose willing, needing, and desirous performances are always organized by political imperatives: as a way of life and an imaginary design, the patriarchal family structures relations of affection and loyalty that emerge from, and coexist with, relations of domination and submission.[36] The ongoing political significance of the family is thus rooted in its gendered form, and Plato's error was not to generalize that form but to allow, through the

[33] Okin, *Women in Western Political Thought*, 189. Okin summarizes what she calls Rousseau's theory of conflicting interests at 176–77.

[34] *Emile*, 363, and in Okin, *Women in Western Political Thought*, 192.

[35] Okin, *Women in Western Political Thought*, 192.

[36] Ibid. In sharp contrast with my argument, Okin concludes that the patriarchal family is a "disaster" as a socializing unity within Rousseau's republican polity (289).

family's abolition, a "civil promiscuity which thoroughly confounds the two sexes in the same employments and in the same labors."[37]

An insistence on the political importance of sexual roles and sensibilities in Rousseau's model family also appears in Joel Schwartz's analysis. Denying that Rousseau's argument introduces a paradox, Schwartz claims that the family supports the polity because the sexual division of labor in the family "[s]trengthens [men], by making them aware of the dependence of their women upon them. A man will hunt more energetically, if need be fight more fiercely, because he provides for and defends two or more people instead of just himself."[38] A modified version of this argument—that man's domestication heightens his commitment to and skills for predatory success—appears in Schwartz's response to Okin, where he proposes that a "natural base" to support "denatured" citizenship appears less contradictory if we recognize in men a natural "solipsistic preoccupation with their individual selves."[39] Women must then combat masculine selfishness by drawing men into a familial sphere of "natural" attachment and care.

These assertions assume that women's interests and needs are synonymous with those of the family, which are seen as distinct from the needs and interests of men, whose dependence arises only as a consequence of being compelled, emboldened, or cajoled to protect and support the family. But, as I have argued throughout, this particular appeal to nature is not sustainable in the context of Rousseau's writings. Clearly, he is as concerned with shoring up women's interest in and need for the family as he is with rationalizing men's. His plea to mothers to forsake their "gay devotion" to the "entertainment of the cities" and "fulfill with a virtuous intrepidity this duty so sweet imposed on [them] by nature" underscores his fear that, even in civil society, women's interests and those of the family might be at odds.[40] In addition, Schwartz's claim that women are by nature more attached to families—that they "are more closely tied to more particular wills than are men"—lacks textual support: this might be Hegel's fundamen-

---

[37] *Emile*, 363.
[38] Schwartz, *Sexual Politics*, 51.
[39] Ibid., 162 n. 21.
[40] *Emile*, 46.

tal premise, but it is not Rousseau's.[41] Similarly, there is little evidence to support the contention of a naturally selfish masculinity.

In the end, the natural dimensions Schwartz reads into the family are instructive not because they clarify Rousseau's republicanism but because they are symptomatic of a desire to sentimentalize the family in the name of a natural sexuality. This is an interpretive move Rousseau anticipates and, indeed, invites: it mystifies the functional basis of the family and ignores the relations of power through which the family is sustained. These are not, pace Schwartz, Aristotelian moments of "ruling and being ruled in return" but embodied dynamics of domination and submission whose inherent instability is the stuff of romance, and of rape. Thus, while Schwartz is surely correct when he emphasizes the difference between a magistrate's feelings toward the citizenry and the father's feelings toward his children, this is not particularly germane: the more fitting rapprochement is between sovereigns and subjects on the one hand, and mother/mistresses and men on the other. But the search for parallels between Rousseau's sexual and political identities can go only so far. Given the slippage and inversion characteristic of role-playing in both domains, it is difficult to know which terms to correlate and at which moment in time. It is more helpful to change the frame of analysis, from one that assumes preconstituted sexual and political differences, to one that traces their emergence as rhetorical effects: *citizen, subject, sovereign,* and *state* are perfect correlatives whose meanings come together and come apart in the interaction of the terms *man* and *woman.*

National Erotics

In making the law beloved and thus safe from the seductions of babbling sophists, Rousseau's sketch of good governance draws also on figurations of erotic desire. In so doing he narrates a *spectacle* of romantic excess whose ability to enthrall is openly acknowledged. Love of *la patrie,* he insists, "is the passion that has produced so many immortal actions whose radiance bedazzles our feeble eyes, and so many men whose ancient virtues pass for fables

---

[41] Schwartz, *Sexual Politics,* 43.

now that love of *la patrie* has become an object of derision" (255). He continues: "The transports of tender hearts appear utterly fanciful to anyone who has not felt them. And the love of *la patrie,* a hundred times more ardent and delicious than that of a mistress, likewise cannot be conceived except by being felt; but it is easy to observe in all the hearts that it inflames, in the actions that it inspires, this fiery and sublime ardor, without which the purest virtue fails to shine" (ibid.). Love of *la patrie,* like love of the mistress, entails spectacular and sensuous experience: feeling it makes it real, and it must be seen to be believed. So, too, patriotism represents a unity of self-interest and duty, of fulfillment and sacrifice, that continues the logic of romantic identification: by "join[ing] the force of *amour propre* to all the beauty of virtue," love of country reproduces the willing performances of masculine lovers, now prostrate before the body of the state (ibid.).

Rousseau takes pains to underscore that these transports are difficult to conceive. In addition to being a particular and consuming identification that defies all reason, patriotic passion feeds on sensational display, and ancien régime Frenchmen have "feeble eyes." The concern is about cultural enervation: the actions and virtues of the ancients, for example, will seem "fabulous" in a monarchical social and political order. This is not to say that monarchical subjects are not mesmerized by political *spectacles* but, rather, that they are subjected to the wrong ones. Thus the language of enchantment is used to characterize both the art of republican governance and the threat to which republicanism must respond. Precisely the contempt with which enervated monarchical subjects view the law leaves them more vulnerable to subjection:

> At such times, when the voice of duty no longer speaks in their hearts, the leaders are forced to substitute the cry of terror or the lure of an apparent interest, by means of which they deceive their creatures [*créatures*]. At such times they must make recourse to all the little and despicable tricks that they call *state maxims* and *cabinet mysteries*. . . . Finally, all the skill of these great politicians is to so bedazzle [*fasciner*] the eyes of those they need, that each one believes that he is working for his interest while he works for *theirs*. (253)

The *spectacle* staged by the corrupt state works similarly to those put on by a republic: each citizen-subject thinks of his own self-interest when he acts on behalf of the state.[42] But in the former, the pursuit of self-interest furthers the king's ends, whereas in the latter, it furthers the good of the whole. The consistent model is of an *amour propre* imagined through relations with a state whose powers inspire awe: the difference between the self-interest of a republican citizen and that of a monarchical subject is whether that power terrifies or seduces. To illustrate the point, *Political Economy* introduces Cato, that citizen-lover whose fabled actions have always dazzled Rousseau's own eyes.

Cato "lived only for [his country] and could not live without it," Rousseau writes. Because he "always carr[ied] his country in the bottom of his heart" and sought happiness "only in that of others," Cato assured that Rome was "virtuous and became the mistress of the world" (255). This political devotion exemplifies the masculine lover, whose *amour propre* is always imagined through the mistress's will: when Caesar stood poised to conquer Rome, Cato chose death over the willful violation of his body politic. This is the "true lover" depicted in *Emile*, a man of "sensual and coarse passion" who is willing "to immolate himself for his beloved."[43] Rousseau elsewhere writes that Cato's true significance is unrelated to any actual historical event: "I do not know if he did anything for his *Patrie*; but I know that he did a great deal for mankind, by offering it the *spectacle* and the model of the purest virtue that ever was."[44] In this same context Rousseau approvingly quotes Seneca: "Behold a *spectacle* worthy of a god intent on his work. . . . [I] see no fairer *spectacle* on earth for Jupiter to behold, should he wish, than Cat[o]."[45] In *Political Economy* Rousseau narratively reproduces this *spectacle*, presenting Cato as a "god among mortals" who can inspire "worthy emulators" to become "the greatest" of contemporary men (255).

The citizen-lover Cato counterpoises the image of the ancien régime bourgeois: "How can love of country take root in the midst of so many other passions that stifle it? And what remains for fellow citizens [*concitoyens*] of a heart divided between avarice, a mis-

[42] See *Social Contract*, 373, quoted in this chapter's opening paragraph.

[43] *Emile*, 391–92.

[44] Rousseau, "Last Reply by J.-J. Rousseau of Geneva," in *Oeuvres Complètes*, vol. 3, 87.

[45] Ibid., 88; from Seneca's *De Providentia* (Rousseau cites this passage in the original Latin).

tress, and vanity?" (260). One hears the twin echoes of Emile's tutor ("a man will serve his mistress no better than he serves virtue") and Lord Bomston ("we serve philosophy worthily only with the same ardor that we feel for a mistress").[46] In these formulations sexual devotion is not in competition with patriotic attachment but provides a rhetorical and experiential model through which it can be imagined, and felt. Cato offers readers a romantic hero whose beloved always incorporates this twofold, sexual and political design, and thus in his stories, Rome plays the part of a woman.

Like the mistress celebrated in *Emile*, the state must maintain the authority to "send her lovers with a nod to the end of the world, to combat, to glory, to death, to anything she pleases."[47] And as we saw illustrated in Rousseau's relationships with Mlles Goton and Vulson, this kind of devotion requires submission: "The government will have a difficult time making itself obeyed if it limits itself to obedience. If it is good to know how to use men as they are, it is better still to turn them into what one needs them to be" (251). Obedience ensures that a man's actions will be in conformity with that which is commanded; but submission guarantees that the movement of his very will always depends on the will of another. When Rousseau rhetorically constructs this servile desire, he does so through romantic figurations. The description of the "real statesman," one who "extends his venerable rule over wills even more than over actions" (250), was first given to us in the portrait of the mistress: hers is the paradigm of an authority "which penetrates to the inner part of a man and is exerted on his will no less than on his actions" (251). Like her, and through her, the republic makes men in the image of citizens, and citizens on the bodies of men.

In these ways, then, Rousseau combines the promise of sexual fulfillment and maternal beneficence with the imperatives of political rule to produce a political erotica that (re)inscribes men's and women's sexual identities onto the body politic. Throughout, I have insisted that these inscriptions cannot be traced to a foundational experiential realm. Families and states, sexuality and political rule, narrative and worldly designs: each pair represents, in Rousseau's account, a mutually constituted truth. This interpreta-

[46] *Emile*, 392; *Julie*, 193.
[47] *Emile*, 393.

tion complicates the conclusions often reached by feminist scholars who read Rousseau as an exemplary theorist of "separate spheres." Joan Landes, for example, draws our attention to the persistent linkages between eroticism and republicanism in the work of Enlightenment thinkers (foremost among them Rousseau), but she sees the relationship as purely negative. Women's growing influence at a time of political instability and change was seen as a threat to nascent republican virtue, she observes, and thus the health of the body politic required their (re)privatization and, with this, the restriction of their erotic powers.[48] More recently contributors to *Eroticism and the Body Politic* have followed Landes's lead in exploring relationships between representations of women's bodies and political conflict in eighteenth-century France. In contrast with Landes, they see ambivalence in the eroticism of the "new" political symbology: while paintings, pamphlets, and caricatures often glorified women's redomestication, their persistent appeal to female eroticism in making the point reiterates women's ongoing power to signify political desires. It also reproduces the feminine body in the image of, and as a site for, political designs.[49]

My reading of Rousseau confirms this ambivalence. My primary concern, however, is not whether his political erotica contributed to women's privatization or, even less, whether or how its ambiguity can subvert male political privilege. Rather, my interest is in how republican identity is constructed through sexual identities, and sexual identities, through political forms, and these are processes whose rhetorical and material moments cannot be readily detached one from the other. Rousseau contributed to the constitution and dissemination of that "new" political symbology; he also contributed to the scripting of a historically emergent romantic love. These contributions converge in the reading practices of Rousseau's public: in his fictional, political, and autobiographical writing, readers encounter a romance that is the story of their lives, as they are lived in the closet, the home, and the state. Which

[48] Landes, *Women and the Public Sphere,* esp. chap. 3, "Rousseau's Reply to Public Women."

[49] Hunt, ed., *Eroticism and the Body Politic.* See in particular essays by Vivian Cameron, "Political Exposures: Sexuality and Caricature in the French Revolution"; and Mary Sheriff, "Fragonard's Erotic Mothers and the Politics of Reproduction."

Republican Performances

> Since everything which enters into the human
> understanding comes there through the
> senses, man's first reason is a reason of the
> senses; this sensual reason serves as the
> basis of intellectual reason. Our first masters of
> philosophy are our feet, our hands, our eyes.
>
> *Emile*

WHAT'S YOUR PLEASURE?

Rousseau frequently rehearsed his uneasiness with imitation. In his brief *De l'Imitation Théâtrale* this uneasiness is couched as an epistemological difficulty rooted in the levels of remove between a general idea, the things made in accordance with that idea, and artistic portrayals of those things. The first is "the original idea, existing by itself; the second is an image of it, the third is an image of the image," and thus at two removes from the "truth."[1] Painters and playwrights exemplify this dangerous art whereby things are depicted "such as they appear to be, and not as they are," but he adds that anyone can "do as much with a mirror."[2] Vain imitations also structure the plot of his early *Narcisse*, in which the beautiful Valère falls in love with his own portrait, retouched as a jest by friends to resemble a woman's.[3] His devout financée Angelique is in on the joke, but she does not unmask the false portrait and insists that Valère choose between her and the woman it depicts. He is redeemed when, on his knees, he admits that she has "vanquished" and that the feelings aroused by his "caprice" are inferior to those she inspires.[4] So, too, in *Julie*'s second preface, the novel's

---

[1] Rousseau, *De l'Imitation Théâtrale*, in *Oeuvres Complètes*, vol. 5, 1197.

[2] Ibid.

[3] Rousseau, *Narcisse, ou L'Amant de Lui-Même*, in *Oeuvres Complètes*, vol. 2.

[4] Ibid., 1015. A secondary plot line involves Valère's sister, Lucinde, and Angelique's brother, Léandre, whose courtship is also endangered and simultaneously preserved by mistaken identities.

instructive value is parsed as a question of representational remove: Is the story a picture that aims to please, or a portrait that aims to represent? While N. fumes that its otherworldly characters sabotage "the common model" necessary to all "tableaux of humanity," R. reminds him that all tableaux require distinguishing between what is essentially true of "the type" (*l'espece*) and what is only of superficial variation.[5] R. and N. thus evince a common commitment to the idea of an original, but no ideas about what might constitute plausible reproductions.[6]

The thematic juxtapositions are familiar—originals and copies, ideas and forms, pleasure and truth—and so are the overdeterminations of Rousseau's textual location. In *De l'Imitation Théâtrale* he is impersonating Plato in a first-person narrative ("The more I think about the establishment of our imaginary republic," it begins) that reworks material from the *Laws* and the *Republic*, with paintings and poems discussed in lieu of plays and actors ("All that I say here about painting is applicable to theatrical imitation").[7] In *Julie*'s second preface he is scripting a dialogue, featuring himself not as the novel's author but as the letters' editor, who wants to believe that they are authentic but has his doubts, and yet who is quite sure they speak truth. And in *Narcisse* he is a playwright whose central prop blurs the distinction between representation as correspondence and as (re)construction: Valère's is a portrait made picture that is, still, a mirror, which pleases because it both does and does not reproduce. To be sure, a plotline that draws on identities counterfeited in the rocky course of love was not Rousseau's original idea: but as a popular theme in seventeenth- and eighteenth-century theater, it was the ideal vehicle and the natural choice for a young would-be man of letters.

It is not enough to attribute these performative paradoxes to the "corrupt" milieux in which they occur. Rousseau suggests this possibility in the preface to *Narcisse*: the absence of "honest folk and good morals" absolves him of contradiction because then "it is no longer a matter of inclining people to do good [*porter les*

---

[5] Second preface, 12.

[6] Daniel Mornet calls this particular discussion "confused" and "vague," unable to offer guidance about the "*vérité humaine*" of the novel; see editor's note in his critical edition of *La Nouvelle Héloïse*, vol. 1, 301.

[7] *De l'Imitation Théâtrale*, 1196, 1199.

peuples à bien faire], it is enough to distract them from doing evil."[8]
He makes this same gesture in both prefaces to *Julie,* and in the
second he has R. refer N. to the sentence just quoted. But so, too,
Rousseau likens *Narcisse* to "illegitimate children one still fondles
with pleasure while blushing to be their father" and *Julie*'s otherworldly characters to "beautiful souls."[9] As undeniable as his flesh
and a holy design, his distractions please because they are true.
Still, the Platonic Rousseau knows that all the dangers of artistic
genius reside in the contrary: they will be taken as truth because
they please. And whether it is ancient Athens or ancien régime
France, nowhere is there a people that does not want its pleasures.
As the paradoxes pile up, it is increasingly difficult to imagine
anything outside these "corrupt" milieux. Aside from his imaginary republic, of course. But there, too, we find a portrait like
Valère's, one that does and does not represent the pleasing truths
of (hetero)sexual difference.

In this chapter I explore the representational practices through
which Rousseau's republican men and women identify their truth
and their pleasure. In so doing I retrace his accounts of performative corruption in the *Letter to d'Alembert* and the *Essay on the Origin
of Languages,* in a manner attentive to the difficulties just rehearsed: I read them not to identify a degenerative cause or moment but to explicate the structural logic through which meanings
are made. In both texts an account of representation is embedded
in a story of moral and social decay. The *Letter to d'Alembert* presents
theatrical practices as inseparable from the public spaces and social relations of a "great city" that Geneva must never let itself
become, while the *Essay on Languages* retraces linguistic representation through a twofold deterioration: from a "natural language"
of gestural symbolization supplanted by utterance, and from a me-
lodious, southern language perverted by calculating languages of
the north. In both texts, the counterfeit identities and interests
made possible by imitative practice reflect political corruption.
Actors and playwrights survive because they are pensioned by the
king, while the opulence displayed in the loges and the poverty
displayed in the pit exemplify monarchical inequalities. And the
features of northern languages, "neither accidental nor arbitrary,"

---

[8] Preface to *Narcisse,* 972.
[9] Ibid., 963; and second preface to *Julie,* 13.

reflect national imperatives: "Of what use would [eloquence] be today, when public force replaces persuasion? It requires neither art nor figures of speech to say *such is my pleasure.*"[10]

If the monarchical pleasures of absolutist rule feed on both theatrical interactions and discursive ineloquence, so, too, they feed on sexual (dis)orders that undermine modesty and enervate audacity. Rousseau has much to say in the *Letter to d'Alembert* about the theatergoer's opportunity for self-distinction, for social aggrandizement, and for the free rein of *pitié* that takes spectators to places they ought not to go; but he has more to say in this piece about the interaction between men and women. Otherwise put: what he has to say about Geneva's civic corruption he offers as a warning about its sexual corruption. This is partly owing to theater's dramatic content: "only romances" succeed on the contemporary stage, he laments, and "love is the realm of women; it is they who necessarily give the law in it."[11] It is also due to the theater's social practices, which afford both actresses and female spectators a publicity inconsistent with *pudeur*. The discussion of republican entertainments in the *Letter to d'Alembert* supports this conclusion: his preferred festivals, sportive competitions, *cercles*, and balls present men and women in a proper sexual order. But these models rely upon the same imaginative design—the same general idea, the Platonic Rousseau might say—that he denounces in the context of the theater. In his republican variations, self-rule is undermined by the confusion of roles, not by role-playing itself, and a sexual publicity is one of its crucial dimensions.

Sexuality assumes a similarly constitutive role in the *Essay on Languages*, which sketches an originary tale deeply reminiscent of the *Discourse on Inequality*.[12] Here the doubled figuration of origins—a primary language of gestures and moans and a "first language" of utterance issuing from the south's "happy climes"[13]—repeats the recursive logic whereby mastery and desire both initiate and consummate social (d)evolution. In the linguistic beginning, there was passion—"Not hunger, nor thirst, but love, hatred,

---

[10] *Essay on Languages*, 428; italics in original.

[11] *Letter to d'Alembert*, 43.

[12] Derrida recapitulates the contemporary debate concerning the date of the *Essay*'s composition and its textual links to the *Discourse on Inequality*; see *Of Grammatology*, 171–72.

[13] *Essay on Languages*, 405.

pitié, anger wrung their first utterings from them"[14]—and every step between that first "barbarism [which] was the golden age" and Rousseau's France, where language provides "only cries for men possessed by the Devil," is marked by the expressive demands of desire. Corruption thus cannot be identified in the move from a *before* to an *after,* but in the practice of one's pleasures. That gesticulating southern barbarian "considered himself master of everything," Rousseau admits, but he neither "knew nor desired other than what was ready at hand"; ever-needy Frenchmen, by contrast, speak a "servile language" whose ineloquence keeps them "scattered" (why assemble when there is nothing "to say to the people but *give money*"?) and unfree.[15] How is republican pleasure possible? In discursive performances that work to "move a young heart [and] repulse an unjust aggressor," in those first communications of a first language whose "songlike" harmonies are well suited to liberty.[16] This means rejecting monarchical declarations of desire—"*such is my pleasure*"—for a consensually nonconsensual version that must always ask: What is yours?

I begin with a reading of the *Letter to d'Alembert* that moves between the text's representation of the theater as a social space and what happens on its stage. In this sense the play's the thing that (re)constitutes the audience, not only by offering it an authentic or distorting, ennobling or debased reflection but also as a site and a structure of interaction. Of particular concern is how this interaction challenges republican sexual dispositions, and most important, *pudeur* or (feminine) modesty. I argue that Rousseau's justification of *pudeur* reiterates the theatricality of its process and form. My conclusion is not, however, that *pudeur* is inauthentic, but that it forces us to move beyond analytic frames organized by dilemmas of authenticity and fraudulence. I illustrate the point in a brief discussion of two, very differently pitched analyses in this vein: Patrick Coleman on Rousseau's republican *spectacle* and Jacques Derrida on Rousseau's dream of language without substitution. By contrast, my reading of the *Essay on Languages* emphasizes the continuity between linguistic practice and theatricality, and thus it underscores the need to begin, and end, with Rous-

---

[14] Ibid., 380.
[15] Ibid., 396, 428–29.
[16] Ibid., 380–81. On languages "favorable to liberty," see chap. 20, 428–29.

seau's *ordre sensible*. I conclude with a discussion of the republican theatricality offered in the closing pages of the *Letter to d'Alembert*.

INSIDE THE CAVE

In the *Letter to d'Alembert* Rousseau presents two, seemingly contrary portraits of theatergoers, one depicting their isolation and the other their promiscuous sociability. The first frames the second: his discussion of the theater begins and ends with an evocation of solitary spectators. "People think they come together in the theatre, and it is there that they are isolated; it is there that they go to forget their friends, neighbors, and relations in order to concern themselves with fables," he begins.[17] But he does not pursue this line, announcing in the next sentence: "But I should have sensed that this language is no longer seasonable in our times. Let us try to find another which is better understood" (16).

He returns to the image of social isolation again as he leaves the discussion of theater and begins his celebration of republican alternatives: "But let us not adopt these exclusive entertainments which sadly close up a small number of people in a gloomy cavern, which keep them fearful and immobile in silence and inaction, which offer their eyes only prisons, lances, soldiers, and afflicting images of servitude and inequality. No, happy peoples, these are not your festivals. It is in the open air, under the sky, that you ought to gather and give yourselves to the sweet sentiment of your happiness" (114). These sequestered and immovable spectators, confronted with shadows and fables that they take for truth, sound familiar. So does Rousseau's urging that they leave the "gloomy cavern" so that the sun might "illuminate [their] innocent entertainments." Like Plato's cave dwellers, Rousseau's theatergoers will resist the claim that what ails them is an imaginary design. Between these two textual evocations, between a picture of people alone together, moved to laughter and tears, and a picture of enfeebled prisoners kept desperate by a *spectacle* of political terror and clamoring for fresh air, is everything Rousseau has to say about the logic, the process, and the content of theatrical *pitié*.

---

[17] *Letter to d'Alembert*, 16. In this section, subsequent references to the *Letter* will be given in the main text.

The space of French comedy and drama, of actresses and play-wrights, of artistic ambition and praise, and of all the gilded hierar-chies of *le monde* at play, is the cave.

The cave is a place without reason (it "has no effect in the the-ater") because it is a place of *pitié*. This is, Rousseau insists, a "ster-ile pity" which "has never produced the slightest act of humanity" (17). Securing for spectators only "vain and empty" emotions, it isolates them because it holds them apart: the staging of pains whose status as feigned we always know arouses a passion that is "pure and without mixture of anxiety for ourselves" (23).[18] Pre-cisely its *un*reality limits the theater's ability to move us in a way that might matter because, as fundamentally unimplicated in the action, we are limited in imagining these suffering, heroic, or ridi-culed unfortunates as our *semblables*. But to imagine that the prob-lem is distance—the isolation of a spectator detached from what afflicts him—is to imagine not *pitié* but its (il)licit obverse, reason: "Reason is what turns man in upon himself [and what] separates him from what bothers and afflicts him."[19] Here it seems the prob-lem of vain emotions stems from the failure of *pitié*: we always retain that reasonable awareness that what's happening on the stage does not *actually* affect our interests. Perhaps it is not that the cave substitutes illusions for reality, but that it demonstrates how to negotiate a distinction between the two.

In chapter one I discussed how Rousseau's notions of self-inter-est and self-love are both situated within the same, sensuous and sentimental logic of pity. What is other and what is *semblable* de-pends on a single movement of identification and detachment through which we imagine, as we feel, the difference. The theater taps into this pitying process, and in such a way that its truths are on display. The capacity to identify profoundly without it *really* mattering, the artistry, talent, and wit through which such identi-fications are forged, and the systematization, if not commodifica-tion, of great deeds as conventional fare: all of these are revealed to the theatergoer. But none of those revelations impinge on the-ater's success: on the contrary, as long as it pleases (and "the prin-

---

[18] David Marshall suggests that Rousseau's critique of the theater is primarily concerned about the form of sympathy it promotes; see *The Surprising Effects of Sympathy*, chap. 4, "Rousseau and the State of Theater," esp. 143–44.

[19] *Discourse on Inequality*, 156.

ciple object is to please" [17]), then spectators will know, and happily forget, those performative truths. In this sense theater requires the spectator's collaboration, and the "halfway" participation in well-staged crimes that Rousseau dares any theatergoer among us to deny is evidence: we watch the clever scoundrel and we care, and "is being concerned about someone anything other than putting oneself in his place?" (43).

The willing suspension of disbelief becomes the willing suspension of will, or rather, a will implicated by some other's actions. This is an odd culpability, but it works on familiar ground: imaginative transgressions, in which representational excess serves as the vehicle for a moral *sensibilité*. Indeed, Rousseau insists that French playwrights' representations pose more dangers to an audience than monstrous deeds themselves: "The massacres of the gladiators were not as barbarous as these frightful plays. One saw blood flow, it is true, but one did not soil the imagination with crimes that make nature tremble" (31). And what imagined crimes surpass public bloodletting in their offense against nature? Those of Agamemnon, Oedipus, Phaedra, Medea, and the other (anti)heroes of ancient Greece, among whom blood lust and bloodletting were familial, if public, affairs. Rousseau is clear: "The general effect of the theater is to strengthen the national character, to augment the natural inclinations, and to give new energy to all the passions" (19). Incest, parricide, infanticide, infidelity, bodily sacrifice: in an ancient republican context these meant one thing, but "deprived of the same motives and concerns, how can the same tragedy find, in your country, spectators capable of enduring the *tableaux* it presents to them and the characters it brings to life?" (31).

Happily, Rousseau remarks, tragedy "such as it exists" is rather far from the tastes of contemporary theatergoers. Not so happily, comedy strikes home every time. While the "enormous beings" that tragedy puts on the stage are unlikely to appeal to Parisian *sensibilités*, the ridiculous and ridiculing characters of Molière's farces are warmly received. These plays not only appeal to the audience's penchant for witty wordplay and charming rascals; they also reassure the audiences of their sophistication, by inviting them to snicker at righteousness and smirk at love's besotting power. Comedies promote the detachment that I have referred to as a failure of *pitié*: ridicule works precisely in the gap between *being* and *seeming to be,* and thus its moral and social effects are particularly dire. If tragedy threatens a theatergoer's *sensibilité* by giving passions free rein on the stage, then Molière's comedy threatens "the whole social order" by making every passion laughable: "How scandalously he overturns all the most sacred relations on which it is founded; how ridiculous he makes the respectable rights of fathers over children, of husbands over their wives, of masters over their servants!" (32). (Rousseau says nothing here about the "sacred" foundations of the state, perhaps because the iniquities "wantonly gathered together" in Molière's comedies delighted the king: Louis XIV intervened on several occasions when their performance provoked censure by the Church, and his patronage kept Molière's struggling troupe in business.)[20]

A republic, by contrast, sustained by passionate attachments between citizens and their state, cannot tolerate the "halfway" criminal participations afforded by comedy: because they are criminal and because they are halfway. Nowhere is this halfway criminality more threatening than in matters of love, which have become "little pleasurable accessories" by means of which comedy entertains. The situation is similar in French tragedy, where playwrights, unable to draw on the "interests of State we no longer have," devote themselves solely to "romances" (43). Inspired by the criminal loves in Greek drama, but far removed from its republican milieu, playwrights give "new energy and new colouring to this dangerous passion." They thus release the "hot blood" (more potent than mere gladiators') that "makes men ungovernable [*indisciplinable*] before having borne the yoke of the laws" (100). In so doing, their sexual representations decouple eros and romance from the ends of the (republican) state. The monarchy, by contrast, is well served by this sexual (dis)order, where all manner of transgressive rule—children over fathers, women over men—amuses an infantile audience more concerned with bon mots than beaux gestes.

This audience made children is in a situation much like the adolescent Emile: "If a young man has seen the world only on the stage, the first way to approach virtue which presents itself to him is to look for a mistress who will lead him there, hoping of course

---

[20] See Howarth, *Molière: A Playwright and His Audience,* 20–22. For an analysis of Molière's comedic aesthetic that offers a nuanced account of his relationship to Louis XIV and his court, see Defaux, *Molière ou les métamorphoses du comique.*

to find a Constance or a Cénie, at the very least. It is thus, on the faith in an imaginary model, on a modest and moving manner, on a counterfeited sweetness, *nescius aurae fallacis*, that the young fool quickly loses himself, while thinking he is becoming wise" (44).[21] As Emile was introduced to Sophie, so the theatergoer imagines the mistress who will secure his virtue. But here the "young fool" lacks the careful guidance of a tutor and is subject instead to the whims and visions of a Molière or a Racine. Worse, he is subject to the seductions of the real thing, inasmuch as he watches women's bodies on the stage. Rousseau offers the contrast of the ancients, whose "in general, very great respect for women" dictated that their virtues be protected from public discussion and their bodies, from public view. And apparently it was not enough that men played all the roles: in Greek drama, Rousseau insists, "the only roles representing girls in love and marriageable girls were of slaves and prostitutes" (45). Such was the strength of republican *mœurs* that even the depiction of a decent woman on the stage constituted an offense to modesty; such was the power of republican imagination that the distance between the representation and the real thing was so tenuously maintained.

In the theater of Rousseau's day, by contrast, social practices continue the sexual (dis)order of ancien régime society, where "the most esteemed woman" is the most seen, the one who "most imperiously sets the tone," the one "whose favor is basely begged for by humble, learned men" (ibid.). Indeed, the staged romance "is even worse" in this regard: "In fact, in *le monde* they do not know anything, although they judge everything; but in the Theater [*la Scène*], learned in the learning of men and philosophers, thanks to the authors, they crush our own Sex with its own talents, and the imbecile Spectators go right ahead and learn from women what they took efforts to dictate to them" (ibid.). Perhaps women's educational deficits and (thus) intellectual limitations still count for something in the salon, but the stage takes away that real disadvantage. And in a milieu that arouses *pitié*, minus the tempering force of *amour propre*, these brilliant and comely displays will be all

[21] *Nescius aurae fallacis*: "(. . .) ignorant of the treacherous breeze" (Horace, *Odes*, I, v. 5). The Pléiade note suggests that Constance refers either to the virtuous maiden in Diderot's *Le Fils Naturel* or to the virtuous spouse in de la Chaussée's *Préjugé à la mode*; see *Oeuvres Complètes*, vol. 5, 1334 n. 10. Cénie is the heroine of a successful comedy by Mme de Graffigny.

the more persuasive, if not as real beings then as plausible variations on the idea of *woman*. Staged romances thus serve "to extend
the empire of the fair sex" because they depict strong heroines,
but also because they display women's passionate and bodily eloquence. Medea's denaturing crime might be mitigated when the
audience sees her rage and her pain. Phaedra's incestuous desire
might appear less criminal if the lust is well played. And the example of political obligation offered by Titus is undermined by the
strength of the heroine in Racine's *Bérénice*: whatever Titus has
chosen to do, at play's end "all the spectators have married
Bérénice" (21–22, 49).

Neither the most brutal displays of love's fury nor the most moving displays of duty's triumph over it can lessen its appeal because
"however love is depicted for us, it seduces or it is not love" (51).
In this theatricality is hardly distinguishable from romantic interaction. Rousseau makes the connection explicit when he asserts
that staged romances will give to women and girls "the same power
over the audience that they have over their lovers" (43). The connection is also evident in his critique of *Le Misanthrope*, whose comedic reversals depend upon a similar passion, the courtly equivalent of true love, namely, the desire to be found clever and
discerning. In subjecting the virtuous Alceste to constant mockery,
Rousseau writes, Molière reassures the audience that a bit of dis-
honesty is far preferable to playing the dupe, and thus he "seduces
by the appearance of reason" (42). Because the comedy must also
appeal to *amour propre* through "chimera, lie, and illusion," its audience also assumes the position of the lover who must be seduced.

But the threats posed by theatrical seductions do not fade when
the curtain falls, and if the fictions on the stage make women's
predicaments and powers felt, the "real" dramas unfolding in the
loges and foyer reveal the practical counterpart to such exposures.
Rousseau's contrast is again the ancient republic, where "there
was no common meeting place for the two sexes," and when occasionally women did attend the theater, "they did not put themselves on display" (81). Since then, it has been a steady decline,
from the invasions of "hoardes of barbarians, dragging their
women with them," to the age of chivalrous performance when
"beautiful Ladies spent their lives in getting themselves kidnapped
by men, with every honorable intention" (82). Once these gallant-

ries began to spread—"especially at the Courts and in the big cities where people take more pride in their refinement"—they were doomed to degenerate into "coarseness." In this way "the modesty natural to women [*au Sexe*] has little by little disappeared" (ibid.).

Yet another fall, from a republican original to a monarchical fraud. But this precipitous history (two paragraphs tell the tale) is preceded by an extended discussion of *pudeur* in which Rousseau stages a dialogic exchange with critics who fight him every step of the way. Central to the story of theater's cultural corruption and monarchy's political decay, the loss of *pudeur* is itself a tragedy in which Rousseau must make his readers believe. In so doing his argument alternates between weighing *pudeur*'s natural and cultural foundations: feminine modesty is the design of one, then the other; it is denied by one, but not the other; it is denied by both; it is confirmed by neither. The increasingly abrupt shifts in position and the increasingly argumentative tone are more disconcerting than persuasive. But the digression never wavers in the form it gives *pudeur*: feminine modesty and shame organize a dynamic of consensual nonconsensuality whose moral meanings take corporeal form. While he appears to be pursuing a question of origins, in practice Rousseau is reiterating a final form, one in which the political imperative of consent cannot be detached from the bodily postures of domination and submission. Whether *pudeur* is a natural or a cultural intention remains obscured by the end of this digression. But what has become clear is how *pudeur* secures "all the charms of love."[22]

"THAT CHARMING SENTIMENT OF SHAME . . ."

Rousseau's previous discussions of "the love interest" and the theater's general effects on manners and morals make passing reference to women's imperiled modesty. But he bears down on the issue only when he takes up the question of the character of actresses and whether their bad example is a "cause" of an abject theater culture. We are off the stage, then, and in the dressing

---

[22] Rousseau, *Lettres Morales*, in *Oeuvres Complètes*, vol. 4, no. 5, 1110: "If the faith of lovers is only a chimera, if the *pudeur* of the female sex consists only of vain prejudices, what would become of all the charms of love?"

rooms, on the boulevards, and in the salons, in order to ascertain actresses' influence, as real women on real men. As Patrick Coleman points out, Rousseau's analysis appears to lose a degree of coherence when he takes up the topic of *pudeur*.[23] The text becomes increasingly argumentative as Rousseau shifts back and forth between its natural and cultural origins. He begins with a question and an answer: "Do you want to know men? Study women." Anticipating that his audience will take this as a truism, he hypothesizes a different reaction if he were to add some unfashionable qualifications:

> But if I add that there are no good *mœurs* for women outside of a withdrawn and domestic life; if I say that the peaceful cares of the family and the household are their lot, that the dignity of their sex consists in modesty, that shame and *pudeur* are inseparable from decency for them, that when they seek men's gaze they are already letting themselves be corrupted by them, and that any woman who shows herself off dishonors herself, I will be immediately attacked by this philosophy of a day which is born and dies in the corner of a big city. (75–76)

Rousseau's narrative provides a polemical voice to this attacking philosophy and its assertion that chasteness is an effect of "social laws" invented to "protect the rights of fathers and husbands" (76). In this voice the essay poses a series of pointed questions: Why blush at nature's needs? Why look for shame in an act "so indifferent in itself"? Why should women be subject to expectations different from men's? Why not learn from the natural example of animals? Rousseau responds by retreating behind a veil of ignorance that hides the "Author's" intentions. Quoting Voltaire—that most notorious of "big city" philosophers—he intones, "your whys, says the God, would never end" (ibid.). Apparently these questions can be answered properly only on high.

But in the next paragraph Rousseau changes course and suggests that he sees reasons for chasteness that have "escaped" the

[23] Coleman, *Rousseau's Political Imagination*, 114. Coleman suggests that the (relative) lack of cogency in this digression is only apparent inasmuch as Rousseau's true aim is to "change the terms of the debate" by replacing the attention to origins (nature versus culture) with an attention to the very possibility of "man's possessing an enduring power of initiative" (115). My disagreements with Coleman are substantial and are presented in detail below.

"great scrutinizers of God's counsels." Foremost among these reasons is that "the shame that veils the pleasures of love from the eyes" anchors "the order of attack and defense." This order is a function not of a difference in desire, he explains, but of different "faculties for their satisfaction": a woman in pursuit of a man might choose one of those times when "victory" just cannot be achieved—perhaps he is "too weak to succumb"—or she might be uninterested at a time when "he needs to be vanquished." In short, because women can never guarantee their "victory," the species itself would be threatened if the roles of "assailant" and "assailed" were reversed (77).

Let us pause, briefly, at this curious and yet familiar move to grasp the significance of male erection, because for some readers it is viewed as evidence that Rousseau's natural scientific (mis)understandings are the primary reason for the form his sexual politics take. Isn't he motivated here by both the physiological asymmetry of human reproduction and a perception of females' naturally insatiable capacity for sex? On the one hand, these claims are suspect in themselves: the first entails a biological knowledge Rousseau may or may not have shared (the importance of male but not female orgasm to conception), and the second has minimal textual support, however resonant it might be in our post-Freudian times.[24] On the other hand, when taken on their own terms, nothing much hangs on either claim because their commitment to distinguish "what is physical in love" ignores Rousseau's representations of desire as an inescapably social and moral problem: while "imagination does not speak to savage hearts," it

---

[24] Laqueur reports that at least until the mid-1800s, it was a common belief that female orgasm was (also) crucial to procreative success; see *Making Sex*, 2–3, 146–48, 181–92. Kofman's interpretation typifies how Rousseau's statements about women's sexual power are read as statements about women's naturally boundless lust; see "Rousseau's Phallocratic Ends," 50–51. In this context Kofman contrasts Rousseau's feminization of libido with Freud's masculinized account, but she concludes that "despite this difference, both appeal to the same 'Nature' to justify the sexual subjugation of women, the essential point of the whole argument" (59n.10). Compare with *Emile*, 694, where women's sexual advantage is credited to "the facility with which [they] arouse men's senses." This is typical of the manner in which Rousseau scares up women's sexual initiative: he always leaves open whether it is men's or women's lustful proclivities that are the problem to be addressed.

is wreaking havoc in the *Letter to d'Alembert*.[25] My point is not that we should ignore what Rousseau's natural bodies convey; on the contrary, the story's central figuration of pleasure and how it is practiced entices us to stare at them. But when he points to bodily signs, it is unhelpful to see these gestures as interruptions of his rhetorical practice. Sometimes he figures the body's natural needs as the uncorrupted contraries of political society, sometimes as its corroboration; in either case, physicality is called to testify to a moral dilemma, here, "the order of attack and defense." So talk of inconstant erections does not take us outside the political realm, any more than Zulietta's malformed nipple did. In both cases, bodily properties confirm that realm's ordering, or disordered, principles: a way of life—a republican freedom or a monarchical subjugation—is imagined through these natural forms.

Consider that Rousseau's narrative quickly reconfigures the question of equal sexual "faculties" into a problem of what the imagination needs: if men and women both expressed themselves without reserve, he postulates, "the passions, ever languishing in a boring freedom, would never have been excited." Romance requires "vain importunity" because it needs mystery and a bit of suspense. And *pudeur* is better than unfettered passion at eliciting desire because its body language is more eloquent: "Its fears, its tricks, its reserves, its timid avowals, its tender and naive delicacy, say better what it believes it hides than passion could have said without it." Indeed, *pudeur* says more because, unlike pure passion, it says "no," and thus it lends more value to what is given, as well as "sweetness to rejection." Resistance and limitation are central to the successful articulation of desire, or at least to the "sweetest sentiments" of a well-fulfilled heart (77).

The voices of reason intervene: "Why, they ask, should what is not shameful for a man be so for a woman?" Perhaps granting that *some* order of "attack and defense" enlivens the game of love (they do not deny *pudeur*'s putative communicative superiority), still, why is it women whose open expressions of desire become criminal? Rousseau's response limns indignation: "As if the conse-

---

[25] See *Discourse on Inequality*, 157–58: "The imagination, which wreaks such havoc among us, does not speak at all to savage hearts; each awaits passively the impulsion of nature, gives himself to it without choice, with more pleasure than frenzy, and the need satisfied, all desire is extinguished."

quences were the same on both sides! As if all the austere duties of women were not derived from the single fact that a child ought to have one [*un*] Father!" (77–78). He stakes the claim for paternity in the hypothesized ("as if") impossibility of justifying *pudeur* on any other ground. The indirection is understandable: he is veering toward just that reason given by his ventriloquized critics at the onset (the social and juridical invention of *pudeur* in order to "protect the rights of fathers and husbands"). But in the next line he retreats back into the mystery of nature: "Even if these important considerations were lacking to us, we would nevertheless still make the same response, and it would still be without reply. Nature wanted it so, and it would be a crime to stifle its voice" (78).

This return to the ground of nature's intention is interrupted by a lengthy footnote that explains in detail the difference between a man's audacity and a satyr's. If one attacks "with violence the charms of a young object [*objet*] who feels nothing for him," Rousseau explains, it is always "scandalous outrage": "it bespeaks a soul without manners [*mœurs*], without refinement, incapable of either love or decency." For the true lover, by contrast, possession without reciprocated desire produces only anger and despair; the real man's audacity thus includes knowing how "to enslave the sentiments before attacking the person." Even then, a shared love is not enough: "consent of the will is also needed" (ibid.). And how does one identify the consenting will of a woman with *pudeur*? One must decipher the bodily signs: "To read it in the eyes, to see it in the ways in spite of the mouth's denial, that is the art of he who knows how to love. If he then completes his happiness, he is not brutal, he is decent [*honnête*]" (ibid.). *Pudeur* requires decent violence and a refined attack: "To win this silent consent [*consentement tacite*] is to make use of all the violence permitted in love" (ibid.).

We have seen all this before (not just the "general idea" but this particular variation: Emile, too, was told to learn to read when Sophie's "heart and her eyes accord what her mouth feigns to refuse").[26] But Rousseau elaborates the (il)logic of women's consent only here, in his critique of theatrical lifestyles and the actresses' "bad example": the verbal articulation of desire and of its absence are equally suspect because *pudeur* always requires the appearance of shame; a man must thus stage an attack in order to

[26] *Emile*, 863.

give voice to her "silent consent," and a woman announces her will through what her body says in the course of the struggle.

Is it not for this reason, Rousseau asks, coming out of the footnote to consider the evidence of *women*'s bodily form, that nature "renders them apprehensive so that they flee, and feeble so that they succumb?" Why do they have a smaller stature, a less muscular form, if they were not destined "to let themselves be vanquished?" (ibid.). Indeed, even a woman's fairer complexion—where a "modest blush can be better perceived"—bears witness to her body's communicative competence. Feebleness announces an intention to submit, fear expresses the desire to be chased, and a delicate skin writes the coincidence of desire and shame all over her face. "Let us move from reasoning to experience," Rousseau concludes, leaving the evidence of women's bodies to survey, in rapid order, the evidence of "big cities," simple mountain folk, and the animal kingdom (female pigeons, for example, which provide a model of "provocations and feeble resistance of an artistry scarcely attainable by the most skillful coquette" [79–80]).

After pausing on the final image of Virgil finding inspiration in a pigeon house, the digression comes to an abrupt close with the announcement that *pudeur*'s origins are not relevant: "If the timidity, *pudeur*, and modesty which are proper to them are social conventions, it matters to society that women acquire these qualities: it matters that they be cultivated in women." He thus ends where his critics began, with a rejection of nature's applicability: "The argument drawn from the example of beasts proves nothing and is not true. Man is hardly a dog or a wolf. It is only necessary in his species to establish the first relations of society to give to his sentiments a morality forever unknown to beasts. Animals have a heart and passions, but the holy image of the decent [*honnête*] and the fair enters only the heart of man" (79). And thus Rousseau closes with his own "holy image" to counter the actresses "odious imitation" of men: "Is there a sight [*spectacle*] in the world so touching," he asks, "so respectable, as that of a mother surrounded by her children, directing the work of her domestics, procuring a happy life for her husband and wisely governing her home? . . . A home whose mistress is absent is a body without a soul which soon falls into corruption; a woman outside her home loses her greatest luster and, despoiled of her true ornaments, she displays herself indecently" (80).

185

Spectacularity is as central to chaste displays as it is to the actresses' wanton crimes: (hetero)sexual desire is aroused by feigned refusals, and naturalizing those refusals is crucial to sustaining the desire. Pity the "sad reasoners," writes Rousseau, "who, in effacing all natural sentiments within themselves, destroy the source of all their pleasures": precisely because it "inflames a lover's desire," that "charming sentiment of shame" *must* be part of nature's design.[27] Thus the pursuit of (hetero)sexual pleasure requires natural actors. This is true of the scenes of domesticity, whose description here is faithful to the portraits St. Preux draws of Julie's rule at Clarens; it is also true of the intimate *spectacle* through which women speak their desire and their will on the surfaces of their bodies. Blushes, glances, palpitations, sighs, gestures, moans: this is the communicative register of a chaste woman, as well as the professional actress. And while both cultivate the art of arousing men's passions by denying their own, there is a difference: while the actress's performative success is inversely related to her audience's languor—the better her display, the weaker their desire to move—the chaste woman's performance elicits action. More, the actress's success on stage promotes her "masculine and firm assurance" (81) when off it, thus doubling her disruptive effects and further immobilizing men. But the woman and the role are always the same for the chaste maiden, and she always makes her lover into an actor.

MASTERS OF PHILOSOPHY

The claim that *pudeur* compels men to act is made by Patrick Coleman, who also insists on the continuity between sexual and political performance and refuses the interpretive closure facilitated by appeals to Rousseau's natural science. He reads Rousseau's complex treatment of the *spectacle* as an effort to forge a new notion of practice, one that avoids the untenable extremes of identification (we are all *semblables*) and critique (every political association is precarious and impermanent).[28] He argues that by inducing

---

[27] *Lettres Morales*, no. 5, 1110. Rousseau's subject is materialist doctrine and the relation between reason and (bodily) sensation; *pudeur* serves as the illustration to which the discussion repeatedly returns.

[28] Coleman, *Rousseau's Political Imagination*, 36–37.

the "thoughtful suspension of thought," the *spectacle* can spur the imaginative and initiative action necessary to a "regenerated political will."[29] The sexual *spectacle* is crucial in this regard, precisely because it concerns man's "enduring power of initiative." Coleman suggests that Rousseau's preoccupation with *pudeur* is at base an effort to "preserve one area of human life in which 'persons who perform' participate in something more significant than the instrumental action of social existence; for Rousseau, it might be said that reproduction offers the only option for genuine, inaugural action, and therefore what [he] means by a public life."[30]

Coleman is well aware that *pudeur* invites trickery and contrivance, and further, that all social-sexual mores require institutional enforcement. Thus he acknowledges up front that the genuineness of sexual initiative is preserved through artifice and that it is limited to men. And yet, when Coleman explains that Rousseau uses *pudeur* to "diffuse the violence of initiative action," he forgets that a critical element of *pudeur* is its inculcation of vulnerability.[31] This nurtured vulnerability is a consistent theme in *Emile*'s educational design for girls, which emphasizes passivity ("the result of [girls'] habitual constraint is a docility which women need all of their lives") and insufficiency ("it is not a question of making her dependence painful [*penible*] for her; it suffices to make her feel it").[32] So, too, the actress's "odious imitation" is an "effrontery" precisely because she is imitating "masculine and firm assurance." In short, *pudeur* does not diffuse violence: it organizes violence along sexual lines, making it central to the enactment of true love. And while this organization might appear to diffuse *women's* potential for violent initiative, that conclusion glosses too quickly the power of the imperious mistress, whose exquisite tyranny is no less central to Rousseau's sexual repertoire than the vulnerability of the virtuous wife.

Clearly, lying prostrate before a severe schoolmistress is not the sort of sexual interaction Coleman has in mind when he directs us to the "genuine, inaugural action" that men's erotic desire both initiates and represents in Rousseau's texts. But these postures

---

[29] Ibid., 15, 36.
[30] Ibid., 115.
[31] Ibid., 117.
[32] *Emile*, 370; I have altered Bloom's translation slightly.

figure prominently in a romance where the difference between savaging and ravishing depends on the right reading of bodily signs, and the "sweetness" of the exchange depends on confounding the (already semantically tenuous) difference. Making sense of this interpretive violence and role reversal requires suspending our own commitments to the authenticity of that "one area of life," in order to consider how, in Coleman's language, the untenable extremes of identification and critique, and the political paralysis they might engender, apply to sexuality as well as citizenship. To secure an authentic practice of citizenship, in other words, is to establish a republican masculinity, and neither that most natural of men, Emile, nor the isolated user of *suppléments*, will escape being typecast. Here Coleman's interpretive commitment to authenticity occludes the necessary fictions that sustain sexual identity, and thus it conceals crucial aspects of the political practice Rousseau envisions for his citizens—"who are, of course, male," as Coleman reminds us.[33]

But sexual identity's status as necessary fiction can never be disclosed. In this sense gender might be that "area of darkness, even of active forgetting, in the symbolic basis of culture" that Coleman suggests is inescapable for Rousseau's citizens.[34] There is textual support for this conclusion in Rousseau's most complete analysis of symbolic systems, the *Essay on the Origin of Languages*, which retraces a first language to the first expressions of erotic desire. Here the emergence of symbolic practice is coincident with the emergence of sexual identity, both of which inaugurate and incorporate the familiar (d)evolutionary process of socialization and political deterioration. In the beginning was a prelinguistic "golden age" in which men and women existed as such only in rudimentary form: "Natural inclinations sufficed to unite them, instinct served in lieu of passion, habit in lieu of predilection, [and] people became husband and wife without having ceased to be brother and sister."[35] Rousseau explains that this situation was unproblematic given the "simplicity of the first morals," a simplicity that precluded the idea of *man*: "Having never seen anything other than

---

[33] Coleman, *Rousseau's Political Imagination*, 116.

[34] Ibid., 36.

[35] *Essay on Languages*, 406. Subsequent references to the *Essay* will be given in the main text.

what was around them, they did not even know that; they did not know themselves. They had the idea of a Father, a son, a brother, but not of a man. Their hut held all their *semblables*; a stranger, an animal, a monster were all the same to them" (396). The transition to fully differentiated sex roles, to the identification of *man* and *woman* and the concomitant institution of incest taboos, occurs with the acquisition of language: the first social intercourse between families, the "first meetings between the sexes," and the first utterances were all coincident (405). There was joy in this development ("the heart ... [f]elt the pleasure of not being alone"), but it also marks the appearance of "new needs" that "force everyone to think of himself and to withdraw his heart within himself" (407). The trajectory is familiar: an expansion of *pitié* and *amour propre*, a proliferation of dependencies and fears, a loss of innocence, pleasure, and freedom. The conclusion seems to be that sexual identity is representative of the losses that make language necessary, and one is only a man or a woman by virtue of one's powerlessness and partiality. This, then, is the darkness at the heart of the symbolic order that must be forgotten if authenticity—of community, self, and authority—can be believed.

This conclusion is reached by Jacques Derrida in his masterful study of the *Essay on Languages*, which traces Rousseau's contribution to a post-Enlightenment "metaphysics of presence." In chapter one I mentioned briefly that Derrida reads Rousseau as exemplary of the Cartesian "dream of a full and immediate presence," a dream that must suppress the very condition of language and consciousness: "contradiction and difference."[36] Of particular interest for our present purposes is Derrida's attention to the terms of this suppression: there is violence, he insists, in the construction of the categories on which autonomy depends, and that violence originates at the level of the symbolic. On this reading, Rousseau responds to the scandalous and unthinkable conclusion that "immediacy is derived" by introducing a series of *suppléments*, those additions and substitutions that make possible the fiction of an unsupplemented—full, self-identical—original.[37] In this series gender is the essential (so to say) *supplément*, and it obtains at the level of the symbolic: masculinity codes the (false) assertion of

[36] Derrida, *Of Grammatology*, 115, 162.
[37] Ibid., 144–57.

189

identity between representation and the thing represented, while the incapacity to assert such identity—a failure ever to constitute that "full presence," to be that *auto* who gives *nomos*—corresponds to the feminine.[38] In this way gender appears to supplement, but in fact constitutes, an autonomy whose status as fiction must be suppressed.

The notion of arche-violence, Derrida's term for the originary suppression of difference that naming requires, offers insight into Rousseau's preoccupation with sexual representations. Women's appearance is more significant than whatever they might "really" be, while men's virtue consists in a unity of the two; the citizen must represent himself, while his wife can (and must) entrust her representation to him: these well-known pronouncements might be thought of as a continuation of gender's linguistic function on the social-aesthetic and political levels. But this approach is of limited help in understanding the material basis and political ends of Rousseau's representative strategy. Consider that the Derridean account locates politics at a "tertiary level" of violence: derived from a first (symbolic) and then second (moral) level of prohibition, political violence "can *possibly* emerge or not (an empirical possibility) within what is commonly called evil, war, indiscretion, rape."[39] Derrida notes the irony of his originary design but not its reiteration of where the truth (or, perhaps, the first lie) resides: in the metaphysics of mind, whose "two inferior levels of arche-violence" are always reflected in political law. But what he figures as anticipated and forever denied by the order of the symbolic is for Rousseau the subject of a political struggle that promises less a dreamy presence than a calculated submission. And its site is the (sexed) body, whose seduction, violation, enslavement, and freedom are neither prior to nor derivative of symbolic practice, but constitutive of it.[40]

Feminist scholars have long recognized how Derrida's (anti)-metaphysical orientation risks treating philosophy, and not bod-

---

[38] Ibid., 175ff. For a critical discussion of Derrida's notion of "the violence of the letter" as it pertains to gender, see de Lauretis, "The Violence of Rhetoric."

[39] Derrida, *Of Grammatology,* 112; italics in original.

[40] For a more sympathetic but not uncritical engagment with Derrida's reading, see Zerilli, *Signifying Women,* chapter two: " '*Une Maitresse Imperieuse:*' Women in Rousseau's Semiotic Republic."

ies, as the critical site of gender's construction.[41] And while Rousseau's insistence that "one is not obliged to make a man a philosopher before making him a man"[42] is hardly a warrant to reject the significance of Enlightenment puzzles to his sexual politics, it does underscore the terms on which Rousseau will work those puzzles: the bodily experiences of creatures who are *sensible* before they think, and whose struggles are always political. But these matters become secondary (if not tertiary) in an analysis that harnesses his sexual politics to a philosophical dilemma. Derrida's concluding observation in *Of Grammatology* is instructive on this score: "Rousseau's *dream* consisted in making the supplement enter metaphysics by force."[43] But when he has "clothed reason in a body" and inscribed the violence of the letter on its surfaces, is it really helpful, or even plausible, to continue to think in terms of metaphysical dreams?

SPEAKING TO THE EYES

The *Essay on Languages* tells a story of philosophical anthropology in which the question of how meaning gets made is inseparable from the question of how humans live together. The *Essay*'s opening paragraph flags the familiar problem of origins ("since speech is the first social institution, it owes its form to natural causes alone") and ties it to the political problem of ends—"language distinguishes between nations; one doesn't know where a man is from until after he has spoken" (375). Then Rousseau poses the question which the *Essay* will attempt to answer: "But what makes this [particular] language be the language of this country and not of another?" Rousseau's story of symbolic practice responds, from the beginning, to a question of political difference. Its nostalgia for a lost immediacy, its exacting discriminations between the spoken and written word, its dream of a wholly gestural society: these compensatory moments in the *Essay* cannot be separated from its narrative of national identity, and the "fall" into language, like the

---

[41] See discussion in de lauretis, "The Violence of Rhetoric," 45ff.

[42] *Discourse on Inequality*, 126.

[43] Derrida, *Of Grammatology*, 315; italics in original.

Discourse on Inequality's "fall" into difference, is always an image of political possibilities and fears.

Such images figure prominently in the remainder of the *Essay*'s first chapter, which is devoted to explaining the power of a nonverbal language of gestures and things: "The most vigorous speech," Rousseau writes, "is that in which the sign has said everything before one has spoken" (376). He illustrates the power of "arguments addressed to the eyes" with reference to characters from ancient history. "They did not say it, they showed it": the tyrant Lucius Tarquin communicating strategy to his son Sextus by decapitating poppies, Alexander sealing Hephaestion's lips by pressing them with his ring, and the Levite of Ephraim rallying the tribes of Israel by sending each a piece of his mistress's dismembered body (376–77). Rousseau ends with an example of "mute eloquence that has at all times had its effect": the orator Hyperides' wordless defense of the courtesan Phrynê, which consisted of exposing her breasts and dissolving into moans at the sight. The effect is always more certain when one speaks directly to the eyes.

The same claim appears in *Emile,* in a discussion of how the student's instruction might be "engrave[d] in his memory in such a way that it will never be effaced."[44] The question prompts a digression on the power of "the language of signs that speak to the imagination," and the imaginative deficit of the modern age, when "men no longer have a hold on one another except by force or by self-interest." Rousseau's point of comparison is the ancient art of persuasion: "One did not say it, one showed it."[45] He offers the same illustrations found in the *Essay on Languages* (minus the Levite's dismembered mistress and Phrynê's bared breasts) before launching into an appreciation of the Romans and their extensive political regalia: "Everything with them was display, show, ceremony, and everything made an impression in the hearts of citizens." He ends his appreciation of ancient persuasion by invoking the murderous scene in the senate: "On the death of Caesar I imagine one of our orators wanting to move the people, exhausting all the commonplaces of his art to present a pathetic description of Caesar's wounds, his blood, his corpse. Antony, al-

[44] *Emile,* 321.
[45] Ibid., 322.

though eloquent, does not say all that. He has the body brought in: What rhetoric!"[46]

But this digression, he hastily adds, "gradually carries me far from my subject"; so in the next sentence he turns back to it, and the body he evokes is Sophie's: "Never reason in a dry manner with youth. Clothe reason in a body if you want to make youth able to grasp it [*lui rendre sensible*]; make the language of the mind pass through the heart so that it may make itself understood." The juxtaposition of Caesar's bloody wounds and Sophie's comely form underscores not only how both belong to the language of persuasive things but also how both require figuration in order to take any shape at all. In other words, both bodies are an image of an image, and the student is no more likely to see some "real" woman's body than he is to see Caesar's. Imagination is the key to all persuasion, and the power of the body's mute eloquence is always a function of what we imagine we are seeing there.

The imagined meaning of bodily things is central to the argument of the *Essay*, which insists that tropes were the first linguistic forms: "Figurative language was the first to arise, literal meaning [*le sens propre*] was found last" (381). The example Rousseau offers is "a savage man" who, in his fear and ignorance, first sees and thus understands all other men as *giants*. Repeated exposure and subsequent comparison provide him with opportunities to see them differently; he thus recognizes *giant* to be a false object. In this way the first transposition of meaning is actually the bifurcation of a first meaning into truth and illusion, and the first sense we make of the world is metaphoric: "That is how the figurative word arises before the literal word does, when passion holds our eyes spellbound and the first idea which it presents to us is not that of truth. . . . Subsequently it became metaphorical, when the enlightened mind recognized its original error, and used expressions [of that first language] only when moved by the same passions as had produced it" (381–82).

The truth of objects that "speak to the eyes" depends, then, on the state of one's passions, a condition generated by the dynamics of *pitié* and *amour propre*. When we imagine ourselves fearful, vulnerable, and small, the world is peopled by giants; when we imag-

[46] Ibid., 322–23.

ine ourselves safe, sound, and human, the world is composed of—larger and smaller, gentler or more fierce—men. Thus the force of visible things is always the force of metaphor, and Horace was correct ("there is no one who doesn't feel the truth of his judgment on this score") that the most eloquent discourses are those most filled with images (377). In speaking to the eyes, they arouse the passions that (re)produce our first, figural truths.

And what are those first, figural truths? In what consists that first language of images that can "persuade without convincing and depict without demonstrating [*rasioner*]"? (383). The answer is provided in a topographical sketch that begins in the "happy climes" of the south and moves to the inhospitable north. In a fertile, generous land, words emerged with "the first ties between families" and "the first meetings between the sexes": "Young girls came to fetch water for the household, young men came to water their herds. Here eyes accustomed to the same objects [*objets*] since childhood began to see sweeter ones. The heart was moved by these new objects, an unfamiliar attraction made it less savage, it felt the pleasure of not being alone" (405–6).

Rousseau gives voice to the obvious objection: "What! Before this time were men born from the earth? Generations succeeded one another without the sexes uniting and without any shared understanding [*sans que persone s'entendit*]?" His answer refers us to those rudimentary families, huddled in their huts and unable to differentiate ("a stranger, an animal, a monster were all the same to them") or identify ("they did not know themselves"): "No, there were families, but there were no Nations; there were domestic languages, but there were no popular languages; there were marriages, but there was no love [*amour*]" (406). Nation, utterance, love: these are the conditions under which sex has meaning. And in warm lands, those conditions are inseparable from ardent passion: "In mild climates, in fertile regions, it took all the liveliness of the agreeable passions to start men speaking." The first language is thus the language of erotic desire, and its first figurations are *woman* and *man*.

Meanwhile, up north, "in those dreadful climates where everything is dead nine months of the year," words emerge in the course of grim and perpetual efforts to survive. A "miserly nature" reverses the south's originary order and instead of passion, language is born of need: "Its first words were not *love me* [*aimez-moi*] but *help me* [*aidez-moi*]" (408; italics in original). National languages continue to reflect the effects of these "physical causes": "French, English, and German are the private language of men who help one another, who deliberate among themselves with cool dispassion [*de sang-froid*], or of excited men who get angry; but the ministers of God proclaiming the sacred mysteries, wise men giving laws to their people, leaders swaying the masses must speak Arabic or Persian" (409). Northern languages figure self-interest and are ideal for negotiation and dispute, while southern languages, by figuring passion, compel political, fanatical loyalty. "Even our fanatics are not true fanatics," Rousseau laments, "they are only knaves or fools." The true fanatic is seductive, and seduced: a man who reads a little Arabic might "smile as he peruses the Koran," but to hear these words delivered by "Mohammed himself" would cause that same man to "prostrat[e] himself and cr[y]: Great Prophet, Messenger of God, Lead us to glory, to martyrdom; we want to conquer or to die for you" (409–10). We have seen this fanatical devotion before, compelled by the skillful mistress who can "send her lovers with a nod to the end of the earth, to combat, to glory, to death, to anything she pleases."[47] But she is not speaking Arabic: her body language alone (re)invokes the same penetrating desire.

Women represent their desire in the language of politics, and political representations speak the language of love. How could it be otherwise in a narrative that identifies (hetero)sexual passion as the first figuration of national languages? To be sure, the *Essay*'s originary scheme intimates that these different threads can be untangled and that, by imagining a prelinguistic world, we can discern an orderly appearance of meanings: perhaps national linguistic identity incorporates a people's natural passions, perhaps women are by nature equatorial. But Rousseau's figurations of gender, language, and nation are simultaneous: the idea of *man* and *woman* and the idea of community are coincident productions of a representative practice whose first task is to give form to our illusions. The image of passionate giants produced by those first, spellbound moments reappears in the political *spectacles* of civic and religious devotions, while wise laws, sacred mysteries, and natural men share an originary desire. In this recursive loop, reminis-

---

[47] Ibid., 393.

cent of the *Discourse on Inequality*, we see the two figural strands bound ever more tightly together: the one that ties language to nation, and to servile or free peoples, the other that ties desire to sexual identity and to natural or perverse social-sexual *mœurs*. In their earliest acts of self-representation—*love me, help me*—men and women are figuring the distinctly political possibilities of their desire.

The passionate topography that maps eros and mastery onto national landscapes also maps sexually differentiated bodies: those "new objects" at the watering hole become visible signs in response to the expressive needs of a linguistic and political order. Foremost among those needs is an "order of attack and defense," a relationship of power and pleasure that characterizes nation, language, and gender. When imagined on a bodily topos, that relationship's republican and despotic possibilities coincide with the meaning of masculine and feminine forms.[48] Greedy kings and diffident subjects thus belong to an economy of pleasure and power whose illiberality is represented on the body of the unchaste women. And the sign of the passionate citizen, the wise law, the sacred mystery, is the mutely eloquent woman who speaks of surrender and rule, need and power, desire and shame, without ever opening her mouth; and in so doing she compels her lover to act. When women and men daily reenact their heterosexual roles, they daily reconstitute an originary and public theatricality that institutes nation, utterance, and love.

To be sure, the multiple meanings of such displays are inescapably metaphoric. The sexual performance of difference, power, and desire transposes meanings we "know" to be (in *le sens propre*) political onto what we "know" to be natural forms, and it is no more likely that we will mistake our lover for our ruler than that we will mistake our *patrie* for our pleasure. Unless, of course, "passion holds our eyes spellbound" and we revert to that first, figural language whose illusions constitute our first representations. These moments of terror and delight are provoked by the language of

---

[48] This assumes that there is nothing wrong with the sign: while Zulietta's malformity signaled well enough her debased condition, Mme d'Epinay's flat chest posed insurmountable problems. "Neither my heart nor my senses have ever been able to see a woman in someone without breasts," Rousseau remarks apropos his tendency to "forget" Mme d'Epinay's sex when he was "near her" (*Confessions*, 412).

persuasive things, the imagined materialities that, by speaking to the eyes, engender political loyalty. Togas, fasces, "crowns of gold or of herbs or of leaves"[49]: to this panoply of republican things Rousseau adds the bodies of men and women. Impressed upon Emile's mind with his earliest sense of self, these images of desire and difference will always return him to his dominant passion, to a world peopled by neither giants nor kings but by citizens. For this reason those images always reappear in Rousseau's republican *spectacles.* Of course, the figural aspects of these representations become apparent as soon as the initiating passion dissipates. But in Rousseau's scenario that moment never comes: perpetually sexualized interaction guarantees that citizens are always acting like men and women, and perpetually politicized sex guarantees that men and women are always (re)enacting a patriotic love.

GETTING A TASTE FOR ONE ANOTHER

The significance for Rousseau of the fete, as both a spectacular and a public event, has been noted by many interpreters.[50] In general, the tendency is to evaluate how it organizes an alternative theatricality, a mode of being and seeing together that unifies and strengthens and, in Starobinski's phrase, "expresses, in the existential realm, what the *Social Contract* formulates in the theoretical realm of law."[51] Even when its regulative functions are acknowledged—community celebration as an opportunity for group surveillance and (thus) for social control—the open-air *spectacle* is figured as a communal self-display in which authenticity pertains to the state of mind it provokes: the "subjective enthusiasm with which an entire people *participates* in the spectacle," as Starobinski puts it, signifies their unity as authors of a social order whose differences in rank and power remain intact.[52] Whether couched in terms of transparency or of a "naturally expressive self," the festival is taken to be an ideal of innocent communication and originary

---

[49] *Emile*, 647.

[50] The festival is discussed at length in Coleman, *Rousseau's Political Imagination;* Starobinski, *Transparency and Obstruction* and Derrida, *Of Grammatology.*

[51] Starobinski, *Transparency and Obstruction*, 96.

[52] Ibid., 100; italics in original.

freedoms whose significance, positive or negative, derives from its location outside politics, before or beyond the rule of law.[53]

But this framing ignores the representative function of republican *spectacles*: to give public form to sexual difference. As both an identity and an imperative to act, this difference inaugurates the very possibilities of "subjective enthusiasm" and "natural" self-expression on which authentic communication would depend. In other words, the emancipatory, illusory, and/or disciplinary dimensions of republican *spectacles* are all similarly dependent on a sexual performativity whose logic does not reduce to any of them. Thus the question of whether the festival suspends social and political differences, whether it provides periodic consolation for their inevitability, or whether it returns us, through fantastical and carnivalesque abandon, to a prepolitical dream obscures the inextricably political dimension of republican representational practices. From this perspective the festival does not interrupt, to challenge or confirm, political principles; it offers an illustration of how those principles obtain in the practice of one's pleasures.

The pleasurable practices of Genevans occupy the final section of the *Letter to d'Alembert*. A republic ought to have "many" *spectacles*, Rousseau begins, "it is in Republics that they were born," and it is among republicans that they serve salutary ends: "To what peoples is it more fitting to assemble often and form among themselves the sweet ties of pleasure and joy, than to those who have so many reasons to love one another and to stay forever united?"[54] He then offers the portrait introduced earlier, of immobile spectators subjected to images of political terror, only to exhort his readers-cum-Genevans to reject those shadowy designs: "No, happy Peoples, these are not your festivals [*fêtes*]!" The open sky and the fresh air are for "pleasures neither effeminate nor mercenary," as "free and generous" as the participants themselves. "But what will be the objects of these [Genevan] *spectacles*?" Rousseau asks, "What will

---

[53] Charles Ellison introduces the model of the "naturally expressive self visible to all in an intimate community" as a "central principle of [Rousseau's] politics"; see, "Rousseau and the Modern City," 518ff. Linda Zerilli reads the festival as a site for the first exchange of words and women, and thus the always imagined moment of a desired *dis*order existing prior to the institution of the law; see *Signifying Woman*, 24–26.

[54] *Letter to d'Alembert*, 114. In this section, subsequent references to *Letter* will be given in the main text.

be shown in them? Nothing, if you please" (115). Nothing, that is, except the citizens themselves, and the sweet ties of pleasure that make them a people.

The promised spontaneity with which the discussion of republicans at play begins—"Plant a stake crowned with flowers in the middle of a square, gather the people together there, and you will have a festival"—is quickly deferred in favor of studied orchestration. The most extensive discussions concern the Genevan *cercles*, public gatherings where women and men met separately to socialize. In both form and function, *cercles* preserve critical features of the theater: they provide amusement and distraction, they bring private individuals together in public spaces, and they reinforce gender roles. So, too, they share some of the theater's disadvantages: the women's *cercles* produce "scandalmongers and satirists," while the drinking that takes place at the men's *cercles* threatens to deprive them of "the noblest of faculties" (97, 99). On the first score, Rousseau emphasizes that women's skill at ridicule can have beneficial effects in a sex-segregated milieu: "For which is better, that a woman speak ill of her husband with her friends, or that she do it with a man in private conversation, that she criticize the disorder of her neighbor, or that she imitate it?" (97). The disciplinary function of these gatherings is made clear when Rousseau compares their "severe observers" to Roman censors. (And not those "infamous informers" who denounced good men in Rome's twilight years, but the citizens of its "great days," who "publicly accused one another out of zeal for justice" [ibid.]). In short, gossip and accusatory and ridiculing talk help to sustain republican political order by policing its sexual borders, and this chorus of "cackling" women shows the political expedience of a very public femininity (ibid.).

On the subject of men's intemperance, Rousseau is less literary and less clear. He concedes that alcohol "alienates [men's] reason for a time, and in the long run, brutalizes it" (99). But the taste for wine, he adds, "is no crime and rarely causes one to be committed." Besides, he adds, most drinkers are "good" men (as well as "upright, faithful, brave, and decent"). And there are national differences to consider, a significant factor when the issue is "an indiscreet state in which the heart is revealed." Drink reveals what is already written there: among people of bad mores (Neapolitans are mentioned in passing) this might be a problem, but with the

Swiss, why fear republican virtue made sloppy and sentimental? (99–100). Finally, however, what seems to matter most, and where Rousseau leaves the discussion, is how intemperance compares with social-sexual promiscuity: "Never has a people perished from an excess of drinking; all perish from the disorder of women" (100). If, then, the men's gatherings risk periodically alienating men's reason, this is still much preferable to the sexual disorder that would follow from the *cercles'* demise.

The *cercles'* advantages extend to men's bodies and their minds. Rousseau's point of contrast is again the salon. While men tend to pace and twitch in those "voluntary prisons" (testimony, he suggests, to their "real need" to get out), in the country *cercles* they will find games, gardens, "a big lake for swimming, [and] the whole countryside open for hunting" (96). The physical invigoration parallels a discursive change: instead of the refined speech through which "the two sexes mutually seduce one another and familiarize themselves, in all decency, with vice," the men's gatherings promote a "less polished" and "rustic," even "vulgar," style, one fit for giving form to weighty words like *virtue* and *patrie* (93, 96).

Recall that the same stylistic characterization was made of *Julie's* early love letters, which also refused the "fancy jargon of the passions" to express heartfelt truths.[55] The *Letter to d'Alembert* repeats and complicates these communicative designs by insisting on the frivolity and superficiality of women's discursive style, and of men's when they write for women. Rousseau's discussion of this problem includes a footnote on women's intellectual and artistic abilities that is, even for him, exceedingly sharp and dismissive:

> Women, in general, do not like any art, know nothing about any, and have no genius. They can succeed in little works which require only quick wit, taste, grace, and sometimes even a bit of philosophy and reasoning. They can acquire science, erudition, talents, and everything which is acquired by dint of work. But that celestial flame that warms and sets fire to the soul, that genius which consumes and devours, that burning eloquence, those sublime transports that carry their raptures to the depths of hearts, will always be lacking in the writings of women;

[55] Second preface, 15.

their works are all as cold and pretty as they are. . . . They do not know how to describe nor to feel even love; only Sappho, as far as I know, and one other woman, deserve to be excepted. (94–95)

He appears to be denying women's capacity for exactly that which his sexual politics demand from them, namely, the passionate excesses of (maternal and connubial) love. It is tempting to read in this denial an intimation of the extent to which women must be made to perform: if incapable of feeling love, perhaps their passion is only ever artifice. But the passage takes on a different tone when read against the argument Rousseau has just made. Imagine, he has suggested, what will be the "temper of a man's soul" when he is "uniquely occupied with the important business of amusing women and spends his entire life doing for them what they ought to do for us" (ibid.). This raises the possibility that a life spent amusing and pleasing others is itself the cause of women's frivolous thinking and stunted emotions. Rousseau derails this potentially problematic train of thought by denying literary excellence to any but Sappho and one unnamed woman.[56]

So, too, his denigration of women's writing parallels his admiration of their other communicative skills: the "celestial flame," "burning eloquence," and "sublime transports" lacking in their words are forever present on their person. Always more "sensible [sensés] than passionate [passionnés]" (94), women's writings lose the figural power of their bodies. This, finally, is the power that must remain harnessed to republican ends, and this harnessing is a key function of every republican *spectacle*. Thus the loss of the *cercles* is imagined as a steady slide into undisciplined self-display. "The two sexes meeting daily in the same place; the groups which will form there for going [to the theater]; the ways of life that they will see depicted, and which they will be eager to imitate; the exposition of the ladies and the maidens all dressed up in their finest and put on display in the loges, like they were in a shop window, waiting for buyers; the affluence of the handsome young who will come to show themselves off": it is highly unlikely that anyone could adopt these practices and "preserve for long the taste of our government," Rousseau suggests (101–2). But citizens are not hermits and "only the most fierce despotism is alarmed at

[56] Rousset suggests that this unnamed "other woman" is Heloise; see his note to the *Letter to d'Alembert*, in *Oeuvres Complètes*, vol. 5, 1365 n. 5.

the sight of seven or eight men assembled, always fearful that their conversation turns on their miseries": "Now, of all the kinds of relations which bring individuals together in a city like our own, the *cercles* form incontestably the most reasonable, the most decent, and the least dangerous ones, because they neither wish nor are able to be hidden, because they are public and permitted, because order and rule prevail in them" (99).

Because their prevailing rule is sex segregation, the *cercles* need a supplement, a well-ordered occasion for the "marriageable young" to "get a taste for one another" under a steady public gaze and in the sobering light of day (117). For this Rousseau introduces "solemn and periodic Balls" that assemble citizens by generational, rather than sexual, difference. Fathers and mothers together enjoy "the sweetest *spectacle* that can touch a paternal heart," while in a separate section the grandmothers and grandfathers observe as "their grandchildren prepare to become citizens" (118). And the citizens-in-training commingle in their social-sexual debut, presenting their masculine and feminine forms to one another, to their families, and to the "Lord Commissioner," a magistrate whose presence serves as a perpetual reminder of the omnipresence of the law. To the latter goes the weighty task of crowning the "Queen of the Ball," a prize title awarded to the "most modestly" behaved of the young women (ibid.). Here, in particularly acute form, we observe the essential theatricality of sexual virtue: distinction is accorded to the best display of a reluctance to display oneself.

And if beauty, rather than "merit," should perchance sway the judges' decision, so much the better: "Having more assaults to sustain, doesn't it need to be encouraged more?" (119). So, too, the "adornment of daughters"—so necessary and problematic in the development of chaste women—is "entirely in its place" at these balls. Any remaining doubt that the content as well as the form of these *spectacles* is public seduction fades when we read that dancing, described as a "decent recreation" and an "inspiration of nature," must be prohibited among the married women: "for to what decent purpose could they thus show themselves off in public?" (118).[57] Here echoing an earlier warning apropos the

---

[57] Rousseau is clear that Emile must take the lead during this courtship ritual: "He is permitted to be his mistress's master" (*Emile*, 790).

theater's unintended effects ("the chaste flames of the mother could inspire impure ones in the daughter"), Rousseau underscores the need to control, or rather to choreograph, the satisfaction of a passion whose arousal he fully intends: "The young, having certain and decent meeting places, would be less tempted to seek for more dangerous ones. Each sex would devote itself more patiently in the interim to occupations and pleasures which are fitting to it, and would be more easily consoled for being deprived of the continual company of the other" (119).

The unifying pleasures of the republican *spectacle* consist in the figural displays of femininity and masculinity. This pertains not only to the maidens and young men but also to the parents and grandparents who, charmed by the "agreeable *spectacle*" of their courting children, also contribute to it by playing the roles of proud and protective fathers, adorning and dignified mothers, and patriotic elders. These performances reproduce citizens in two ways. First, they bring about the marriages through which the state is repeopled and which, because they are unions born of the children's free choice (masquerading as their *natural desire*), "maintain the body of the people better in the spirit of its constitution" (119–20). Second, these performances reproduce citizens through the "sweet impressions" they engrave in every heart: "These balls, thus directed, would resemble less a public *Spectacle* than the gathering of a big family, and from the bosom of joy and pleasures would be born the preservation, the concord and the prosperity of the Republic" (120). The spectacular communication of their joy and their pleasure returns republicans to their first language, to their earliest figurations of a world in which *family, man,* and *woman* are the indelible signs of *la patrie*.

The topographical history of this originary moment offered in the *Essay on Languages* reappears as autobiography in the final scenes of the *Letter to d'Alembert*. There Rousseau lovingly recalls a scene from his Genevan youth, a spontaneous dance performed by citizen-militia in the town square. The joy and skill of their performance (as well as the stirring anomaly of seeing "military pomp in the bosom of pleasure") produced a "very lively sensation" that soon spread throughout the town, bringing women to the windows and then into the square, and "half-clothed" children running from their beds (123). The dancing stopped with the appearance of women and children: "Now there were only embraces, laughs, *santés* and caresses." Rousseau's father gives voice to the illusion, and it comes in the form of an imperative: "My Father, embracing me, was seized with a trembling which I think I still feel and share: 'Jean-Jacques,' he said to me, 'love your country. Do you see these good Genevans? They are all friends, they are all brothers. Joy and concord reign in their midst. You are Genevan; you will one day see other Peoples; but even if you should travel as much as your Father, you will never find their likes'" (124). The imagined moment of origin figures nation, family, and love together in an orderly performance of public desire. And it is these first pleasurable practices of gendered self-display and witness that sustain the republic: as a way of life, as an identity, and as an idea.

The sustenance comes not only through remembrance but also through repetition. The theatricality, the figural language, and the heady excesses of passion that characterize republican *spectacles* are all central to the daily interaction of Rousseau's men and women. Whether they are dancing in the village square or trysting in the chalet, republicans constitute themselves as a free people by sharing the pleasures of their mutual bondage, and they reproduce their state as they reproduce their sex. In previous chapters I have pointed to that coincident reproduction in Rousseau's figuration of individual life stories; in the *Essay on Languages* and the *Letter to d'Alembert* this coincidence is writ large, in the representational practices of different nations. The pleasures of speech, of self-display, of images that horrify and enchant: on Rousseau's telling, all of these reflect and give form to sexual identity, and always to political effect. So, too, these accounts reveal the quotidian regularity with which sexual and political identities are reproduced. Passion and servility infuse our every utterance and our everyday roles.

This routinization of the sublime truths of *la patrie* and sexual difference follows precisely Rousseau's formula for the "true constitution of the state." This is how he presents what I will call cultural law in the *Social Contract*:

> To these three sorts of laws [political, civil, criminal] is joined a fourth, the most important of all, which is engraved neither in marble nor in bronze, but in the hearts of the citizens, it is the true constitution of the state; everyday it takes on new force; when other laws grow old or die away, it revives them or takes their place, preserving a people in

the spirit of its institution and imperceptibly [*insensiblement*] substituting the force of habit for that of authority. I am speaking of *mœurs*, customs, and especially of opinion, a part of the law unknown to our politicians but on which depends the success of all the others; a part with which the great Legislator secretly occupies himsel[f]. (394)

The everyday force of mores, customs, and "especially" opinion produces habitual truths. We have seen Rousseau inscribe this cultural law on the bodies of his male and female characters, and invite his readers to self-inscribe through the pleasurable practices of reading, and watching, as his figurations take shape. Republican *spectacles* generalize these habituating encounters by engraving the pleasing truths of government and family on the heart of every participant: thus the *Letter to d'Alembert's* emphasis that they constitute "an important component of the ruling order [*police*] and good mœurs" (119). The festival that comes as an interruption, a consolation, or an extrapolitical reverie is a critical site for organizing the daily practice through which a people, without reflection or intention, reproduce their state.

The uncommonness of the *spectacle* seems to preserve the possibility of a moment of, if not genuine democracy, then genuine pleasure. Promising, in the formulation of the *Essay on Languages*, the experience of "pleasure and desire merged into one," the festival represents the collective expression of a fulfilled, indeed, a self-fulfilling, people. But if, as I have suggested, these spectacular moments continue Rousseau's politics, then their fulfillment continues the relationships of willed submission that self-governance requires. This is not to say that the pleasure is not genuine but only that its anticipated or remembered object—the unity of a selfsame people—incorporates relations of power and difference. And this is just what we would anticipate in a consensually nonconsensual regime, where rule no longer proceeds through the king's pronouncement of his pleasure but through the regular assembly of citizens who must represent their own. The perennial appearance of the Lord Commissioner should not distract us from a more general truth: in every way that matters, they are doing it by themselves.

In the following chapter I take up a singular example of the expressive demands of a republican people and the language of love that they speak. The story to which I turn, *Le Lévite d'Ephraïm*, moves between natural idylls, village squares, battlefields, and a festive gathering of maidens. In these very public places, political and sexual practices coalesce in a blood-drenched *spectacle* that celebrates the identity of a free people. These collective expressions of joy duplicate and discipline the acts of submission performed within the romantic dyad. This is the submission so complete that it embodies the very faculty of will. Who they are, what they want, and how they get it become self-evident truths for citizens whose deepest—earliest, embodied—desires the state had always fulfilled. Bearing out the conclusion of the *Letter to d'Alembert* that "there is no pure joy other than public joy, and the sentiments of nature reign only over the people" (124), the story of the Levite exemplifies a republican romance that weds pleasure to power, and gives form to that union on the bodies of women and men.

Making Rhetoric Matter

> On the death of Caesar I imagine one of our
> orators wishing to move the people; he exhausts
> all the commonplaces of his art to present a
> pathetic description of Caesar's wounds, his
> blood, his corpse. Antony, although eloquent,
> does not say all that. He has the body brought in:
> What rhetoric!
>
> *Emile*

AGONIES AND ECSTASIES

The *Essay on Languages* argues that discourse always draws force
from its correspondence with material things, and in the end,
moral and political persuasion needs a sensational language.
Rousseau's stories feed this literary sensibility: in them, bodies
generate narrative. What they say, and what is said about them,
becomes intelligible within his grammar of sexual and political
interaction. This is the grammar of consensual nonconsensuality,
a logic of power and pleasure that articulates the sovereignty of
the willing subject by means of its own servile desires. That this
sovereign will belongs, ultimately, to the body politic is the persuasive truth of a republican *sensibilité*: citizens love the law as they
love one another, with the deepest sensation that the two are inseparable. And indeed they are: the masculine audacity, the feminine chastity, and the filial and parental devotion through which
men and women speak their embodied loves are all the design of
a republican political order, and the self-narration of Rousseau's
citizens always takes the form of a romance.

But true romance is never without its agonies. Perhaps the feeling isn't mutual, perhaps interests conflict. Rousseau writes the
necessity of such possibilities into his erotic "order of attack and
defense": women's *pudeur* promises the suspense and struggle that
true love requires because it keeps consent uncertain. He also

writes this uncertainty into the social contract: "If there were no different interests, one would scarcely feel the common interest, which would never encounter any obstacle; everything would proceed on its own and politics would cease to be an art" (371). This note, attached to the *Social Contract*'s discussion of the difference between a general will and the will of all, points beyond the inevitability of conflicting desires to the benefits, procedural and *sensible,* of political disagreement: common interests are known as such, and take on a properly majestic cast, when they are compared with partial, particular concerns. An artful politics consists in the display of difference and the staging of opposition that secure the self-evidence of a general will. Here, too, the genius of the artist is to evoke what is essentially true of "the type" through skilled depictions of its superficial variations, and in portraying these agonal performances, the artist-cum-seducer "makes use of all the violence permitted in love."[1]

This violence and this love are the subject of *Le Lévite d'Ephraïm,* a story of romantic and political agony whose narrative is driven by a sensational language of things. This "poem in prose," as Rousseau called it, was never published during his lifetime, although he had planned to do so in a volume that would include the *Essay on the Origin of Languages* and *De l'Imitation Théâtrale.*[2] The companion texts are fitting. I indicated previously that the Levite appears in the first chapter of the *Essay on Languages* as an example of the efficacy of communicating through material means: the Levite, Rousseau concludes, accomplished with a dismembered corpse what "in our day [would] turn on lawsuits, debates, perhaps even jokes."[3] And while *Imitation Théâtrale* confirms the conclusion of the text's Platonic original apropos the dangers of the poet's art, it does so with a familiar ambivalence. In its last paragraph the text compares the rejection of poets to a wise man who, "smitten by the charms of a mistress [and] seeing her ready to abandon her virtue, breaks off the sweet chain, albeit with regret, and sacrifices his love to reason and duty."[4] Among those who have known

---

[1] *Letter to d'Alembert,* 78.

[2] *Oeuvres Complètes,* vol. 2, 1920, vol. 5, 1537. The reference to the *Lévite* as a "poem in prose" appears in its first preface; see Rousseau, *Le Lévite d'Ephraïm,* in *Oeuvres Complètes,* vol. 2, 1205.

[3] *Essay on Languages,* 377.

[4] *De l'Imitation Théâtrale,* 1211.

the "seductive attractions of Poetry" since childhood, however, an occasional indulgence might have no more dire effect than to return citizens to "our first loves": "We would forever tell ourselves that there was nothing serious or useful in this dramatic display [*appareil*]; in occasionally lending our ears to Poetry, we would secure our hearts from being abused by it, and we would not endure its troubling order and freedom, neither in the interior Republic of the soul nor in that of human society."[5] If not precisely a rehabilitation of illusory transports, these final images of poetry arming citizens against their own unreason (and doing so in the manner of the sacrifical mistress) makes *Imitation Théâtrale* an apt complement to Rousseau's own poetic offering.

And like *Imitation Théâtrale*, the *Lévite d'Ephraïm* is a mimetic text: it offers an embellished retelling of the last three chapters of Judges, a story of the shattering and then the recomposition of the twelve tribes of Israel. In its entirety the Book of Judges concerns the period that begins with the Israelites' conquest of Caanan and ends just prior to their unification under monarchical rule, the story told in 1 Samuel. A recurrent theme in Judges is crisis and how to manage it: Judges' stories chronicle the many natural, social, and communicative disasters that befell the federated tribes, and how they were saved by the divinely inspired guidance of judges, men and on occasion women whose temporary leadership often took a military form.[6] The Israelites in this period are not without modes of governance (Mosaic law as well as edicts issued by popular tribal assemblies governed social relations and appeals for justice),[7] but their status as a political community is unclear: when Yahweh alone is sovereign, one might speak of either anarchy or divinely ordained self-rule. This twofold possibility had long been deftly exploited by supporters and critics of monarchical privilege, each of whom saw in Judges a fitting image of life without kings: a chaotic time of transgression and brutality, or a prepolitical golden age of audacious individualism.[8]

[5] Ibid.

[6] The Hebrew is *shofet* and has a range of political and administrative connotations. See *The Anchor Bible: Judges*, 5–7.

[7] Ibid., see introduction, 10–11, 26.

[8] Kirstie McClure's timely insistence on this point helped to clarify my thinking about the text as a whole.

Rousseau, I will argue, saw a bit of both: or, rather, his vision combined monarchy's ennobled prehistory with the force of its worldly sovereignty. His story shows no hints of the Israelites' imminent demand for a king ("that we may be like all the nations, and that our king may judge us, and go out before us, and fight our battles," 1 Sam. 8:20). On the contrary, it ends with the portrait of an Israel unified and ruled by the power of its people's will. In this republican variation, natural, social, and communicative crises structure a narrative of political (re)constitution in which an otherworldly power—the unerring, unbending, and often anguishing rule of a will that encompasses the whole—materializes in and on the community of believing citizens. Its closing scene, in which a "cry of joy [arises] from amidst the People," recalls the purely public joy of Rousseau's remembered Genevan *spectacle* and, like it, the Israelites' fete of unity defends, as it celebrates, a life without earthly kings.

This is not, to be sure, a life without agonies, and the story abounds with obstacles crucial for making the common interest felt. Those obstacles consist in sexual and familial desires that challenge republican rule. But the challenge is not in the content of these various desires; rather, it is the manner in which they are pursued. Instead of mutual pleasures we are shown narcissistic pursuits, and instead of the real man's audacity, we are witness to the satyr's. And the result is a brutal violence exceeding "all that love permits." In this story, the rapacity of kingly desire assumes a popular form, and thus citizens confront its lustful disfigurement on the face of a *semblable*. The Israelites' survival as a self-ruling people then depends on the reconstitution of their disfigured brothers, which means they must be (re)integrated into a republican "order of attack and defense." The story's closing scene testifies to the republic's self-restorative power as the disobedient Benjamites turn from rapists to seducers, and forgo the violence that love does not permit in favor of the violence that it does. And when dancing maidens freely choose submission to their suitors, the exquisite severity of the general will is redeemed: love of *patrie*, *famille*, and *semblable* inspire the bodily surrenders upon which a republican order depends. In this way the obstacles that a republican romance confronts are best seen not as the partial and particular desires of individuals that must be overcome but as artful displays of passion that cry out for state discipline.

THE STORY AND TWO DEFERRALS

Rousseau's *Lévite d'Ephraïm* is generally faithful to the plot line of the story told in Judges 19–21, although its divergences are significant. In its barest particulars his version is as follows: a Levite from the mountains of Ephraim has fallen in love with a beautiful maiden from Bethlehem and taken her to his bucolic retreat, where he plans to live with her in mutual joy and sweet isolation. But she soon tires of him and flees to her ancestral home. The Levite promptly goes to fetch her. During the course of their journey back to the Levite's home, they stay the night in the town of Gibeah, where they are given lodging by an old man who is also, originally, from the town of Ephraim. During the night the house is attacked by young men from the tribe of Benjamin who lust after the beautiful Levite and demand that the old man send him out. Horrified that the laws of hospitality might be broken, the old man tries to offer them his daughter instead. But the Levite intervenes, refuses to let the young daughter go, and sends out his companion instead.

The young Benjamites promptly brutalize and rape her. In the morning, after finding her dead on the doorstep, the Levite cuts up the corpse and sends one piece to each of the leaders of the twelve tribes. The tribes gather to hear the Levite's story, after which the leaders take a collective oath never to allow their daughters to marry into the murderous tribe of Benjamin; they then set out to destroy the Benjamites in battle. Many thousands of men from every tribe are killed in the war that ensues, and the Benjamites are almost completely annihilated: only six hundred men remain when the unified tribes call a halt to the battles. The leaders realize that destroying this tribe would inevitably mean annihilating their kinsmen, who are still, regardless of their crime, God's people.

So the victorious unified tribes resolve to save the Benjamites, which means finding wives for the survivors while still honoring the collective vow against intertribal marriage with them. When

211

the leaders learn that the people of Jabès had refused to send soldiers during the war, they instruct four hundred of the Benjamite men to seize that town's maidens; we are told that the disobedience of the Jabès people justifies the town's destruction. The Benjamites are advised to abduct the last two hundred virgins from the town of Shiloh, where an upcoming festival will leave them isolated, dancing in a grove.

But no sooner is the abduction under way than the Shiloh maidens' cries attract the attention of their townsmen, who come running to their defense. The tribal elders step in and try to persuade the Shiloh community that their young women must be taken by the Benjamites in order that the tribe might survive. Everyone is moved by the plight of the Benjamites, except the fathers of the maidens, who remain outraged by their daughters' coercion. The crowd finally agrees that the young women should decide their own fate. Here Rousseau introduces the characters of Axa, a Shiloh virgin and daughter of the man who orchestrated the plan to rescue the Benjamites, and Elmacin, her fiancé. When Axa chooses to forswear her own desire and give herself to a Benjamite, the spectacle first moves Elmacin to accept her decision and pledge himself to a spiritual (read celibate) life, and then the other Shiloh virgins to imitate her. The narrative concludes: "With this touching display, a cry of joy arose from amidst the people; Virgins of Ephraim, through you Benjamin shall be reborn! Blessed be the God of our fathers! there is still virtue in Israel."[9]

It is an understatement to say that this tale of political and social crises is shot through with dilemmas of sex and desire. Indeed, the interpenetration of, on the one hand, questions of communal identity and security and, on the other, questions of sexuality and eroticized violence makes it difficult to settle upon the subject of this story: is Rousseau depicting the perilous disruptions of homosexual desire, the multiform process of women's subjugation, or the concomitantly fragile and overpowering prerogatives of collective need writ *sensible* in the language of lost loves? Perhaps one should avoid making such a choice. Surely the *Lévite* is "about" all of these things, not to mention a range of possible subjects in excess of authorial intention and historical situation. And yet, the

---

[9] *Le Lévite d'Ephraïm*, 1223. All subsequent page references to *Lévite* will be given in the main text.

temptation is still to pursue a thematic foundationalism, to retrace the path of corruption and redemption that will elucidate the story's narrative logic. Which desires motivate and which are compensatory, what eludes communal norms and what can be recuperated by or contained within them, what is authentic and what is perverse: attending to the process and the power of the story's unfolding entices the reader into thinking in terms of these relationships of priority, if not causality.

I want to resist making these moves inasmuch as *my* motivating desire is to consider how the story uses (hetero)sexuality to instantiate the complexity and paradox of republican political agency. This sovereignty that resides in individuals by virtue of their ability to alienate it will always frustrate originary tales and orderly designs. So, too, its dependence on the people's "sublime ardor" makes rule by sovereign law an affair of the heart, and freedom a function of passion. From this perspective, what constitutes authenticity and what constitutes perversion—of identity, desire, or need—cannot be assessed at any distance from the politics that emerge through that differentiation. From this perspective, sexuality is not the subject of political intervention or control but is itself a politics: Rousseau's organization of desire *is* his organization of sovereignty. This formulation harkens back to the claim I made in chapter three that heterosexuality can be seen as an argument, a sensuous demonstration of the logic of consensual nonconsensuality. My analysis here builds on that suggestion by showing how, in the *Lévite*'s polemical politics, sexual means achieve republican ends.

To elucidate these structural dimensions of the story, I focus on its tortured version of consent rather than on its (re)constitution of natural and unnatural, or authentic and corrupt, desires. In fact, the appeals to natural design prominent in many of Rousseau's writings are almost absent in this account of internecine strife. Perhaps because the characters must be able to recognize one another as *semblables*, he avoids the oppositions that frame his attack on monarchical regimes and their corrupt social-sexual order. Here the narrative resolution depends on a political preservation of the whole, which requires that its multiform desires conform not to nature but to a republican political logic in which the agreement to be ruled means that "no" sometimes means "yes." This is a disorienting world of desires that blur into aversions,

213

subjects that fade into objects, and will that bleeds into submission. And although sustaining real distinctions between these terms means, indeed, everything, we miss an opportunity to explore the political process of their constitution and the political utility of their collapse if we read this story as one of corruption, usurpation, transgression, repression, or any other degenerative process through which something unaffected is made otherwise.

But this means reading Rousseau against the grain of his own self-presentation. Because while the story does not make use of a degenerative scheme, it does use the familiar tropes of innocence and culpability that tempt readers to see it as a symptom of the author's own psychic state. And Rousseau seems to be inviting just this move: he introduces the text in two (incomplete) drafts of a preface by appealing to the dramatic circumstances of its composition. This originary drama is recounted in detail in the *Confessions*. On June 8, 1762, ensconced at the Montmorency estate of the Maréchal and Mme de Luxembourg, Rousseau learns that the Paris *parlement* is considering condemnation of the recently published *Emile*. He reports that he had difficulty sleeping that night and thus spent most of it reading an entire book from the Bible, "the book that ends with the Levite of Ephraim and which, if I am not mistaken, is the book of Judges, for I have never looked at it again since that time."[10] The story had a strong effect on him, he continues, and plunged him into "a kind of dream" from which he was abruptly awakened by a messenger carrying the news of his imminent arrest.

The next morning Rousseau fled for Swiss territory and during the trip, "solely to amuse myself and without any hope of success," he composed the first three (of four total) Chants of the *Lévite d'Ephraïm*: "If it is not the best of my works," he remarks, "it will always be the most cherished."[11] The image is striking: Rousseau scribbling away in an open carriage as he barrels toward the border, on the run from monarchical injustice, if not the more insidious and obscure "conspiracy" to which he increasingly attributed his woes. Similarly striking is his appeal to the *Lévite* as evidence of the quality of his character. He writes in the first preface to the piece, "If ever any just man deigns to take my defense in compen-

---

[10] *Confessions*, 580.
[11] Ibid., 586.

sation for such outrages and libels, I want only these words as praise: 'in the most cruel moments of his life he wrote *Le Lévite d'Ephraïm*'" (1206). And the second preface consists entirely of a recapitulation of the text's sensational origins (1206–7).

These factors loom large for Thomas Kavanagh, whose reading of the *Lévite d'Ephraïm* retraces its "structure of denigration centering on victimage and violence which is the core of a macrotext including not only Rousseau's autobiographical works, but the major themes of his political writings."[12] In Kavanagh's view the story reproduces a consistent narrative theme: self-proclaimed innocence in conflict with community, where violence and victimage are the inevitable effects of an "agonizing dialectic" that yokes together the individual who demands justice and a social order that can never satisfy the demand.[13] Kavanagh's interpretation relies heavily on what he calls Rousseau's "psychic investment" in the text, because "only against this background" can the story's pivotal representation—"in the fullest sense of the word, the return of the repressed"—come into view.[14] This repressed desire, whose apparent absence is an effect of the work itself, becomes intelligible within the context of Rousseau's own psychic and emotional economy: the story represents a mode of self-understanding and self-overcoming.

Rousseau's personal investment in this text certainly intensifies the reader's interpretive choice: is the *Lévite* symptomatic of a logic of self-narration, a dream logic in which Rousseau's own fears and desires are key to deciphering the text, or is it symptomatic of problems of representation more generally, problems that structure political and textual, as well as individual, practices? Does the story give form to the author's own victimization and witness, or to the inescapable violence that sovereignty, in any form, entails? Again, the choice seems strained: one option veers toward a solipsism with minimal worldly regard, the other toward a generality, if not universality, that obscures particular instances of the narrative project. But if these options represent contrived extremes, still there is a choice to be made concerning the point

---

[12] Kavanagh, "Rousseau's *Lévite of Ephraïm*," 148. See also his *Writing the Truth*, especially chap. 5, "The Victim's Sacrifice."

[13] Ibid., 141.

[14] Ibid., 148.

of textual entry, and my concern is that a biographically driven reading misses the implications of Rousseau's parallel presentations of personal, sexual, and political crises. A dream logic that assumes multiple and inconstant identities never confronts *as such* the paradoxes to which the idea and on my reading the practice of republican sovereignty give rise: thus it risks reducing an institutional imperative to the play of signification. Further, this logic seems ill-equipped to grapple with the materiality of his affective displays: while Rousseau's perceived victimization and women's depicted evisceration might well be consonant, approaching the text from the first perspective risks framing the second as a political, perhaps poetic, casualty rather than as a political and definitely poetic target.

Finally, my concern is that if we assimilate Rousseau's characters to his self-portraiture, and their interactions to his quest for personal vindication, it becomes increasingly easy to conclude that the most profound consequences of his politics are in one's head. Variations on this conclusion surface regularly in political theoretical interpretations, often figured as a question of "inner domination."[15] Alternatively conceived as the emasculating, occasionally liberating, demands of reason or as the erasure of any critical space for reflection, the tendency is to see in Rousseau's prescriptions an agenda for internalizing the conflict that a consensually derived politics will inevitably encounter.[16] My emphasis on the imaginative dimension of political consciousness and the role of *pitié* in Rousseau's republicanism seems to reinforce this tendency, inasmuch as it points to the significance of emotional and cognitive designs. But I have also claimed that the sense Rousseau's republicans make of their needs, desires, and government is a worldly event, one staged through institutions and rituals that work on their bodies as well as their minds. In the end, perhaps

[15] Cassirer's reading of Rousseau as a proto-Kantian offers a classic formulation of this problem and its resolution; see *The Question of Jean-Jacques Rousseau*. M. E. Brint's reading of *Narcisse* is exemplary of more recent moves toward conceptualizing the problem as one of self-estrangement; see his "Echoes of *Narcisse*." Brint concludes that "inner domination" is Rousseau's solution to the problem of perpetually destabilized identity (633).

[16] William Connolly is particularly pithy on this point: "Rousseau withdraws politics from the general will and relocates it quietly inside the selves which make these general laws"; see *Political Theory and Modernity*, 58.

the interpretive choice turns less on whether one begins inside or outside the knowing subject—be it Rousseau, be it his republicans—and more on how one envisions the relationship between inside and outside: is it the relationship of dream to reality, template to canvas, little Republic to large, or consciousness to life?

My own choice on this score reflects a commitment to attend not only to the materiality of affective practice but also to the power obtained by these practices when they are conceived as private intentions. This is the power of the freely willed action, which can evade the issue of its own political dependencies insofar as it appears to be the consequence of individual, moral judgment. Similarly, a politics inaugurated by individual will, like the desire that emerges from a natural body, always lays claim to the legitimating power of its sovereign origins. Even the intention represented by the dream reiterates the authority of an extrapolitical individuality: justice and injustice alike become images of fantasized reversal and recollection. In these ways political critique can come to depend upon an assessment of inner states—perhaps the consciousness was false, the consent was coerced, or the desire was artificial—while the particular, political relations that sustain and collapse those differences go undetected. We are back at those distinctions whose contingency must be recognized if they are to mean anything at all; and again, this contingency is political, textual, and historical, not simply psychic. Thus, in deferring an individualist reading of the *Lévite* I do not mean to suggest that the story ignores personal pathos, any more than it ignores competing and incommensurable needs. Rather, my interest is how it absorbs both pathos and incommensurability into a language of republicanism, and in this way reinforces Rousseau's political vision by appeal to the very signs of its tragic, and even obscene, dimensions.

DILEMMAS OF DESIRE

The final three chapters of the Book of Judges open and close with statements that underscore the unruled and unruly context in which the Levite's story unfolds. Judges 19:1 begins, "And it came to pass in those days, when there was no king in Israel, there was a certain Levite," while Judges 21:25 closes the story and the

217

book thusly: "In those days there was no king in Israel; every man did that which was right in his own eyes."[17] These statements, slight variations on which appear twice in earlier chapters of Judges, foreshadow the peoples' repudiation of Yahweh: there *was* a king in Israel, but his authority as such was not recognized.[18] Rousseau's version announces lawlessness only at its beginning, and in such a way that Yahweh's authority is not at issue. After two introductory paragraphs that offer highlights of the "unspeakable crimes and castigations more terrible still" to be recounted, the story begins: "In the days of liberty when no one ruled over the Lord's people, it was a time of license where each person, recognizing neither magistrate nor judge, was his own master and did whatever seemed good to him" (1208–9). The stage-setting continues: "Israel, still scattered over the fields, had few large towns and the simplicity of its *mœurs* made the empire of law superfluous; but all the hearts were not equally pure, and the vicious found the impunity of vice in the security of virtue."

The vision of dispersed families, simple mores, and the nascent threat of trespass recalls the "golden age" of the *Discourse on Inequality*. Although clearly intended to represent a moment prior to the establishment of the state, this early society is an important step in that direction. Both its loose kinship associations and its "duties of civility" characterize an emergent political community that, although importantly precontractual, is not without norms and modes of justice.[19] The *Discourse on Inequality* describes these norms and modes: "Morality beginning to introduce itself into human Actions, and everyone, prior to Laws, being sole judge and avenger of the offenses he had received, the goodness appropriate to the pure state of Nature was no longer what was appropriate to a nascent Society; it was necessary for punishments to become more severe in proportion as the occasions for giving offense became more frequent; and it was up to the terror of vengeance to take the place of the restraint of Laws."[20]

---

[17] *The Holy Bible*, King James Version. All subsequent scriptural citations are taken from this edition.

[18] See Boling's commentary at 17:6, 18:1, 19:1, and 21:25, in *The Anchor Bible: Judges*.

[19] *Discourse on Inequality*, 170.

[20] Ibid., 170–71.

This tenuously golden age is evocative of the *Lévite*'s setting, which is sketched through a similar mix of innocence and impending doom. After situating the story at the time of law's superfluity, Rousseau introduces his title character by way of a nostalgic fantasy: "During those short intervals of calm and equality which remain forgotten because no one commanded others and no one did wrong, a Levite from the mountains of Ephraim saw in Bethlehem a young maiden who pleased him" (1209). Of course, this pleasant beginning comes as sharp contrast to the two introductory paragraphs, where Rousseau's announced intention to offer a "picture" of a woman's "shredded and palpitating limbs" and of the subsequent "civil wars" illustrates his claim that courage will be required of the reader: "At such crimes, he who averts his gaze is a coward, a deserter of justice; true humanity will face them [*les envisage*] in order to know them, to judge them, to detest them" (1208). Alerted from its opening line to the story's gruesome cast, readers fix their gaze upon the initial portrait of bliss, knowing it to be mere preface. And it is indeed blissful: in a marked departure from the biblical version, Rousseau dwells on the image of the Levite's sylvan home and the natural backdrop (turtledoves, roses, streams) of his all-encompassing love. (Rousseau's plans for publication indicate that the first chant was to include an illustration of the lover and his beloved in an Edenic setting, an ancient musical instrument visible in the foreground.)[21]

As in the *Discourse on Inequality*, the prefatory bliss marks a time when liberty and license have yet to be meaningfully differentiated. So, too, the *Discourse*'s persistently oblique appeal to a natural touchstone for that differentiation appears in the *Lévite*: the authority of Yahweh, indeterminately combining natural and moral law, offers a general form—some "original idea"—for notions of duty, disobedience, and transgression. His authority serves as a referent for the tribes as they conceive obligations, first to preserve the Benjamites and second, to honor their collective oath to withhold their marriageable daughters. Yahweh himself remains outside the action, although he is several times called upon by the united tribes. But unlike the biblical original, where he

---

[21] See "Notes and Variations," *Oeuvres Complètes*, vol. 2, 1926. Recall that "crude musical instruments" appear in the *Discourse on Inequality*'s "golden age" as well (171).

twice instructs his supplicating subjects to attack, Rousseau's Yahweh articulates his displeasure, even suggesting that the tribes' Benjamite "brothers" be left "in peace" (1218).[22] So, too, he admonishes the people for their "unjust vows" (1220). But it is not, finally, Yahweh's will or might that dictates the fate of the twelve tribes, any more than it is natural law that dictates the fate of the *Discourse*'s protorepublicans; their fate depends on their own fitful realization of who they are and how that shared identity and interest override tribal particularity, both particular transgressions and particular retributions. The consolidation of community on which Rousseau ends his story—the cry of joy and blessing that arises "from the midst of the People"—begins when the tribes gather to learn of the Benjamites' crime. Brought together by the Levite's graphic advertisements, the heretofore scattered tribes are now referred to as "the People of God," "the Lord's People," and then simply "the People" (1216–17).

The final scene in which "the People" appear offers readers what the *Social Contract* attributes to the compact's transformative power: "a moral and collective body composed of as many members as there are voices in the assembly."[23] Similarly reminiscent of a contracting community is the formula of shared *mœurs* and familial identity that sustains the Israelites' devotion to a common cause: the cultural law engraved on their hearts brings them back to their first duties. And like citizens who would resist the general will, the *Lévite*'s surrogate republicans will find themselves "forced to be free." On occasion this entails the perverse logic of destroying in order to save, for example, the massacre of the townsfolk of Jabès; and on occasion the enforcement of freedom plays out through individual wills and sensate bodies, for example, the virgins of Shiloh. This last case offers a brutal embodiment of the paradox of republican freedom, that liberty requires submission. "What?" cry out the fathers who have rushed to the aid of their daughters. "Will the daughters of Israel be subjugated and treated like slaves under the eyes of God? Where is the liberty

---

[22] The tribes are told to attack at Judges 20:23 (where the people, rather than Yahweh, refer to the Benjamites as "brothers") and 20:27.

[23] *Social Contract*, 361. See also 359, where, in a response to Grotius, Rousseau writes: "Before examining the act whereby a people elects a king, it would be good to examine the act whereby a people is a people; For this act being necessarily prior to the other, is the true foundation of society."

of God's people?" (1222). Here women assume a starring role as exemplars of the tribes' status as a free people, and as (re)enactors of its political will. And the moment when the *Social Contract* invokes the founding act—the performative alienation whereby individual power is ceded to a general will—the *Lévite* presents a nubile maiden, Axa, falling "half-dead" into the arms of her Benjamite ravisher and inspiring the other maidens to imitate her (1223). Otherwise put, the people's freedom and their republican possibilities are affirmed when an exemplary woman consents to be raped.

This final, bodily manifestation of a general will, to which I will return shortly, is preceded by numerous examples of how women secure social structure, and in each case the functional and symbolic aspects of their bodies interpenetrate. At various points they appear as offering or shield (Levite's beloved to the men of Gibeah), as epistle (her dismembered corpse), as consolation and plunder (the Jabès virgins), and as oblation (the Shiloh virgins). But these objectifications do not adequately capture the importance of women to this political drama, where the emergence of a general will is chronicled through sexual and procreative crises. The plot unfolds around two dilemmas of desire: the first involving a failure to sustain mutual (heterosexual) attraction, the second involving nonmutual and (thus?) socially disorganizing (homosexual) desire.

The action originates in the Levite's relationship with a woman whom the biblical original refers to as his concubine and whom Rousseau takes pains to paint as a wife *manquée*: in a speech made by the Levite and in the only note to the text Rousseau conjectures that Mosaic law must have prohibited their marriage (1209).[24] The Levite proposes that she come to live with him anyway: "We will be united and free; you will be my happiness and I will be yours." Her response is mute but effective: "The young maiden smiled; they were united, and he took her into his mountains" (ibid.). But she soon tires of their retreat and "escapes" to her family home. The biblical version says, "His concubine played the whore against him, and went [u]nto her father's house" (Judg. 19:2); Rousseau writes, "the young woman became bored with the Levite, perhaps

[24] See also Rousseau's more extended discussion of this issue in a first draft of the footnote, 1922.

because he left her nothing to desire" (1210).[25] Bucolic abundance and uninhibited love satiate; and as forewarned in *Emile*, the result is a waning of romantic interest. The Levite's mistress leaves him to retrieve what Rousseau suggests is an impossibility: "She believed that she would find [with her family] the innocent pleasures of her childhood, as if she were of the same age and the same heart" (ibid.). What was imagined as mutual fulfillment ends in boredom and a futile escape into nostalgia, and what was planned as self-sufficiency becomes a forlorn solitude. The subsequent threat to and (re)constitution of the political community follow on this twofold failure of (heterosexual) desire and interdependence.

The second dilemma arises in the town of Gibeah. Ready to bed down in a public square, the Levite and his concubine are offered lodging by an old man. Because he is also, like the Levite, from the tribe of Ephraim, the old man insists it is his duty to provide for them. When the Levite is later besieged in the old man's home, the Benjamites' sexual passion is signaled as a problem of hospitality.[26] The Bible says that the townsmen cried out to the old man, "Bring forth the man that came into thine house, that we may know him" (Judg. 19:22). Rousseau's version is, "Give us this young stranger whom you received into your home without [our] leave, so that his beauty might pay the price of this refuge and he might atone for your temerity" (1213). The text explains that their passion had been aroused earlier when they first saw the Levite, but because of a "lingering respect for the most sacred of all

[25] Both English and French translations of the relevant verse (Judg. 19:2) vary with respect to how the concubine's behavior is characterized: some have it that she was adulterous and slatternly, others that she was angry, even wronged. In the face of conflicting textual sources, Robert Boling suggests that irritation or anger is the more likely intention because "it is odd that a woman would become a prostitute and then run home" (*Anchor Bible: Judges*, 273). He concludes with the more compelling observation that "as Israelite law did not allow for divorce by the wife, she became an adulteress by walking out on him" (274). We do not know which translation Rousseau used, but in my perusal of eighteenth-century French Bibles, the most frequently used verb is *paillarder*, roughly translated as "to play the whore." Kavanagh discusses this question of translation and Rousseau's variation at 152 n. 3 in his "Rousseau's *Le Lévite d'Ephraïm*."

[26] Boling's commentary on this passage suggests something similar: "[T]he initial and determinative offense is a violation of the law of hospitality" (*Anchor Bible: Judges*, 276).

places, they did not want to lodge him in their homes in order to violate him." Their plan was to violate him later in the public square (1214). The old man implores them to understand his duties as a host—"Do not violate sacred hospitality!"—and tries to give them his daughter as a substitute. In the biblical version the men refuse the offering and the Levite then offers them his concubine; in Rousseau's version the Levite prevents the "generous old man" and his daughter from leaving the house and wordlessly hands over his "beloved companion" instead. The Benjamites immediately set upon the "half-dead young girl" and "tear into her without *pitié*" (ibid.).

Rousseau makes minimal recourse to nature when he depicts the Benjamites' homosexual desire. A direct reference appears only once, when the old man tells the Benjamites that their demands will "outrage nature" (ibid.). But the men themselves are described as "without yoke, without brake, without restraint" when they come after the Levite, and Rousseau's prose strips them of their masculinity only in describing the concubine's brutalization. After accusing them of "destroying your kind [*espèce*] by the pleasures intended to reproduce it" (a line that recalls *Emile*'s prognosis for a world without feminine *pudeur*: "the human race would perish by the means established to conserve it"),[27] Rousseau's narrative turns toward the now-violated concubine: "Alas! She is already dead! Barbarians, unworthy of the name of men [*le nom d'hommes*]; your howling resembles the cries of the horrible Hyena, and like it, you devour cadavers!" (1215). These predators are unsexed by their "ferocious desire" for the concubine, not the Levite, and it is their satyric audacity in the pursuit of pleasure that constitutes their crime.

Rousseau's minimal attention to whether homosexual desire is (un)natural is noteworthy but not unusual. On this score the tone he strikes in the *Lévite* is similar to what one finds in the *Confessions*. There, in a story of his stay at a Turin hospice, Rousseau describes his reaction to the sexual overtures of an older neophyte, a Moor, with equal parts amazement and disgust. Laying claim to an extraordinary naïveté, he writes that he was neither angry nor indignant at the man's behavior, "for I did not have the least idea what

---

[27] *Emile*, 694.

it was all about."[28] His principal distress seems to have been aesthetic: "I could not understand what was the matter with the poor man . . . [a]nd truly I know of nothing more hideous for someone of cold blood to see than that obscene and foul demeanor and that terrifying face on fire with the most brutal lust; I have never seen another man in that state, but if we appear like that to women, they must indeed be fascinated not to find us detestable [*en horreur*]."[29]

Rousseau writes that he recounted the incident publicly and in great detail, and as a result, the hospice director rebuked him for making a fuss over nothing. He explained to Rousseau that the Moor's actions were "forbidden [like] fornication, but for the rest, the desire [*intention*] was not an offense to the person who was its object, and there was nothing to be bothered by in having been found attractive." Rousseau is so struck by this straightforward approach, as well as by the "natural manner" of an ecclesiastic listening in on the discussion, that he decided "this was no doubt an accepted practice [*usage admis*] in the world."[30] Thus his personal, intense dislike for the whole business, which he takes pains to underscore, is not expressed as moral outrage: despite an abundance of fitting tropes—desire, religion, age, nation—the language of transgression is absent. Rousseau is disgusted—"especially by what I saw"—and the disgust colors his perception of its "apologist," but there is no mention of nature's perversion or corruption.[31] Perhaps most striking are the lessons he recalls taking from this experience: first, to be disabused of his naïveté and remain on guard against future overtures and, second, to esteem women more highly. "It seemed that I owed them, in sentiments of tenderness, in personal homage, the reparations of my sex, and the most ugly of she-monkeys [*guenons*] became in my eyes an adorable object through the memory of that false african."[32]

Homosexual desire is treated less as a moral challenge to the natural order than as an opportunity to shore up an engendered social organization: precisely because he sees in the Moor's "foul

---

[28] *Confessions*, 67.

[29] Ibid.

[30] Ibid., 68.

[31] Ibid. In addition to the wretched face of masculine lust, "what Rousseau saw" was the man's ejaculation; see 67.

[32] Ibid., 69.

demeanor" the face of a *semblable*, Rousseau renews his commitment to heterosexual fantasy. (Still, there is some ambiguity: is this a felt need to make "reparations" through tenderness or to avoid at any cost another terrifying encounter with masculine desire?) So, too, in the *Lévite* the Benjamites' lust initiates dilemmas of social order—intertribal versus intratribal identities and public versus private space—and in both cases, the affirmation of boundaries requires the affirmation of heterosexual desire. But the social disorder threatened by this homosexuality pales in comparison to the crisis precipitated by its heterosexual substitution. The brutalization of the concubine marks the challenge to the community's unity and will, that "intrigue and partial association" Rousseau condemns in the *Social Contract*.[33] When messengers are sent to the Benjamites demanding that the culprits be turned over, the tribe refuses and rushes to defend Gibeah, "resolved to fight alone against the reunited people." What began as a challenge to hospitality is transformed into a challenge to collective security, through an act that defies the norms of heterosexual consensuality. Resolution to the crisis will thus turn on a reiteration of those norms, and that means a repeat performance of women's sexual-political consent: the concubine spoke eloquently, if wordlessly, the outrage of rapacious domination, and her similarly eloquent sisters will recuperate the people's freedom.

ACTING FREE

In the second half of the *Lévite*, dilemmas of desire give way to maternal crises as the realization that the Benjamites must be preserved quickly reduces to the imperative to find them mates. And while here the problem appears to be simple reproduction, the drama of missing mothers is signaled in the opening paragraph when Rousseau introduces the Benjamite tribe as the "sad child of pain who caused your mother's death" (1208). The mother in question is Rachel, who died giving birth to the tribe's namesake and founder, her second son Benjamin (Gen. 35:17–19). The symbolic legacy of its origin foreshadows the tribe's later procreative crisis, both of which implicate women as critical sites of social con-

---

[33] *Social Contract*, 371.

tinuity and order: their bodies are critical to making members *and* meaning for the collectivity.

This convergence of symbolic and material performance is in certain respects illustrative of Gayle Rubin's influential analysis of gender as a function of kinship structure.[34] As her analysis makes clear, procreative strategies are always questions of how cultural and social systems are imposed on the natural world, one aspect of which is the body itself. Thus women's "natural" desires—for men, for children, for familial continuity and care—are emblematic of a social system whose purposes always predate and exceed them. And indeed, in the *Lévite* precisely an obstruction to the "traffic in women" threatens the security of intertribal relations: the tribes' oath never to allow marriage between their daughters and the Benjamites interrupts the normal patterns of exchange. The problem which then confronts them is how to honor their vow and still make the necessary transactions. Rousseau's resolution of this problem illustrates Rubin's claim that men are the "exchange partners" and thus the beneficiaries of the social organization that such exchanges secure.[35] But his account also underscores women's agentic capacity in a way that Rubin's seems to preclude. From a political perspective, the central issue is how women's capacity to want and to will figures in the constitution of a republican community. It is thus not only the systemic imperatives of a social order that constitute women as *objects,* as in Rubin's account. They are also constituted as desirous, willing *subjects* through the political imperatives of republicanism: in their transformation from maidens to wives, the Israelite women recapitulate the process of moral and social maturation experienced by Julie and Sophie. My goal in retracing that process is not to adjudicate the reasonableness of these characters' decisions but to lay bare the social, sexual, and narrative structures through which moral decision making assumes worldly form.

The Israelite maidens become Benjamite wives in two separate incidents. In the first, simultaneously keeping their oath and preserving their "brothers" prompts the unified tribes to massacre an entire town. The disobedience that authorizes the massacre is uncovered only as a consequence of the tribes' intention to get

[34] Rubin, "Traffic in Women."
[35] Ibid., 174.

around their vow: "To elude such a cruel oath [and] contemplating new carnages, they took a census of the army to see if, despite the solemn obligation, any of them had failed to show up, and they found no one from Jabès" (1220). The tribes do not raid Jabès for women; rather, they exterminate the entire community: "men, women, children, excepting only the virgin daughters." In this sense the Jabès maidens are indeed objects of exchange, made plunder, whose will and desire are apparently irrelevant to the transaction. But Rousseau's description of these events leaves little room to doubt their iniquity. Explaining the position of the Jabès townsfolk with respect to the civil war, Rousseau writes: "Less concerned with punishing the crime than with spilling fraternal blood, [they] refused vengeances more atrocious than the transgression, without considering that the violation of an oath and desertion from the common cause are worse than cruelty" (1220). The subsequent executions are called "murders," which Rousseau describes with a ferocious detail found nowhere in Judges. And there is no pretense of justice in the delivery of the Jabès maidens, who are compared to "prey." The section describing their nuptial embrace "by hands dripping with the blood of their kin" ends with the following, astonishing lament: "Oh (female) sex, always a slave or a tyrant, whom man oppresses or adores, and yet whom he can make happy or be happy [with] only by allowing to be his equal" (1221).[36]

In the second incident, and unlike the first, a raid is precisely what is required because the people of Shiloh have done nothing to warrant punishment. Here honoring the tribes' vow *requires* that the women be taken against their townsmen's will: consent on the part of the men of Shiloh would put them in opposition to the collective oath. The sociopolitical imperative repeats a formula familiar from the *Social Contract*: the sanctity of the common cause requires overcoming individual wills, and yet the autonomy of those willing subjects is confirmed precisely in its negation. Men's wills are here manifest in their right to exchange and withhold women, and it appears that respecting their sovereignty entails violating women's bodies. But Rousseau's narrative complicates this conclusion. When the people of Shiloh, gathered together for

---

[36] The original reads: "*Sexe toujours esclave ou tiran, que l'homme opprime ou qu'il adore, et qu'il ne peut pourtant rendre heureux ni l'être, qu'en le laissant égal à lui.*"

a public festival, realize what is happening, they rush to defend the women. They stop only after the village elders "make their voices heard, and the people, moved by compassion for the Benjamites, become concerned on their behalf" (1222).[37] The text is explicit that only the fathers remain steadfast; they insist that their daughters be allowed to decide their fate in an appeal to the crowd that makes a direct connection between the women's situation and the liberty of all. The crowd's assent to the fathers' proposal hinges on the recognition that the demands of equity outweigh compassion for the Benjamites: "Divided between justice and pity, the assembly finally decides that the captives would be set free and decide for themselves what to do" (ibid.).

At this point Rousseau has strayed far from the biblical version, which covers the whole incident with "And the children of Benjamin took them wives, according to their number, of them that danced, whom they caught: and they went and returned unto their inheritance, and repaired the cities, and dwelt in them" (Judg. 21:23). This terse denouement is followed by two brief verses, one of which recounts the subsequent dispersal of the Israelites, "every man to his tribe and to his family," and the second of which consists in the statement, quoted earlier, that this was a time without kings, when "every man did that which was right in his own eyes." Rousseau's elaborations, by contrast, provide both a closing scene of social unity and a familial and sexual *spectacle* in which the recognition of women's wills confirms the beneficent coercion of the common cause.

The scene begins when the Benjamites are forced to set the women free. Whereas earlier they had openly attacked (and "the chase animated [the women's] color and the ravishers' ardor"), they must now "try to replace force with means more powerful over [the women's] hearts" (1222). The savaging becomes courtship. Extending their arms in a gesture of escort, the Benjamites present their case: "Daughters of Shiloh, will you be happier with someone else? Are the last of the Benjamites unworthy of persuading you?" In the face of this coy display, Axa throws herself into her mother's arms, all the while throwing "furtive" looks at her betrothed, Elmacin, who responds with an inarticulate cry. Axa's Benjamite ravisher witnesses this wordless exchange: "He guesses

---

[37] From this point on Rousseau writes in the present tense.

all, he moans, and then ready to withdraw, he sees Axa's father arrive" (1223). Her father speaks directly to her: "You know my heart; I love Elmacin, he was to be the consolation of my old age: but the welfare of your people and the honor of your father must outweigh him. Do your duty, my daughter, and save me from disgrace among my brothers." Never denying her right to choose, he suggests instead that only her rightful choice will save the community, as well as his pride. These words by themselves do not affect her, "but lifting her eyes, she meets those of her venerable father; they say more than his mouth; she makes her choice." Her wordless gesture of consent echoes the concubine's earlier surrender: "half-dead, she falls into the Benjamite's arms." Elmacin, meanwhile, calms the agitated crowd by responding to Axa's choice with his own vow to remain celibate and enter a religious order ("Because I cannot be yours, I will never be another's") while the Shiloh maidens, as if struck "by a sudden inspiration," imitate Axa's sacrifice (ibid.). The virgins, the crowd sings out, have saved the people of Israel.

With this Byronic, if not bathetic, display Rousseau brings to a close the quintessential republican romance. We have retraced its logic before: because the community must express a general will both engendered and endangered by individual desire, enforcing that will entails the coincidence of fulfillment and coercion. This twofold experience of sovereignty and subjection is formally acknowledged in the *Social Contract*'s description of its citizen; the *Lévite* dramatically enacts these paradoxical relations through sexual performances that simultaneously recognize and refuse individual will, and in so doing, (re)structure the community. Further, the culminating moment of this freely chosen submission is located in women's bodily performances, where its sacrifical dimension is most vividly on display. But the men also experience deferred desire: the Levite, the old man of Gibeah, Axa's father and fiancé, and, of course, the lustful young men of Gibeah are all denied satisfaction. My point is not to equivocate on who suffers the most but to underscore that the grammar of sexual interaction is also the grammar of political interaction, and when the Shiloh virgins accept their ravishers, they hold in place a political community whose foundation is consent to the terms of one's domination.

But now the problem of authenticity—here, of will and choice—seems inescapable. After all, in the *Social Contract* men's bifurcated sovereign-subject identity is said to enable genuinely autonomous action; in what sense can women in the drama sketched here be anything more than what Rubin calls "semi-objects," in distinction to the "subject" position occupied by male exchange partners?[38] By insisting on the significance of women's agency in this drama, I am perhaps as guilty as Rubin finds Lévi-Strauss to be, whose late acknowledgment that "even in a man's world, [a woman] is still a person" and thus a generator of signs, rouses her disgust. When Lévi-Strauss writes that women's dual role as sign and as agent explains why "the relations between the sexes have preserved [a]ffective richness, ardor and mystery," Rubin is dumbfounded that he is "presenting one of the greatest rip-offs of all time as the root of romance."[39] But I am arguing that Rousseau demonstrates how romance consummates the rip-off, and how women's status as generator of signs is crucial to a social system organized by sexuality and is emblematic of a political order that is always, in the final instance, coercive.

For this reason the issue of women's agentic capacity cannot be understood in any simple opposition to a sociopolitical regime that misrepresents them: what they feel, choose, imagine, and desire—how they might act by and for themselves—becomes unintelligible when wrenched from worldly context. In this sense the conditions that compromise women's autonomy also make that autonomy intelligible. Of course expressions of will in the *Lévite* are wholly gendered: that women will play their roles properly is guaranteed by a femininity that finds permeable the line between coercing and courting and that values devotion to fathers and others over self. And this is paradigmatic of republican citizenship; Rousseau would much prefer that his republicans freely choose to be forced, rather than force them to be free. When, then, I propose that we recognize Axa's performance as a consent to be raped, I am only pushing to their (il)logical limit the principles of the "true constitution" engraved on republican hearts. Because the pleasures intended to reproduce citizens also reproduce their

[38] Rubin, "Traffic in Women," 176.

[39] Ibid., 201. Rubin quotes Lévi-Strauss from *The Elementary Structures of Kinship*, 496.

230

self-subjection, any claim about the authenticity of their desires and their wills must perforce be staked in a field of oxymoronic convergence, where coercion and consent, sacrifice and gain, and pleasure and pain often cohere.

How to reconcile the twofold position of citizens—as political agents and objects of political control—is at the core of Rousseau's politics. A failed reconciliation drives the plot of the *Discourse on Inequality*, while the promise of its success frames the *Social Contract*: "Man is born free and everywhere he is in chains. . . . [H]ow did this change take place? I do not know. What can render it legitimate? I believe I can resolve that question."[40] What renders this enslavement legitimate, finally, is neither its contractual foundation (a key moment in the *Discourse on Inequality*'s degenerative tale) nor its ability to engender happiness (happy slaves are everywhere in monarchical regimes) but its ability to sustain a unity of need and desire that allows, indeed forces, citizens to be self-subjecting. Rousseau does not equivocate: it is a passionate bent that ties self-satisfaction to the ends of the state. I am suggesting that this bending takes place through a *sensibilité* engraved upon hearts and bodies in the language of masculine and feminine identity. "It is certain," Rousseau writes in *Political Economy*, "that in the long run people are what the government makes them."[41] In the stories he tells, what they are made to be are men and women, political subjects whose very experience of willing unites desire and submission as inseparable elements of fulfillment.

The troubling slippage in the *Lévite* between will and force does not vitiate individual autonomy; on the contrary, such confusion is definitive of it. To be sure, this remains suspiciously paradoxical as a logical proposition. But Rousseau does not intend his citizens to reason it out; rather, he intends them to feel it. Like the Legislator, Rousseau's aim is "to persuade without convincing" through repeated narration of a romance that writes republicanism into the people's daily practices.[42] Like Lycurgus, who "ceaselessly" showed the Spartan his *patrie*, "in his laws, his games, his home, his loves, his feasts," Rousseau keeps the inconceivable truth of

[40] *Social Contract*, 351.
[41] *Political Economy*, 251.
[42] *Social Contract*, 383.

republican self-rule forever in view.[43] This is not, finally, possible through the *Social Contract*'s image of the honorable lawbreaker, proudly accepting punishment as the hallmark of his freedom. It is possible through the image of love, whose "miracle," Rousseau has discovered, is that it can "make us find pleasure in suffering."[44]

SOVEREIGN REPRESENTATIONS

The *Lévite d'Ephraïm*'s account of a republic's incorporation depicts a sex-gender system in motion. From the Levite's initiating, obsessional love to the final act of group surrender, the story gives form to a general will through expressions of sexual and familial desire. The sacrifices that the general will requires are here assimilated to the narrative conventions of a romance: lovers must struggle, with the world and with themselves, before confirmation and consummation of their love can be achieved. That unreciprocated desires both precipitate the crises and set the stage for their resolution confirms the republican cast to this romance: freedom entails a pathos whose eloquence is itself inspirational. In this story, the Israelites are "forced to be free" not by denying their individual desires but by realizing those desires through the body politic. And this is possible only insofar as they act like men and women, creatures who have always pursued, refused, and authorized pleasure through the practices of a consensual nonconsensuality.

This grammar of sexual interaction is finally what makes legible the sovereignty of a people without kings. As I suggested earlier, the story's status as political parable offers conflicting interpretive possibilities: a primitive state whose excesses and strife anticipate the need for firm rule, or a state of nature whose hardships pale in comparison to subsequent monarchical depredations. Rousseau's interpretation offers us a state of nature with a firm rule. This rule comes not from Yahweh or from natural law but from a will whose power and right are manifest on the body of the people. Indivisible and inalienable, unerring but, on occasion, misguided, this general will signals a sovereignty that is, miraculously, precontrac-

---

[43] *Government of Poland*, 957.
[44] *Julie*, 245.

tual.[45] And again, we find that the miracle is love: it is in playing their parts as (hetero)sexual men and women that the Israelites move inexorably toward the consolidation of their community. From the early obstructions that make the common interest felt, to Axa's forced freedom and its captivating effects, the characters are doing, if not what comes naturally, then what is engraved upon their hearts and inspired by their romantic visions.

In this way, Rousseau organizes sovereignty through a libidinal economy. Spectacular and *sensible*, this organization of desire introduces power, subjection, and rule through the people's pursuit of pleasure. Their sovereignty emerges in public gatherings perversely reminiscent of those featured in the *Letter to d'Alembert*: dancing and dead bodies, manly and satyric audacity, and the rituals of marital courtship together make the Israelites the only objects of every public display. These gatherings also recall the observation in *Essay on Languages* about the communicative practices of a free people. "Any language in which one cannot make oneself understood by the assembled people is a servile language." This is the case in countries where "neither art nor figures of speech are needed to say, *such is my pleasure*"; but in Mediterranean climes the language of fanaticism encourages mutual, public seductions.[46] The Levite's is such a land, and in his story Rousseau persistently brings the bodies in. Their pitiable agonies do not resist sovereignty: they make sovereignty worldly, visible, ecstatic, *sensible*.

The *Levite*'s sensational language of desire responds directly to the communicative dilemma outlined in the *Social Contract*, where the problem of political rationality is framed as a problem of representation:

> Sages who want to speak to the common herd in their own language rather than in the common vernacular cannot make themselves understood. For there are a thousand ideas that are impossible to translate into the language of the people. Overly general views and overly distant objects are equally beyond its grasp; each individual, appreciating

---

[45] See *Social Contract*, Book II, chap. 1 ("That Sovereignty Is Inalienable"), chap. 2 ("That Sovereignty is Indivisible") and chap. 3 ("Whether the General Will Can Err"), 368–72. On the necessity of sovereignty's contractual basis, see Book II, chap. 4 ("On the Limits of Sovereign Power"), 375.

[46] *Essay on Languages*, 428–29.

only the governmental plan that relates to his particular interest, has difficulty perceiving the advantages he should derive from the continual privations that good laws impose. For a nascent people to appreciate sound maxims of politics and to follow the fundamental rules of statecraft [*raison d'Etat*], the effect would have to become the cause; the social spirit that should be the work of that [political] institution would preside over the institution itself; and men would be, prior to the laws, what they should become by means of those laws.[47]

The language capable of bridging the chasm between immediate interest and long-term desire is a first, figural language of passion: it makes the threatening appear inviting, the monstrous appear natural, and the human, divinely inspired. Its spirit can preside over the founding to the extent that in those founding moments, the people are kept "spellbound" by the moving drama of their earliest loves and agonies. In the *Social Contract*, this language is put into "the mouths of the immortals" by a legislator whose ventriloquism is the "true miracle": Judaic and Islamic laws, Rousseau suggests, "still proclaim today the great men who dictated them."[48] In the *Lévite* this language takes a material form, and it is spoken by the Israelites themselves. In both cases those "thousand ideas" and complex concepts that resist the vernacular become accessible not as general and distant propositions but as heartfelt truths, fanatically expressed.

The precision necessary to distinguish accurately between similar yet shifting terms is thus abandoned in favor of figural excess. Consider again the *Social Contract*'s multiple names for the "public person that is formed through the union of all the other persons": *city, republic, body politic, state, sovereign, power, people, citizens, subjects.*[49] A political treatise works to articulate the distinctions between these terms, precisely to clarify the general idea to which they all refer. The *Lévite d'Ephraïm*, by contrast, effaces these distinctions in its recounting of the spectacular performances of a "sublime ardor" that always defies reason. We have seen from the beginning how the discourse of republicanism moves through passionate terrain: from Emile's and Rousseau's early figurations of love and rule, to the various "golden age" primitives who see mon-

---

[47] *Social Contract*, 383.
[48] Ibid., 384.
[49] Ibid., 361–62.

sters before they see men (and who come to see the difference as they come to see women), the path to citizenship follows a rocky course in which identities and distinctions are a function of imaginative transgressions. When citizens gather to express the will that is collectively theirs, they speak this "first language" of passionate violation and redress, a language of *citoyen* and *citoyenne* sustained by metaphoric excess.

Isn't It Romantic?

THE REPUBLICAN romance I have teased out of Rousseau's writings raises questions for various feminist perspectives on his work and for feminist approaches to canonical political theory more generally. Among readers attuned to the politics of gender, the importance Rousseau accords to romantic and familial relations invites analyses of how those relations represent both power asymmetries and ethical alternatives. When feminist readers are focused on issues of citizenship and social justice, they underscore the diminished opportunities for women that Rousseau's familial vision seems to require. Approaches attentive to the devaluation of women's moral and social labor, by contrast, are apt to find that same vision a resource for challenging the atomistic model of the citizen attributed to liberal political theory. A third, sometimes overlapping, interpretive frame that emphasizes how women connote disruption—of sexual, political, and symbolic order—will interrogate the fantasies and fears embedded within Rousseau's domestic ideal. In every case, the tendency is to view the relationship between femininity and republicanism as oppositional: the maintenance of Rousseau's public spaces requires that women be relegated to the private. But the reading I have developed over the course of this book suggests we move cautiously in accepting that conclusion.

Certainly Rousseau disapproved of the public women of the ancien régime: the *salonnières* and actresses, to say nothing of bourgeois Parisiennes, posed threats to the institutional and interactive schemes of republican society as he imagined it. So, too, the almost total absence of women in the *Social Contract*, even in its discussion of families, is remarkable. And yet, recall their occluded presence in the text's final note, where Rousseau argues for civil marriage by decrying the consequences when this power is left to religious men: "Is it not clear that they alone will dispose of inheritance, offices, the Citizens, the State itself, which could not

236

endure if composed solely of bastards?"[1] This juridical figuration incorporates women's bodies as objects, rather than subjects, of political regard; but the situation is less clear when we turn to other texts. As I have argued over the course of this study, whenever Rousseau narrates his republican characters—at play, in battle, or learning to be citizens and men—he deploys a language of familial and erotic relations that reiterates women's significance to his political scheme. Their significance is due in part to the economic, social, and reproductive labor they perform, but it also arises from the representational resources women provide for depicting passion, difference, and nature, aspects of human existence seen as central and often threatening to a community founded by convention. In both instances, Rousseau's narrative takes shape as it attaches to women's bodies—sites, as well as signs, of the new republican order. By inscribing the intricate, uncertain, and thoroughly alluring possibilities of an autonomous will on women's bodies, Rousseau naturalizes and eroticizes the consensual nonconsensuality authorized by the contract: men and women continuously reenact it, in their everyday (hetero)sexual practice.

To the extent this is a thoroughly habituated practice—a common vernacular of masculinity and femininity that organizes *mœurs*, laws, and everyday bodily presentation—public assemblies can safely be turned over to warriors, athletes, and voters who are happy to "give only their own opinion" without discussion or debate.[2] But these singularly masculine performances are atypical in Rousseau's stories, and, contrary to the accepted wisdom, women appear regularly in his public sphere.[3] The circulation of the stories themselves makes up one such sphere, circumscribed by a literary public: women's contributions, as characters and readers, are critical to the social and political ends of his novel, plays, memoirs, and didactic and cultural essays. And as we have seen, Rousseau composes women's political participation textually, in his de-

---

[1] *Social Contract*, 469. Rousseau's last-minute decision to suppress this note, and its subsequent reappearance in posthumous editions of the *Social Contract*, are generally attributed to the anti-Protestant climate in France; see the Pléiade commentary, *Social Contract*, 1506–7, and Vaughan's note, *Political Writings of Rousseau*, 2:133.

[2] *Social Contract*, 372.

[3] See, for example, Landes, *Women and the Public Sphere*, 67, 89.

pictions of republican *spectacles*. His (re)compositions of Sparta are a telling example: he borrows extensively from Plutarch's account of the celebrated republican original, but he also recasts that account, eliminating any mention of the homosexuality or pedophilia that characterized public sexuality in that city-state.[4] He also makes no mention of Spartan women's cross-dressing, which, together with their domestic confinement, is presented by Plutarch as a strategy to nurture and contain heterosexual desire.[5] (But isn't *this* romantic? Consider that Rousseau tells us he fell in love "for the first and only time" when he saw Sophie d'Houtedot galloping toward him in men's clothing. He explains that while he is generally not fond of "masquerades, I was taken by this one's romantic air, and this time, it was love.")[6] We are not, of course, surprised to discover the imperfection of the Spartan original, but neither should we be surprised by his "corrections" that allow him to imagine women's participation: without the restraint that their material presence imposes, a rhetoric of self-rule spurred by the figural excesses of eroticism might lead citizens to act queerly.

The proposition that women be seen as political actors in Rousseau's republican drama appears implausible only if one takes the gestures of silent and introspective voters to be definitive of action. But, as I have suggested, the voting citizen remains almost unnarrated in his writings; much more numerous and detailed are his descriptions of citizenship as public gathering and self-display. These descriptions extend the spaces and the dispositions that count as political. They also complicate our understanding of how the general will is realized. The electoral image given in the *Social Contract* is famously nondeliberative, presenting readers with detached, pensive individuals who resemble nothing so much as the isolated theatergoers of the *Letter to d'Alembert* (or, perhaps, Rawlsian rational actors behind their veils). By contrast, the *spectacles* that I have examined over the course of this book cast citizens as ardently interactive, perpetually reconstituting their interests and their polity with illocutionary zeal. Here we find an alternative version of discursive will-formation, a version unchastened by the stern demands of impartiality: public seductions and brutalities,

---

[4] See Plutarch, *Plutarch's Lives*, vol. 1, "Lysurgus," 59–90.

[5] Ibid., 74.

[6] *Confessions*, 439.

individual and collective expressions of passion, and inspired imitation are the communicative idioms through which the general will is made known. And at the center of this democratic polemic is the repeat performance of tacit consent: the unutterable made eloquent through "half-dead" women.

In insisting that there is agency in these "half-dead" women—Axa's consent, Julie's mastery, even the "sweet tyranny" of Sophie's right to say no—I make no claims about the resistant or subversive capacities they might retain. Such matters remain central to some feminist readings of canonical figures, where the goal is to consider how different political regimes and rationales preclude or perhaps enable women's speech, and, conversely, how women's voices give rise to alternative political visions.[7] However, in this book, my primary interest has been to parse the communicative and, ultimately, the imaginative structures that give political and sexual desires a coincident form. From this perspective, the question of what counts as an authentic consent or a sincere desire, or even as an act of subversion, is secondary to the project of identifying the logic and the rhetoric—which is to say, the articulating structures—that make choice, desire, and power intelligible. Rousseau's writings show how romantic love serves as one such logic; further, they show how sexed bodies perform the rhetorical operations that persuade us of the logic's inexorable truths. Thus I have read the blushing, adorned, voluptuous, malformed, and dismembered bodies of women that reappear throughout his work as a political symbology that makes (republican) sense of bodily expressions, and my analysis has remained trained on the communicative register that these bodily expressions establish, rather than on the truths they do or do not represent.

To pursue the issue of whether the representation of women's consent in these stories is truthful or empowering would require access to a position within the articulating structures that shape that truth and power; only Julie, Axa, and Sophie have that access, and, of course, they are all creatures of Rousseau. Returning to the self-evidence of his authorial control might suggest that we are now standing on the precipice of the text, ready to plunge into a historical reality it may or may not represent. My intention is

---

[7] For a recent study of Rousseau along these lines, see Marso, *(Un)Manly Citizens*.

otherwise: Rousseau's romances remain significant because they have provided and continue to provide narrative, thus conceptual, resources for making sense of our own notions of consent, desire, power, law, and will. The question, then, is not one of accurate representation but of constitutive design.

The insights and provocations of much contemporary feminist criticism touch on many of Rousseau's ongoing concerns. Inasmuch as his republican romance encompasses relations both sexual and political, narrative and material, its political horizons remain vast and close at hand. The bodily and institutional form Rousseau gives to consensual nonconsensuality helps to flesh out contemporary models of compulsory heterosexuality, for example. In Adrienne Rich's germinal account, this term identifies heterosexuality as a social imperative, best viewed as an institution whose enforcement mechanisms range from ostracism and ridicule to disfigurement and death.[8] But Rich's formulation tends toward ahistorical, even essentializing, universalisms, and her notion of a "lesbian continuum," introduced to reclaim the emancipatory potential in "a range [o]f woman-identified experiences," suggests an uncritical decoupling of sexuality and gender.[9] Rousseau provides some historical specificity to Rich's notion of a heterosexual imperative: his writings suggest that the emergence of romantic love, as an ideology and a cultural ideal, constitutes a moment, if not of this imperative's origin, then of its generalization, authentication, and penetration across increasingly large sectors of society.

Perhaps as salient is Rousseau's attention to the cultural and epistemological dimensions of compulsory heterosexuality: while Rich highlights the everyday and exotic brutalities that discipline women's desire, Rousseau narrates the pity and sensuality that sustain political imperatives as pleasurable. And perhaps his *éducation sensible* speaks also to the proposition that lesbianism be figured as a desexualized continuum: his narrative regularly exploits the instability of gender identities—sensitive men and magisterial women are stock characters in his erotic *spectacles*—but it masters these political and representational ambiguities every time, by bringing sex (back) in. (It is easy enough to imagine Julie and

[8] Rich, "Compulsory Heterosexuality and Lesbian Existence," esp. 637–40.
[9] Ibid., 648.

Claire as exemplary candidates for such a continuum, but why not St. Preux as well?) For this reason I have avoided adjudicating between sex (as an organic object), gender (as the social elaborations of that object's meaning), and sexuality (as the expressions of that object's desire) throughout my analysis. These terms are indispensable for designating interpretive fields, but Rousseau's perennial return to bodily materiality—for a "literal" account of moral and social difference and for a means of enacting republican ends—suggests that their strict differentiation carries as many risks as does their collapse.

The importance of sexuality to Rousseau's republicanism and, in particular, to his account of consensual rule, makes his work a powerful resource for thinking the operations of gender and governance together. Here, too, his narratives complicate how other contemporary feminist critics understand intimacy and publicity, desire and duty, as convergent or divergent terms. In Catharine MacKinnon's analyses, for example, sexuality emerges as the "linchpin" of women's oppression, sustained as such through the power of the liberal democratic state.[10] Examining, in turn, the multiple social domains that constitute women's sexuality as existing for and through men's desires, MacKinnon paints a picture of objectification that has appeared, to the eyes of some critics, totalizing and censorious: Where is the space for interpretive complexity—of politics and pleasure—in this picture? Why do some women's expressions of pain and rage serve as evidence, while others' expressions of pleasure are self-evidently corrupt? The feminist debates generated by MacKinnon's work encompass a wide range of issues, but agency remains a consistent point of contention: some argue that it is impossible within her framework, while others argue that is naively, and inequitably, bestowed.[11]

Rousseau's romantic design frames these issues somewhat differently. On the one hand, it suggests that the claim to a dispositive (because satisfying, reflective, or heartfelt) desire is never evidence of something beyond systemic political affects; to the con-

[10] See MacKinnon, "Feminism, Marxism, Method, and the State," 19, and *Toward a Feminist Theory of the State.*

[11] For representative positions on this issue, see the essays in *Pleasure and Danger,* ed. Carole Vance; and Joan Scott, "Experience." A chronology and critical analysis of feminist antipornography activism are the subjects of several essays in *Sex Wars.*

trary, a dispositional claim signals a site for political analysis and critique. Further, Rousseau's romance suggests that this disposition is sustained through juridical and cultural practices whose indeterminacy provides less a counterweight to some essentialized experience than the opportunity for its narrative construction: consent is always inflected with coercion, love's pleasures with its pains, and romance with sweet sorrow in a sensibility that can accept the dangers of (compulsory) heterosexuality as normative.

But, on the other hand, Rousseau never wavers in his insistence that consent, however rarefied, is pivotal to his republicanism. It sustains a heterosexual desire rooted in the sensations of wielding and surrendering power, and it reflects a political desire rooted in the sensations of love. In Rousseau's sexual politics, women's consent, like the consent of the citizen, remains critical to the successful romance, and thus its constitutively compromised dimensions cannot be evidence of its "always already" fraudulent content: the juridical, bodily, and narrative forms that constrain consent also make it intelligible, and the notion of a consensuality purged of any coercive effects remains as chimerical as true love. These constraining forms likewise enable pleasures that remain complexly interwoven with relations of power; for this reason, a sexuality purged of all servile and imperious desires would be as unworldly as it is inconceivable. When MacKinnon suggests that, under current conditions of sex oppression, feminine sexuality "*is* its own lack," she seems to concede just this point;[12] but in her pursuit of juridical reform, she reveals her own attachment to worldly designs. A perverse implication emerges from my reading of Rousseau: if law and (hetero)sexual desire are mutually constituting, then reforming the one entails assuming the postures of the other. This is not a claim about how desire must inevitably feel, any more than it is a claim about what the law will inevitably proscribe: the Rousseau who appears in this book contributes very little to the pursuit of such natural, psychological, or legal truths. My claim, rather, is that the capacity for autonomy obtains in coincidentally sexual and political practices, and cannot be abstracted from them.

[12] MacKinnon, "Feminism, Marxism, Method, and the State," 20; italics in original.

Whether such abstractions reflect emancipatory or apologetic intentions, they risk losing sight of the institutional and bodily conditions that make consent meaningful to us. I have argued that Rousseau's account shows how those conditions might obtain in the romance of republican men and women, citizens and lovers whose desiring performances generate autonomy as their effect. And while this conclusion raises the specter of a vicious circularity—a failure to secure origins that undermines both a democratic self-understanding and the possibility of its critical transformation—we can relieve this logical tension by returning to the framework of the performative: the grounds for consent are established only through its enactment, and in a very concrete way we (re-)create the possibility of moral and political designs through our practices. This perspective sheds light on a central and often ignored paradox of the *Social Contract*: Rousseau introduces a cost-benefit analysis that counts moral freedom among the acquisitions that come only with the making of the contract, but the decision to contract is itself incomprehensible without the moral capacity for consent.[13] Does it follow from this that Rousseau's democratic ideal is chimerical? Or does it perhaps underscore the need for another approach to his narrative, one that takes Rousseau's metaphoric excesses seriously in order to see how they are produced by his efforts to differentiate literal from figurative, cost from benefit, and origin from end? Rousseau's ardent defense of paradoxes reminds us that not all circles are vicious: they can also be hermeneutic, a moment when the political and the poetic work together.

The very concrete ways that we re-create moral and political possibility must thus include an interpretive practice that attends to *how* narrative makes sense, of and on the world. What remains singularly instructive about Rousseau's narratives is how their generative powers (re)turn us to the mute realm of material things, where the modern dilemma of governance is given a sensuous, bodily form. This is the dilemma of conventional authority, best articulated in all its severity by Hobbes: in the final instance sovereignty must be based on consent, but governmental authority that is not absolute is no authority at all (and on Hobbes's telling, it is usually not much of a government). His solution is to insist that the contractors' choose freely to alienate completely their powers,

---

[13] *Social Contract*, 365.

and in the process he evacuates the notion of consent: "Fear is the passion to be reckoned on." Whether I agree with a gun to my head or as a result of prudential reasoning, in either case I have consented.[14] For interpreters with a wide range of political commitments, Rousseau represents a substantial improvement: however deeply flawed his republican solution, they argue, at least he remains committed to the ideas of individual political freedom and a genuinely popular sovereignty. A reading that attends to his narrative constructions, as well as their representational effects, suggests that he does not reject the Hobbesian dilemma: he resituates it. For Rousseau, erotic desire is the "passion to be reckoned on," and to the degree we perform as his republican men and women, rulers can be confident of citizens' prudential, and passionate, consent.

This is not to say that, for Rousseau, sex can replace the gun, any more than, for Hobbes, brute force is sufficient to maintain sovereign power. On the contrary, both of them recognize state violence as the limiting condition for a consensual nonconsensuality that demands daily repeat performances. In Hobbes this everyday subjection is sustained through reverence for an earthly power, glory, and mystery whose narrative origins are scriptural: neither the subjects' hearts nor their heads, but their souls must bear the marks of political inscription.[15] And for this insight into the strategic importance of a Christianized state, Rousseau offers Hobbes his only words of praise: "It is not so much what is horrible and false in his political theory as what is just and true that has made it hateful."[16] But Rousseau knows that the narrative resolutions of such passion plays will always take place in another world, and that what is represented in them will always exceed material and sensuous confirmation. His stories, by contrast, keep the awesome power of consensual nonconsensuality in this world, where its mystery continues to inspire acquiescence despite being everywhere on display. The romantic failure chronicled in these stories' denouements—Julie drowns, Sophie strays, and Cato loses his mistress, thus his life—is not sufficient to wrench sensitive readers from their narrative absorption: modern men and women do not believe in happy endings, but they do believe in love.

[14] Hobbes, *Leviathan,* 111.

[15] Ibid., 380–82, and part 3: "Of a Christian Commonwealth," 409–625 (the longest of the book's four sections). See discussion in Herzog, *Happy Slaves,* 100–101.

[16] *Social Contract,* 463.

Works Cited

The Anchor Bible: Judges. Trans. Robert Boling. Vol. 6a. Garden City, N.Y.: Doubleday, 1975.

Aristotle. *Politics.* Trans. Carnes Lord. Chicago: University of Chicago Press, 1984.

Armstrong, Nancy. *Desire and Domestic Fiction: A Political History of the Novel.* New York: Oxford University Press, 1987.

Attridge, Anna. "The Reception of *La Nouvelle Héloïse.*" *Studies on Voltaire and the Eighteenth Century* 120 (1974): 227–67.

Austin, J. L. *How to Do Things with Words.* 2d ed. Cambridge: Harvard University Press, 1975.

Barker-Benfield, G. J. *The Culture of Sensibility: Sex and Society in Eighteenth-Century Britain.* Chicago: University of Chicago Press, 1992.

Benhabib, Seyla. "On Hegel, Women and Irony." In *Feminist Interpretations and Political Theory*, edited by Mary Lyndon Shanley and Carole Pateman, 129–45. University Park: Pennsylvania State University Press, 1991.

Brint, M. E. "Echoes of *Narcisse.*" *Political Theory* 16 (November 1988): 617–35.

Burgelin, Pierre. "Sur l'éducation de Sophie." *Annales de la Société Jean-Jacques Rousseau* 35 (1959–62): 113–37.

Butler, Judith P. *Bodies That Matter: On the Discursive Limits of "Sex."* New York: Routledge, 1993.

———. *Excitable Speech: A Politics of the Performative.* New York: Routledge, 1997.

———. *Gender Trouble: Feminism and the Subversion of Identity.* New York: Routledge, 1990.

Cameron, Vivian. "Political Exposures: Sexuality and Caricature in the French Revolution." In *Eroticism and the Body Politic*, edited by Lynn Avery Hunt, 90–107. Baltimore, Md.: Johns Hopkins University Press, 1991.

Casanova, Giacomo. *History of My Life.* Trans. Willard Trask. New York: Harcourt Brace and World, 1966.

Cassirer, Ernst. *The Question of Jean-Jacques Rousseau.* Bloomington: Indiana University Press, 1963.

Coleman, Patrick. *Rousseau's Political Imagination: Rule and Representation in the Lettre à d'Alembert.* Geneva: Librairie Droz, 1984.

Connolly, William E. *Political Theory and Modernity.* Oxford: B. Blackwell, 1988.

Crocker, Lester. "*Julie* ou La Nouvelle Duplicité." *Annales de la Société Jean-Jacques Rousseau* 36 (1963–65): 105–52.

Darnton, Robert. "Readers Respond to Rousseau: The Fabrication of Romantic Sensitivity." In *The Great Cat Massacre and Other Episodes in French Cultural History*, 215–56. New York: Basic Books, 1984.

de Beauvoir, Simone. *The Second Sex.* Trans. H. M. Parshley. New York: Knopf, 1953.

de Lauretis, Teresa. "The Violence of Rhetoric: Considerations of Representation and Gender." In *Technologies of Gender: Essays on Theory, Film, and Fiction*, 31–50. Bloomington: Indiana University Press, 1987.

de Man, Paul. "Metaphor (Second Discourse)." In *Jean-Jacques Rousseau*, edited by Harold Bloom, 194–214. New York: Chelsea House, 1988.

Defaux, Gérard. *Molière ou Les Métamorphoses du Comique.* France: Klincksieck, 1992.

Derrida, Jacques. *Of Grammatology.* Trans. Gayatri Spivak. Baltimore, Md.: Johns Hopkins University Press, 1976.

Derrida, Jacques, and Christine V. MacDonald. "Choreographies: An Interview with Jacques Derrida." Edited and translated by Christine V. MacDonald. *Diacritics* 12:2 (Summer 1982): 66–76.

Duggan, Lisa, and Nan D. Hunter. *Sex Wars: Sexual Dissent and Political Culture.* New York and London: Routledge, 1995.

Ellis, Martin B. *Julie, or La Nouvelle Héloïse: A Synthesis of Rousseau's Thought.* Toronto: University of Toronto Press, 1949.

Ellison, Charles. "Rousseau and the Modern City: The Politics of Speech and Dress." *Political Theory* 13 (November 1985): 497–533.

Ellison, Julie. *Cato's Tears.* Chicago: University of Chicago Press, 1999.

Elshtain, Jean Bethke. *Public Man, Private Woman: Women in Social and Political Thought.* Princeton, N.J.: Princeton University Press, 1981.

Fermon, Nicole. *Domesticating Passions: Rousseau, Women, and Nation.* Hanover, N.H.: University Press of New England, 1997.

Foucault, Michel. "Governmentality." In *The Foucault Effect: Studies in Governmentality*, edited by Graham Burchell, Colin Gordon, and Peter Miller, 87–104. Chicago: University of Chicago Press, 1991.

———. *History of Sexuality*, vol. 1. Translated by Robert Hurley. 1978. New York: Vintage Books, 1980.

Hegel, Georg Wilhelm Friedrich. *Phenomenology of Spirit.* Trans. Arnold V. Miller. Ed. J. N. Findlay. Oxford: Clarendon Press, 1977.

———. *Philosophy of Right.* Trans. T. M. Knox. London: Oxford University Press, 1967.

Herzog, Don. *Happy Slaves: A Critique of Consent Theory.* Chicago: University of Chicago Press, 1989.

Hobbes, Thomas. *Leviathan.* Ed. Michael Oakeshott. New York: Collier Books, 1962.

The Holy Bible. King James Version. New York: James Pott and Co., 1912.

Horowitz, Asher. *Rousseau, Nature, and History.* Toronto: University of Toronto Press, 1987.

Howarth, W. D. *Molière: A Playwright and His Audience.* Cambridge: Cambridge University Press, 1982.

Huizinga, Jakob Herman. *The Making of a Saint: The Tragi-comedy of Jean-Jacques Rousseau.* London: H. Hamilton, 1976.

Hunt, Lynn Avery, ed. *Eroticism and the Body Politic.* Baltimore, Md.: Johns Hopkins University Press, 1991.

Jed, Stephanie H. *Chaste Thinking: The Rape of Lucretia and the Birth of Humanism.* Bloomington: Indiana University Press, 1989.

Jones, Vivien, ed. *Women in the Eighteenth Century.* London: Routledge, 1990.

Kavanagh, Thomas. "Rousseau's *Lévite of Ephraïm.*" *Eighteenth Century Studies* 16, no. 2 (Winter 1983): 141–61.

———. *Writing the Truth: Authority and Desire in Rousseau.* Berkeley: University of California Press, 1987.

Keohane, Nannerl. " 'But for Her Sex . . .': The Domestication of Sophie." *University of Ottawa Quarterly* 49, (1979): 340–400.

Kofman, Sara. "Rousseau's Phallocratic Ends." In *Revaluing French Feminism: Critical Essays on Difference, Agency, and Culture,* edited by Nancy Fraser and Sandra Lee Bartky, 46–59. Bloomington: Indiana University Press, 1992.

Kristeva, Julia. *Powers of Horror: An Essay on Abjection.* Trans. Leon S. Roudiez. New York: Columbia University Press, 1982.

Laclau, Ernesto, and Chantal Mouffe. *Hegemony and Socialist Strategy: Towards a Radical Democratic Politics.* Trans. Winston Moore and Paul Cammack. London: Verso, 1985.

Laclos, Choderlos de. *Les Liaisons Dangereuses.* Ed. Yves Le Hir. Paris: Garnier, 1995.

Landes, Joan B. *Women and the Public Sphere in the Age of the French Revolution.* Ithaca, N.Y.: Cornell University Press, 1988.

Lange, Lynda. "Rousseau and Modern Feminism." In *Feminist Interpretations and Political Theory,* edited by Mary Lyndon Shanley and Carole Pateman, 95–111. University Park: Pennsylvania State University Press, 1991.

———. "Rousseau: Women and the General Will." In *The Sexism of Social and Political Theory,* edited by Lorenne Clark and Lynda Lange, 41–52. Toronto: University of Toronto Press, 1979.

———. "Women and the 'General Will.' " *University of Ottawa Quarterly* 49 (1979): 401–11.

Laqueur, Thomas Walter. *Making Sex: Body and Gender from the Greeks to Freud.* Cambridge: Harvard University Press, 1990.

Lévi-Strauss, Claude. *The Elementary Structures of Kinship.* Translated by James Harle Bell, John Richard von Sturmer, and Rodney Needham, editor. Boston: Beacon Press, 1969.

Locke, John. *Second Treatise of Government: Two Treatises of Government.* Ed. Peter Laslett. Cambridge: Cambridge University Press, 1960.

Lucan. *Lucan's Civil War.* Translated by P. F. Widdows. Bloomington: Indiana University Press, 1988.

MacKinnon, Catharine. "Feminism, Marxism, Method, and the State: An Agenda for Theory." In *Feminist Theory: A Critique of Ideology,* edited by Nannerl O. Keohane, Michelle Z. Rosaldo, and Barbara C. Gelpi, 1–30. Chicago: University of Chicago Press, 1982.

———. *Towards a Feminist Theory of the State.* Cambridge: Harvard University Press, 1989.

Mandeville, Bernard. *The Fable of the Bees, or Private Vices, Publick Benefits.* 2 volumes. Indianapolis: Liberty Press, 1988.

Marshall, David. *The Surprising Effects of Sympathy: Marivaux, Diderot, Rousseau, and Mary Shelley.* Chicago: University of Chicago Press, 1988.

Marso, Lori Jo. *(Un)Manly Citizens: Jean-Jacques Rousseau's and Germaine de Staël's Subversive Women.* Baltimore, Md.: Johns Hopkins University Press, 1999.

McKeon, Michael. *The Origins of the English Novel, 1600–1740.* Baltimore, Md.: Johns Hopkins University Press, 1987.

Morgenstern, Mira. *Rousseau and the Politics of Ambiguity: Self, Culture, and Society.* University Park: Pennsylvania State University Press, 1996.

Mornet, Daniel. "Les Enseignments des Bibliothèques Privées." *Revue d'histoire litterarire de la France* 17 (1910): 449–96.

Mullan, John. *Sentiment and Sociability: The Language of Feeling in the Eighteenth Century.* Oxford: Clarendon Press, 1988.

Okin, Susan. "Women and the Making of the Sentimental Family." *Philosophy and Public Affairs* 11 (Winter 1982): 65–88.

———. *Women in Western Political Thought.* Princeton, N.J.: Princeton University Press, 1979.

Pateman, Carole. " 'The Disorder of Women': Women, Love and the Sense of Justice." *Ethics* 90 (1980): 20–34.

———. *The Problem of Political Obligation: A Critique of Liberal Theory.* Cambridge: Polity Press, 1985.

———. *The Sexual Contract.* Stanford, Calif.: Stanford University Press, 1988.

———. "Women and Consent." *Political Theory* 8 (May 1980): 149–68.

Persius. *The Satires of A. Persius Flaccus,* edited by Basil L. Gildersleeve and Otto Jahn. New York: Harper and Brothers, 1875.

Plutarch. *Plutarch's Lives.* Ed. Arthur Hugh Clough. 2 vols. London: J. M. Dent and Sons, 1929.

Ravven, Heidi M. "Has Hegel Anything to Say to Feminists?" *The Owl of Minerva* 19 (Spring 1989): 149–68.

Ray, William. "Reading Women: Cultural Authority, Gender, and the Novel. The Case of Rousseau." *Eighteenth-Century Studies* 27 (1994): 421–47.

———. "Rethinking Reading: The Novel and Cultural Stratification." *Eighteenth-Century Fiction* 10 (1998): 151–70.

Rich, Adrienne. "Compulsory Heterosexuality and Lesbian Existence." *SIGNS: Journal of Women in Culture and Society* 5 (1980): 631–60.

Rubin, Gayle. "Traffic in Women: Towards a 'Political Economy' of Sex." In *Toward an Anthropology of Women,* edited by Rayna Reiter, 157–210. New York: Monthy Review Press, 1975.

Schiebinger, Londa. "Why Mammals Are Called Mammals: Gender Politics in Eighteenth-Century Natural History." *American Historical Review* 98 (April 1993): 382–411.

Schwartz, Joel. *The Sexual Politics of Jean-Jacques Rousseau.* Chicago: University of Chicago Press, 1984.

Scott, Joan. "Experience." In *Feminists Theorize the Political,* edited by Judith Butler and Joan W. Scott, 22–40. New York: Routledge, 1992.

Sheriff, Mary. "Fragonard's Erotic Mothers and the Politics of Reproduction." In *Eroticism and the Body Politic,* edited by Lynn Avery Hunt, 14–40. Baltimore, Md.: Johns Hopkins University Press, 1991.

Shklar, Judith N. *Men and Citizens: A Study of Rousseau's Social Theory.* London: Cambridge University Press, 1969.

Starobinski, Jean. *Jean-Jacques Rousseau, Transparency and Obstruction.* Trans. Arthur Goldhammer. Chicago: University of Chicago Press, 1988.

Strong, Tracy. *Jean-Jacques Rousseau and the Politics of the Ordinary.* Thousand Oaks, Calif.: Sage, 1994.

Taylor, Charles. *Hegel.* Cambridge: Cambridge University Press, 1975.

Thomas, Paul. "Jean-Jacques Rousseau, Sexist?" *Feminist Studies* 17 (Summer 1991): 195–217.

Todd, Janet. *Sensibility: An Introduction.* London: Methuen, 1986.

Vance, Carole S., ed. *Pleasure and Danger: Exploring Female Sexuality.* Boston: Routledge and K. Paul, 1984.

Watt, Ian P. *The Rise of the Novel: Studies in Defoe, Richardson and Fielding.* London: Chatto and Windus, 1957.

Weil, Eric. "Jean-Jacques Rousseau et sa Politique." *Critique* 56 (January 1952): 4–28.

Weiss, Penny A. *Gendered Community: Rousseau, Sex, and Politics.* New York: New York University Press, 1993.

Wexler, Victor. " 'Made for Man's Delight': Rousseau as Antifeminist." *American Historical Review* 81 (February 1976): 266–91.

Wilson, Arthur M., Jr. "Sensibility in France in the Eighteenth Century." *French Quarterly* 13 (1931): 35–46.

Wirz, Charles. "Note sur *Emile et Sophie, ou Les Solitaires.*" *Annales de la Société Jean-Jacques Rousseau* 36 (1963–65): 291–301.

Wollstonecraft, Mary. *A Vindication of the Rights of Women.* Buffalo, N.Y.: Prometheus Books, 1989.

"Women in the Beehive: A Seminar with Jacques Derrida." In *Men in Feminism,* edited by Alice Jardine and Paul Smith, 189–203. New York: Methuen, 1987.

Zerilli, Linda M. G. *Signifying Woman: Culture and Chaos in Rousseau, Burke, and Mill.* Ithaca, N.Y.: Cornell University Press, 1994.

Index

Abelard, 127–28

Adventures of Telemachus (Fénelon), 82. *See also* Fénelon; Telemachus

Agamemnon, 176

Alceste (*Le Misanthrope*), 179

Alexander, 192

amour de soi, defined, 30

amour-propre, defined, 31, 35

Anchor Bible: Judges, 209, 222n

ancien régime, social-sexual mores of, 15, 75, 82, 107, 178; and theater, 164, 177

Angelique (*Narcisse*), 169 and n

Antony, 193

Aristides, 138

Aristotle, 8n, 24–26, 163

Armstrong, Nancy, 105n

Attridge, Anna, 103n, 105

Austin, J. L., 11

Axa (*Le Lévite d'Ephraïm*), 212, 221, 228–30, 233, 239

Barker-Benfield, G. J., 18n

de Beauvoir, Simone, 74n

Benhabib, Seyla, 53n

Benjamin, tribe of. *See* Benjamites

Benjamites, 210–12, 220–23, 225–26, 228–29

Bérénice (Racine), 179

Berman, Marshall, 160n

blood, 11, 34, 151, 177, 207, 224, 227

Bloom, Allan, 7n, 10n, 60n

blush, 83, 171, 185, 186. *See also* complexion

body, as material sign, 11–12, 17, 25–26, 73, 76, 136, 183, 185, 192, 196, 201, 221, 237. *See also* blood; blush; body politic; brain; breast(s); complexion; erection; eye(s); hand(s); heart(s); knee(s); language, materiality of; lips; mouth; nipple; *sensibilité*; skin

body politic: depicted in *Discourse on Political Economy*, 150–52, 155–56, 163–64; depicted in *Social Contract*, 145–48

Boling, Robert, 222n

Bomston, Edward (*Julie*), 108n, 109–10, 112–13, 123, 125–26, 129–30, 166

Bousset, 133

brain, 151–52

breast(s), 10, 24, 33, 130–31, 192, 196n. *See also* breast-feeding; nipple

breast-feeding, 156, 157–58

Brint, M. E., 216n

Brutus, 138

Burgelin, Pierre, 83n

Butler, Judith, 9 and n, 21n

Caesar, 47, 138, 165, 192–93, 207

Cameron, Vivian, 167n

Casanova, Giacomo, 26 and n

Cassirer, Ernst, 4, 216n

Cato, 165–66, 244

de Chantal, Jeanne, 139 and n

Cicero, 81n, 82n

citizen(s): and articulation of general will, 238–39; depicted in *Discourse on Political Economy*, 142, 152–55, 159–60, 163–166; depicted in *Social Contract*, 4–5, 144–45, 163; libidinal economy of, 233; and masculinity, 153, 207; reproduction of, 203; and self-display, 197. *See also* Benjamites; body politic; consensual nonconsensuality

Claire (*Julie*), 109–10, 114 and n, 115, 118–20, 125–26, 142, 241

Coleman, Patrick, 11n, 173, 181 and n, 186–88, 197n

comedy, 176–77, 179

complexion, 64, 76, 118, 126, 131, 185. *See also* blush

Confessions (Rousseau), 5n, 18–19, 24, 72n, 132–43, 214, 223

251